The English Vicars Apostolic

1688-1850

Nicholas Schofield & Gerard Skinner

FAMILY PUBLICATIONS · OXFORD

ISBN 978-1-907380-01-3

Published by
Family Publications, Denis Riches House
66 Sandford Lane, Kennington
Oxford OX1 5RP, UK
www.familypublications.co.uk

Printed in England by
Cromwell Press Group, Wilts

TABLE OF CONTENTS

Introduction... 5

I - The London District (1688-1850) 14

John Leyburn (1688-1702) 15
Bonaventure Giffard (1703-34)................................ 19
Benjamin Petre (1734-58) 24
Richard Challoner (1758-81)................................... 31
James Robert Talbot (1781-90)................................ 44
John Douglass (1790-1812)..................................... 50
William Poynter (1812-27) 57
James Yorke Bramston (1827-36) 64
Robert Gradwell (Coadjutor) (1828-33) 71
Thomas Griffiths (1836-47).................................... 76
Thomas Walsh (1848-49) 82
Nicholas Wiseman (1849-50) 84

II - The Midland District (1688-1840) and Central District (1840-50) . 87

Bonaventure Giffard (1688-1703)............................ 88
George Witham (1703-16) 94
John Talbot Stonor (1716-56) 96
John Hornyold (1756-78)....................................... 102
Thomas Joseph Talbot (1778-95)............................ 106
Charles Berington (1795-98)................................... 110
Gregory Stapleton (1801-02).................................. 113
John Milner (1803-26).. 118
Thomas Walsh (1826-48) 129
Nicholas Wiseman (Coadjutor) (1840-47) 133
William Bernard Ullathorne, OSB (1848-50)............. 137

III - The Eastern District (1840-50) 139

William Wareing (1840-50)..................................... 140

IV - The Northern District (1688-1840)...................... 143

James Smith (1688-1711)....................................... 144
George Witham (1716-25) 147
Thomas Dominic Williams, OP (1725-40)................... 149

Edward Dicconson (1741-52) 152

Francis Petre (1752-75) 155

William Maire (Coadjutor) (1768-69) 157

William Walton (1775-80) 159

Matthew Gibson (1780-90) 162

William Gibson (1790-1821) 165

Thomas Smith (1821-31) 169

Thomas Penswick (1831-36) 172

John Briggs (1836-40) 175

V - The Northern District (1840-50) 177

Francis George Mostyn (1840-47) 178

William Riddell (1847) 180

William Hogarth (1848-50) 183

VI - The Lancashire District (1840-50) 186

George Hilary Brown (1840-50) 187

James Sharples (Coadjutor) (1843-50) 191

VII - The Yorkshire District (1840-50) 194

John Briggs (1840-50) 195

VIII - The Western District (1688-1850) 197

Philip Michael Ellis, OSB (1688-1705) 198

Matthew Prichard, OSF (1713-50) 204

William Laurence York, OSB (1750-70) 208

Charles Walmesley, OSB (1770-97) 211

William Gregory Sharrock, OSF (1797-1809) 216

Peter Bernardine Collingridge, OSF (1809-29) 219

Peter Augustine Baines, OSB (1829-43) 223

Charles Michael Baggs (1844-45) 234

William Bernard Ullathorne, OSB (1846-48) 239

Joseph William Hendren, OSF (1848-50) 244

IX - The Welsh District (1840-50) 248

Thomas Joseph Brown, OSB (1840-50) 249

General Bibliography 254

Picture Credits 256

INTRODUCTION

Part of the inspiration for this book was provided in the summer of 2007, when I was asked to preach an annual retreat to some Carmelite sisters and given generous hospitality in the nearby 'Bishop's House'. This may not sound particularly unusual, except that the convent stood in the cathedral compound of Abu Dhabi and the 'Bishop's House' was the residence of the Vicar Apostolic of Arabia, Paul Hinder OFM Cap. The Apostolic Vicariate cares for the Catholics of Bahrain, Oman, Qatar, Saudi Arabia, the United Arab Emirates and Yemen – an area of some 1.2 million square miles with a flock of at least 2 million, served by about sixteen parishes and fifty-five priests.

As I gave my conferences in the sweltering heat and saw at first hand the work of the Vicar Apostolic, I began to think of the Apostolic Vicariates in England and Wales, first established during the reign of James II and eventually replaced in 1850 by the restored system of diocesan government. I noted some similarities between the two, especially in the need for discretion and the lack of resources, although in many ways the Catholic community in the Arabian Peninsula (with the exception of Saudi Arabia) enjoys greater freedom albeit within a well-defined framework. An English Catholic of the eighteenth century, still burdened by the penal laws, would have shared Bishop Hinder's comparison of his flock with the Church of the Roman catacombs, hoping for the day when they could come out into the open.

What, then, is a Vicar Apostolic? The title was in use as early as the fourth century but acquired its modern meaning in 1622, when Gregory XV established Propaganda Fide to look after missionary territories and adopted the Vicars Apostolic as one of the main forms of ecclesiastical government in these areas. Such a leader was in bishop's orders but exercised authority not in his own name but in the name of the Pope.

Mgr Ronald Knox described the English Vicars as 'emissaries from Rome, personally responsible to the Holy See – as if this island had been some newly discovered territory in the Pacific, whose inhabitants were mere beginners in the faith.' The dependent nature of the Vicars Apostolic meant that some critics, Catholics included, saw them as un-English. In 1790, for example, Sir John Throckmorton argued for a diocesan hierarchy: the current Pastors 'are now alien, you will make them Englishmen; they are dependent, you will make them free; they are foreign emissaries, you will transform them into English Bishops.'[1]

The status of the Vicars Apostolic was not well-defined in the early modern period, long before the codification of canon law, and boundaries were established gradually as queries about jurisdiction were sent to Rome. In 1669, for example, the Vicar Apostolic of Fo-Kien (China) asked the Holy See if he was equal to a diocesan bishop regarding the power of jurisdiction and the answer was negative. Government by the Vicars Apostolic was seen as provisional, even if it lasted for several centuries until such a time that the local church was 'mature' enough to form a diocese and stand on its own as part of the Universal Church. The restoration of the Hierarchy in 1850 meant, in Knox's mind, that England and Wales stopped being 'a Crown Colony of the Triple Tiara' and achieved 'dominian status at last.'[2]

There had been different solutions to the shepherding of the English Catholic community following the Reformation. The last of the Marian bishops, Thomas Goldwell of St Asaph, died in 1585, having spent his final years in Rome as a Theatine and having failed in his proposed missions to England. Shortly afterwards the founder of the English Colleges of Douai and Rome, William Allen, was named Prefect of the English Mission, but the Cardinal was never able to visit his native country in this role. In 1598, four years after Allen's death, the Pope appointed George Blackwell as Archpriest of the secular clergy of England and Scotland. However, his perceived sympathy for the Jesuits meant that his appointment was not recognised by a vocal group of secular clergy (the so-called 'Appellants'), some of whom were promptly suspended. Blackwell's support for an Oath of Allegiance introduced after the Gunpowder Plot drew criticism from St Robert Bellarmine and the Pope himself and he was eventually replaced by George Birkhead (1608-14) and then William Harrison (1615-21).

---

[1] B. Ward, *The Dawn of the Catholic Revival in England, 1781-1802* (1909), i, 227.
[2] R. Knox, *Occasional Sermons* (1960), 296.

Shortly before his death, the last of the Archpriests sent an appeal to Rome for an English bishop to restore unity and discipline within the Church and administer the sacrament of Confirmation. In 1625 Urban VIII appointed a single bishop to act as Vicar Apostolic of England: the appropriately-named William Bishop, who had been condemned to death in 1583 but then freed from the Marshalsea prison. The first Vicars Apostolic did not prove a great success: Bishop died nine months after his appointment and his successor, Richard Smith, caused so much dissension that he was first suspended from office and then forced to flee to France, spending part of his exile under the protection of Cardinal Richelieu. Once again there was no resident bishop in the country and administration passed to the Chapter (later known as the Old Brotherhood) that had been founded by William Bishop, though with uncertain canonical standing.

When the Catholic James II acceded to the throne, he encouraged the Pope to restore government by a Vicar Apostolic. The first appointee, John Leyburn, travelled the length and breadth of England administering the sacrament of Confirmation. In 1688 his single Vicariate was divided into four Districts, each with its own bishop. A modern historian has called it 'one of the few hours of sunlight during the troubled months of James' reign.'[3] In 1840 Gregory XVI doubled the number of Districts, in recognition of the growing numbers and confidence of English and Welsh Catholics.

Though beyond the scope of this book, it is worth comparing this arrangement with the other two of the British Kingdoms. In Ireland, the Catholic hierarchy essentially remained intact, though it suffered much persecution. Indeed, one Archbishop of Armagh and Primate of All Ireland, St Oliver Plunkett, was martyred at Tyburn in 1681. On the other hand, Scotland's break with Rome occurred in 1560 and Catholics in that Kingdom initially came under the English Archpriest or Vicar Apostolic. In 1653 Scotland became an Apostolic Prefecture and, in 1694, an Apostolic Vicariate, the first bishop being Thomas Joseph Nicolson. In 1727 the Vicariate was divided into Highland and Lowland Districts and, exactly a century later, reorganised into Eastern, Western and Northern Districts. The Scottish Hierarchy was not restored until 1878.

Comparisons can also be made with the rest of Protestant Europe. Catholics in the Protestant Netherlands, for example, were governed by the Vicars Apostolic of the Dutch Mission between 1592 and 1725,

---

[3] E. G. Rupp, *Religion in England 1688-1791* (1987), 181.

when the States General expelled the bishop from the Republic. Leadership was thereafter provided by the Apostolic Nuncio in Brussels, until Pius IX re-established the Archdiocese of Utrecht, with four suffragan Secs, in 1853. The faithful in Protestant Germany were originally covered by the Apostolic Vicariate of the North, which also included much of Scandinavia. Up until its suppression in 1930, territory was added and subtracted. For example, in 1709 a new Vicariate of Upper and Lower Saxony (Hanover) was formed, which was eventually divided between the dioceses of Hildesheim and Osnabrück by Leo XII in 1824. When the Elector of Hanover became King George I of Great Britain in 1714, he would already have been used to dealing with Vicars Apostolic.

The world of the English and Welsh Vicars Apostolic was very different from that of the so-called 'Second Spring'. Take the example of the bishops in the London District. Dressed in sober lay dress and living discreetly in a town house (an address that in the eighteenth century was frequently changed), their lives could not have been more different from their confreres in Catholic Europe. Persecution and anti-Catholic feeling was a constant threat: Giffard was imprisoned five times, Talbot faced trial twice and Challoner only narrowly escaped the Gordon Riots. Their freedom to exercise their ministry was limited. Many were buried without vestments or signs of their office, with their hands lying simply by their sides. Challoner was bishop for fifty years but never once ordained a priest, for there were then no seminaries on English soil and priests were ordained overseas. Douglass was the first to openly wear a pectoral cross, though only in the privacy of his home and without wearing a cassock. His successor, Poynter, normally wore a brown suit and Joseph Silveira recalled the astonishment produced the first time the bishop walked from his room at St Edmund's to the chapel in his episcopal cassock in 1817. His usual dictum, however, was 'Church dress for Church use, Sir.'[4] The Vicars Apostolic were not *ancien régime* prince bishops and, in actual fact, their effective power was limited by the relative independence of the regulars, the hard-headedness of many seculars and the complex nature of canon law. Despite such obstacles, though, the extent of the jurisdiction of the London Vicars Apostolic was technically very great since it included the Catholics of the British colonies, including the West Indies and North America.

---

[4] B. Ward, *History of St Edmund's College Old Hall* (1893), 222.

On one level, the story of the Vicars Apostolic is one of heroism and devotion. Who can fail to be impressed by the likes of Bishops Giffard or Challoner? However, the reader will also be struck by the many disagreements and controversies that dominated their lives. There were divisions within the Church, such as the almost constant tensions between the secular and regular clergy (especially the Jesuits). There were conflicts over rival jurisdictions and differing visions for the English Church. With the prospect of Catholic Relief, there was much debate over the nature of any agreement with the State – should there, for example, be a government veto on the appointment of bishops and what sort of oath should be made before the taking of public office? This was not a new issue, for in the final years of Elizabeth's reign a group of clergy (the so-called 'Appellants') had approached the Government seeking accommodation and denying links with 'Fifth Columnists' or plotting Jesuits. The same desire for Catholics to become an accepted part of the nation, even if this meant a degree of compromise, was to be found two hundred years later.

Simmering beneath the spirited discussions of the Catholic Committee and Cisalpine Club was the question of who exercised leadership over the Catholic community – the lay grandees, who for centuries had acted as patrons, or the increasingly confident Vicars Apostolic. It would be easy to say that the latter won and that the way was thus paved for the restoration of the Hierarchy. However, calls for a diocesan structure had differing motives. For the bishops it gave them greater dignity and authority. For the clergy it promised tenure as parish priests rather than missioners (though this was not granted until 1917). For the leading laity it pointed towards a 'gallicanized' Church that was more acceptable to their fellow countrymen, with English Bishops rather than Vicars Apostolic seemingly overly dependent on Rome.

Long before the days of a Bishops' Conference, there was a marked lack of unity among the bishops, although by the beginning of the nineteenth century they were occasionally meeting together. A modern Catholic may be startled by the very public feuds between them, fuelled by the fiery personalities of Stonor, Walmesley, Milner and Baines.

The Vicars Apostolic are sometimes represented as living in a stagnant period of decline, almost as if they were waiting for the advent of Wiseman, Newman *et al.* to lead the English Catholics into the 'Second Spring'. This book hopes to do two things: firstly, to make the Vicars

Apostolic better known to a general readership and secondly to remind modern Catholics of the debt owed to them, for these bishops laid the foundations of the modern Church in England and Wales.

There have been books and articles on them before, of course. There are useful summaries of many of the Vicars Apostolic in both the *Dictionary of National Biography* and the recent *Oxford Dictionary of National Biography*. The last thirty years have seen individual studies of Giffard (J.A.Williams, 2003), Challoner (Eamon Duffy (ed.), 1981), Baines (Pamela Gilbert, 2006) and Ullathorne (Judith Champ, 2006). William Maziere Brady, an Irish convert and Roman correspondent for *The Tablet*, published his *Annals of the Catholic Hierarchy in England and Scotland* in 1877. This claimed to be based on extensive research in the Vatican archive and contains much useful (though sometimes inaccurate) information. A series of magisterial volumes produced by two Presidents of St Edmund's, Ware chronicled the Vicars Apostolic of the century before the restoration of the Hierarchy: Edwin Burton's *Life and Times of Bishop Challoner* (1909) and Bernard Ward's *The Dawn of the Catholic Revival in England 1781-1803* (1909), *The Eve of Catholic Emancipation 1803-1829* (1911) and *The Sequel to Catholic Emancipation 1829-1850* (1915). A booklet edited by Dom (now Abbot) Aidan Bellenger, *Fathers in Faith* (1991), usefully focussed on the bishops of the Western District. The earlier period was covered by Dom Basil Hemphill's instructive *The Early Vicars Apostolic of England 1685-1750* (1953). The author had originally intended to write 'a history of all the Vicars Apostolic (1685-1850), but in that form it proved too cumbrous.'[5]

The English Vicars Apostolic attempts to do exactly that, though hopefully not in a 'cumbrous' form. By its nature, this volume is also something of a 'stop gap' for much work still needs to be done in this area and many of the Vicars Apostolic, perhaps most notably Stonor, Milner and Walsh, still await a detailed study. Though some of the bishops are well-documented, others have left only a scant record, due in part to the discretion they had to exercise in their ministry, or have come down to us surrounded by a hagiographic haze. Many important records have failed to survive, such as the papers relating to the Western District destroyed at the time of the Gordon Riots.

This book is arranged in a similar way to our *English Cardinals* (Family Publications, 2007), with each subject standing alone and arranged in

---

[5] B. Hemphill, *The Early Vicars-Apostolic of England, 1685-1750* (1954) ix.

chronological order and (in this case) by District. The history of each of the Vicariates can thus be followed or the life of an individual Vicar Apostolic, chosen at the reader's discretion. In the case of bishops who were translated to other Districts, their career is continued under the relevant section. Coadjutors who died before succeeding as Vicars Apostolic are included for the sake of completeness. However, it was decided not to include the two Vicars Apostolic of England appointed in the 1620s, since they belong to an earlier period and have been treated comprehensively elsewhere.

Fr Skinner and I would like to thank Dr Judith Champ, Revd Dr Stewart Foster and Dr James Hagerty for reading the draft of this book and making invaluable suggestions. We are also indebted to the following for advice, encouragement, permission to use pictures in their possession or taking photographs of various portraits: Cardinal Cormac Murphy-O'Connor, Archbishop Vincent Nichols, Bishop Arthur Roche, Abbot Aidan Bellenger, Abbot Geoffrey Scott, Lord Camoys, Lord Petre, the Hon. Georgina Stonor, Mgr Mark Crisp, Mgr Martin Hayes, Mgr Nicholas Hudson, Fr Jerome Bertram, Fr Paul Keane, Fr Richard Whinder, Br Bartholomew Preston OSB, Sr Mary Joseph OSB, Dr Peter Doyle, Dr James Kelly, Dr Meg Whittle, Duncan Gallie, Sue Gill, Stefan Kaminski, Philippe Lefebvre, Chris Long, Colin Mason, Claudia Primangeli, Pat Salter and Chris Smith.

Fr Nicholas Schofield

THE FOUR
DISTRICTS
1688-1840

THE EIGHT
DISTRICTS
1840-1850

ABBREVIATIONS

The following abbreviations are used throughout the book in the footnotes:

AAW   Archives of the Archbishop of Westminster

Anstruther   Godfrey Anstruther OP, *The Seminary Priests* (4 vols, 1968-77)

Brady   W. Maziere Brady, *Annals of the Catholic Hierarchy in England and Scotland AD 1585-1876, With Dissertation on Anglican Orders* (1877)

Burton   Edwin Burton, *The Life and Times of Bishop Challoner, 1691-1781* (1909)

CRS   Catholic Record Society

Dawn   Bernard Ward, *The Dawn of the Catholic Revival in England, 1781-1802* (1909)

Eve   Bernard Ward, *The Eve of Catholic Emancipation: being the History of the English Catholics during the first 30 years of the 19th Century* (1911-12)

Hemphill   Basil Hemphill, *The Early Vicars-Apostolic of England, 1685-1750* (1954)

Milburn   David Milburn, *A History of Ushaw College: A Study of the Origin, Foundation and Development of an English Catholic Seminary with an Epilogue 1908-1962* (1964)

Sequel   Bernard Ward, *The Sequel to Catholic Emancipation* (1915)

Schiefen   Richard J. Schiefen, *Nicholas Wiseman and the Transformation of English Catholicism* (1984)

St Edmund's   Bernard Ward, *History of St Edmund's College* (1893)

The London District
(1688-1850)

The London District consisted of the counties of Bedfordshire, Berkshire, Buckinghamshire, Essex, Hampshire, Hertfordshire, Kent, Middlesex, Surrey, and Sussex, together with the Isle of Wight and the Channel Islands. It thus comprised the present-day dioceses of Arundel and Brighton, Brentwood, part of Northampton, Portsmouth, Southwark and Westminster. After the realignment of 1840, the London District lost the counties of Bedfordshire and Buckinghamshire to the new Eastern District.

The Vicar Apostolic of London fulfilled an important role due to his presence in the nation's capital, where Catholicism thrived and the extraterritorial Embassy chapels were able to maintain fine liturgical and musical establishments. As the British Empire developed, the London Vicar Apostolic also exercised jurisdiction over Catholics in many of the colonies. However, under the penal laws he was carefully watched by the authorities, perhaps more so than the other Vicars Apostolic, and was frequently forced to change his address.

John Leyburn

1620-1702
Titular Bishop of Adrumetum (1685)
Vicar Apostolic of England (1685-88)
Vicar Apostolic of the London District (1688-1702)

The Leyburn (or Leyburne) family of Cunswick Hall, not far from the Westmorland town of Kendal, were prominent Catholics. The bishop's uncle, George Leyburn, was the first English-born chaplain to Queen Henrietta Maria and also President of the English College, Douai (1652-70); a great-uncle, James, had been hanged, drawn and quartered at Lancaster in 1583 for holding to the papal supremacy.

John Leyburn was born at Cunswick in 1620, the fourth son of John Leyburn and Catherine Carus. He studied at Douai from 1633, although the details of his formation and early years as a priest are unclear due to a lack of documentation. He may have remained at the college as professor and studied for the prestigious doctorate at the Sorbonne. Between 1640 and 1645 he acted as travelling tutor for Francis Browne, the future fourth Viscount Montague. Leyburn was connected to the Montague family through his great-uncle, the martyr James Leyburn, who was a first cousin of the first Viscount Montague's sister-in-law, Anne Dacre.

By 1652 Leyburn moved to Paris as secretary to Richard Smith, Bishop of Chalcedon and second Vicar Apostolic of England, who was also closely connected to the Montagues. Smith's six years of episcopal governance in England were turbulent, marked by a fierce conflict with the regulars, and he withdrew to Paris as something of a failure, having been reprimanded by the Pope. He initially lived with Cardinal Richelieu but by the time Leyburn joined his household, he was residing in a property adjoining the house of the English Augustinian Canonesses on the Rue des Fosses

Saint Victor, which the bishop had helped to establish. Leyburn remained in this post until March 1655, when the bishop died and was buried before the High Altar in the Canonesses' church.

On returning to England, Leyburn acted as chaplain to the third Viscount Montague, whose family was based at Cowdray House and Battle Abbey in Sussex and Montague House in Southwark. It was clear that the priest's star was rising. As early as 1657 he was recommended to Rome as a possible bishop, although no appointment was made. He joined the Chapter of the English Secular Clergy, which had much authority over ecclesiastical affairs in the absence of a resident bishop, and in 1668 became its Secretary. This appointment put him against his uncle George, the President of Douai, who did not consider the Chapter as validly erected. The following year, Leyburn was mentioned in a list of candidates for the episcopate prepared by the Chapter in the event of a hierarchy being restored and he was described as 'a Professor of Theology, a Doctor of the Sorbonne and a Catholic of great piety, charity and prudence, although he had spent some time away from the Church in his youth and one of his brothers was "a very great puritan".'[1]

Despite his differences with his uncle, Leyburn succeeded him as President of the English College at Douai in May 1670. According to Canon Agretti, the Belgian Minister Apostolic who came to England to investigate the state of the underground Church, Leyburn 'evinced before me great submission towards the Holy See, although he desires not the Presidency, inasmuch as he is placed more commodiously in the house of Viscount Montagu, who, they report, has great affection for him.'[2] The Leyburn connections at Douai were to continue when his nephew, Nicholas, became Vice-President in 1673 – the third generation of the family to hold high office at the college.

In 1676 John Leyburn moved to Rome to act as secretary and auditor to the newly created English Dominican Cardinal, Philip Howard. In 1679 the Cardinal became Protector of England and the following year Protector of the Venerable English College, beside which he lived with Leyburn in a newly-built *palazzo*.

In 1685 the Catholic James II succeeded to the throne and it seemed only a matter of time before Catholic bishops would be appointed. Leyburn was recommended by both the King and Cardinal Howard as the new

---

[1] Brady, 141.
[2] Ibid., 142.

Vicar Apostolic of England and the Pope gave his approbation on 6 August 1685. On 9 September Leyburn was consecrated Titular Bishop of Adrumetum in Rome by Federico Cardinal Baldeschi Colonna. He arrived triumphant in London the following month, together with the new papal nuncio, Archbishop Ferdinand d'Adda: the first time Catholic bishops had set foot in the country since 1629. Leyburn cut a distinctive figure in London, walking around 'in a long cassock and cloak, with a golden cross hanging to a black ribbon about his neck; [he] goes in a chair or sedan but his train is not held up.'[3]

Leyburn was given lodgings at Lincoln's Inn Fields and a royal pension of £1000 a year. He reduced the number of districts into which the Apostolic Vicariate was divided from six to four, and chose Vicars General and Rural Deans for each of them. However, despite their assistance, it was up to Leyburn to make a country-wide visitation and administer the sacrament of Confirmation for the first time in nearly fifty years. In his great tour of the North in 1687 the bishop confirmed an impressive 20,859 Catholics and was even greeted by the Anglican Bishops of Durham and Chester as he made his progress, the latter being an old friend. In the month of September he travelled round Lancashire and confirmed vast numbers: 1,143 at Preston and Tulketh, 1,182 at Ladyewell and 1,252 at Wigan.

In January 1688 four new Vicariates were created by Blessed Innocent XI and Leyburn became the first Vicar Apostolic of the London District. The four bishops signed a Joint Pastoral, proclaiming the beginning of a new era. If the Catholic Faith had previously been a private and discreet affair, the bishops wrote, 'now you are in Circumstances of letting it appear abroad, and of edifying your Neighbours by professing it publicly, and living up to the Rules prescribed by it.' However, they were careful to note that 'the memory of past hardships which you have suffered from some among them, may be apt to create provoking animosities, and the Liberty you now enjoy may possibly tempt you to insult those who formerly abridged you of it; but it must be your care to prevent or suppress all such irregular Motions.'[4]

Leyburn was a realist and tried to restrain the zeal of the King in promoting the Catholic cause. In 1687 James had instructed the Fellows of Magdalen College, Oxford, to elect a Catholic, Anthony Farmer, as President. They refused, stating that Farmer was an unsuitable candidate.

---

[3] A. Clark, *Life and Times of Anthony Wood*, (Oxford Historical Society, vol. 26, 1894), iii, 171.
[4] Hemphill, 22-23.

When they rejected also the King's alternative candidate, Bishop Parker of Oxford, James decided to strip them of their fellowships. Parker was appointed President but died soon afterwards and was replaced by the new Vicar Apostolic of the Midland District, Bonaventure Giffard. Leyburn disapproved of this imprudent move and persuaded the King to restore the fellows, leading Lord Macaulay to describe the bishop in his *History* as 'a wise and honest man'.[5]

At the Revolution of 1688, Leyburn tried to flee to the continent with Giffard, but they were both seized at Faversham. Hours later the King himself was captured and brought through the town. Leyburn, now a septuagenarian, was conveyed to the Tower, where he remained until July 1690. On release, he remained quietly in London, discreetly ruling over his District. His remaining years saw frequent alarms, especially during periods of anti-Catholic panic. Such was his peaceful conduct that the authorities kept an eye on his movements but largely left him alone. Leyburn was small of stature and a skilled practitioner of Latin, who had acquired the character of being both wise and polite. He enjoyed warm friendships beyond the Catholic community and, on account of his keen mathematical interests, was on friendly terms with Descartes and Hobbes.

Despite the uncertainty of his later years, Leyburn lived to the ripe old age of 82 and established a tradition of longevity that was followed by many of his successors in the London District. He died in London on 9 June 1702 but the whereabouts of his final resting place is (surprisingly) unknown.

Further Reading

J. A. Hilton et al. (eds), *Bishop Leyburn's confirmation register of 1687* (1997)

---

[5] T.B. Macaulay, *The Works of Lord Macaulay Vol. 3: History of England* (1905), 77.

BONAVENTURE GIFFARD

1642-1734
TITULAR BISHOP OF MADAURA (1687)
VICAR APOSTOLIC OF THE MIDLAND DISTRICT (1687-1703)
VICAR APOSTOLIC OF THE LONDON DISTRICT (1703-34)

For his early life and ministry as VA of the Midland District, see pp. 88-93

In 1703, following the death of Bishop Leyburn the previous year, Bonaventure Giffard was transferred from the Midland to the London District. At the time of his predecessor's death, efforts were being made to appoint a coadjutor and the Pope indicated that he wanted George Witham, the English bishop's agent in Rome, to succeed Leyburn. Witham proved reluctant to move south and suggested Bishop James Smith, who also refused the offer. This was perhaps understandable for life in the capital was precarious, especially since an Act had recently been passed offering a £100 reward for securing the conviction of a Romish priest. Giffard duly accepted the position and he seemed the obvious choice, for in the closing years of Leyburn's life he had frequently been in London, confirming at the Hammersmith convent and writing on Leyburn's behalf to Propaganda Fide, the Roman Congregation with responsibility for non-Catholic countries. George Witham succeeded Giffard in the Midland District.

Life in the capital was indeed full of dangers and the new Vicar Apostolic was several times in prison and often on the run, using aliases such as 'Joseph Giffard', 'Joseph Leveson' and 'Fowler'. In September 1704 he was arrested while living near Red Lion Square but absconded and became little more than a fugitive. Early in 1705 Giffard wrote to the President of Douai that he feared ending his days behind bars at Hurst Castle in Kent and that he was 'forced as yet to lie very quiet.'[1] In a letter to Rome he noted that he had been 'tossed about by continual perturbations and perils, so as scarcely to find any where a place to rest with safety.'[2] By 1706 he had found protection with the Venetian Ambassador and in a letter of October 1714 says that he had been imprisoned three times and, since May of that year, had had to change his address fourteen times.[3] Five years later the bishop reflected 'I was consecrated on the Feast of St Athanasius, and a good priest told me even then, by way of prophecy, that I might likely have him for my pattern, and copy him in his persecutions.'[4] It is little surprise that Giffard found relief in his visitations of country missions and houses, where, he once noted, 'I can be amongst friends and relations ... with much ease and comfort.'[5]

Giffard had to deal with much poverty – the poverty of his priests, some of whom went to prison for debt, and the poverty of his flock, to whom he was generous with alms and for whom he sponsored a number of charities, including the Benevolent Society of St Patrick (established 1704) and the Aged Poor Society (1708). He managed to attract donations from wealthy Catholics and channelled some of these towards the rebuilding of Douai College and the establishment of a Mass centre in his native Wolverhampton. The bishop was wont to give away two-thirds of his money and once wrote of himself that 'one poor garret is palace, cathedral, table of audience, dining room, bedchamber and often kitchen,' though as long as he could preach 'would not change my condition for that of the greatest Cardinal.'[6]

Giffard's concerns extended far beyond the boundaries of the London District. On two occasions he found himself responsible for the Northern District, after the death of its bishop and, towards the end of his life, he had to intervene once again in that District following a dispute over fasting during which one of the factions appealed to the Vicar Apostolic of London. Giffard also kept an eye on the Western District, which had no resident bishop between 1688 and 1715. Although Bishop Ellis had resigned in 1705, it took eight years to find his successor, partly due to Giffard's own intervention in the process. He strenuously

---

[1] AAW (Archives of the Archbishop of Westminster), Paris Seminary Collection, no. 247.
[2] Brady, 151 (quoting a letter of Giffard to Cardinal Sacripanti, 7 February 1706).
[3] AAW B37, Ep. Var. 5/67 (Giffard to Mayes, 7 October 1714).
[4] Hemphill, 48-49.
[5] AAW B34, Ep. Var. 2/46 (Giffard to Mayes, 10 April 1718).
[6] AAW B34, Ep. Var. 2/48.

wanted to avoid a bishop from a religious order, reflecting an antipathy common to many secular priests, and promoted the cause of his brother, Andrew, who had, as it happened, no interest in the position. Giffard occasionally set foot in the Western District: in 1711, for example, he visited the important Catholic centre at Wardour in Wiltshire, where he met the Jesuit chaplain, Thomas Fairfax, formerly a Fellow at Magdalen. The bishop permitted the translation to the chapel of the bodies of Ss Primus and Secundus, which had been given to Lord Arundell's mother by Pope Alexander VII – an example of the splendour that could sometimes be found in the houses of wealthy, well-connected Catholics. On another occasion, he seems to have travelled as far west as Cornwall to administer the sacrament of Confirmation.

The Vicar Apostolic of the London District also had an unformulated jurisdiction over Catholics in the scattered British Colonies, parallel to the similar responsibility exercised over the Colonies by the Anglican Bishop of London. This was a confused area of canon law, assumed by the Vicariate since London was the capital of the nascent Empire but not specified in the 1688 Bull setting up the London District. The matter was only formalized by Propaganda in 1757. An early instance of Giffard's involvement in the Colonies was his approval of a regulation regarding the observance of holy days in Maryland in 1722. The following year he delegated the power to grant matrimonial dispensations and other matters to the Maryland missionaries. He also allowed them to use privileges enjoyed in England, such as the Office of St George with an octave, since they were 'part of and belonging to the London District.'[7] Responsibility over the Colonies was not a privilege that the Vicars Apostolic guarded jealously, though these distant territories could be a useful location to send troublesome priests.

Little wonder, then, that by the second decade of the eighteenth century Giffard began looking for a coadjutor. In 1715 his Vicar General, John Talbot Stonor, together with his well-connected friend, Thomas Strickland, tried to seize power by claiming that Giffard was senile and neglected his episcopal duties. The venerable bishop fought back, writing: 'I thank God I am yet strong and enjoy better health than when I was only 30 years old.'[8] However, in March 1716 Stonor gained faculties to administer the London District if Giffard was absent or unable to rule. Strickland, meanwhile,

---

[7] Burton, ii, 124.
[8] Hemphill, 54-57.

tried to act as a go-between between the Government and the Catholic community, involving both a bettering of conditions for Catholics and the swearing of an oath of allegiance to the new Hanoverian monarch, George I. When his grand plan failed, due in large part to the lack of support from his co-religionists, Strickland launched a vicious vendetta in the summer of 1719 and tried to engineer the arrest of some leading Catholics, including Giffard. It would have been the bishop's fifth period of imprisonment but he was tipped off and managed to escape.

In November 1719 Giffard sent three names to Propaganda for the office of coadjutor: Lawrence Mayes (the Roman Agent), Robert Witham (President of Douai) and Henry Howard (brother of the Duke of Norfolk and nephew of Cardinal Howard). Giffard's preference was for the latter, since he had a good pedigree and was thought to be acceptable to both seculars and regulars. Despite further interference from Stonor, Rome confirmed Howard's appointment as coadjutor in September 1720. Tragically, the bishop-elect contracted smallpox and died at the early age of thirty-three, eleven days after the proposed date of his consecration. A scion of another Catholic family, Benjamin Petre, was finally appointed in his place, although he proved to be a reluctant bishop and, much to Giffard's exasperation, repeatedly tried to resign.

Despite his many vicissitudes and the on-going accusations of Jacobitism and Jansenism (he was deemed too 'soft' on clergy suspected of this heresy), Giffard was respected as a committed pastor and a true survivor. He was highly regarded as a spiritual director, as revealed in his letters, and he was a keen adherent of the spirituality of St Francis de Sales. His last years were spent at Stafford House and then the chaplain's residence attached to the Hammersmith convent, where he was allowed some peace at the end of his long labours. He had indeed become a relic of past times – living into the reign of George II, he could still speak of his father, killed in the service of Charles I.

Giffard died at Hammersmith after a long illness on 12 March 1734, aged 91, and was buried in Old St Pancras Churchyard, his heart meanwhile being sent to the English College, Douai, for interment beneath the choir of the chapel. In 1907 the Giffard Vault at St Pancras was opened. The coffins of the two most recent burials (Bishop Douglass and Rev George Chamberlayne) were put to one side and four complete skeletons were discovered, their wooden coffins having long since perished. These were identified as Bishops Giffard and Petre together with Andrew and Anne

Giffard, the bishop's siblings. It was noted at the time that 'the facial outline of the skulls of the Giffards was markedly like the portrait of Bishop Bonaventure at St Edmund's.'[9] The bones from the four bodies were placed into one coffin and finally buried in the chapel cloister at St Edmund's, Ware, on 28 November 1907. A memorial tablet was erected to Giffard in Magdalen College chapel in 1989.

Further Reading

J. A. Williams, 'Bishops Giffard and Ellis and the Western Vicariate, 1688–1715', *Journal of Ecclesiastical History*, 15 (1964), 218–28

J. A. Williams, 'Our Patriarch: Bishop Bonaventure Giffard, 1642–1734: an introductory sketch', *Recusant History*, 26/3 (May 2003)

B. C. Foley, *Some People of the Penal times* (1991)

L. Brockliss, G. Harriss, and A. Macintyre, *Magdalen College and the Crown: Essays for the Tercentenary of the Restoration of the College, 1688* (1988)

---

[9] *The Edmundian*, December 1907, 9.

BENJAMIN PETRE

1672-1758

TITULAR BISHOP OF PRUSA (1721)
COADJUTOR TO BISHOP GIFFARD (1721-34)
VICAR APOSTOLIC OF THE LONDON DISTRICT (1734-58)

Benjamin Petre is overshadowed by his immediate predecessor and successor in the London District. He is remembered as the ever-reluctant bishop and even as something of a 'wet blanket'. However, contemporary accounts also speak of his ability and zeal, especially as coadjutor to Giffard. He was already an old man in eighteenth-century terms when he succeeded to the London District but had the foresight to appoint a young, extremely able coadjutor to help him shoulder his burdens. Moreover, despite living in semi-retirement on his family estates, his rule was marked by some important developments in the life of the English Catholic community.

The bishop belonged to a junior branch of the principal Catholic family in Essex. Indeed, it was largely because of his aristocratic pedigree and private income that he was chosen as Giffard's coadjutor in 1721. Born at the family house of Fidlers near Writtle, Chelmsford on 10 August 1672, Benjamin Petre was the eighth and youngest son of John Petre and his third wife, Frances White,[1] the granddaughter of the Earl of Portland. Her brothers, Thomas and Jerome, were members of the circle of the Duke of York (later James II). In fact, Thomas White (a Dominican) performed the marriage by proxy of the Duke and his second wife, Mary of Modena, in 1673 and after the restoration of the English Dominican Province in

---

[1] Several works list his mother as Elizabeth Pincheon, John Petre's second wife. However, D. Shanahan has shown that his father's Will, dated 18 August 1685, proves that Benjamin was the son of his third wife.

1688 became Provincial. Jerome White briefly served Mary of Modena until his death in November 1674, leaving Frances 'my jewel of diamonds given me by prince Renaldo,' who was the Duchess' uncle.[2] In later life, Petre used his mother's maiden name as his alias.

On the Petre side of his family, Benjamin could claim as his great-great-grandfather Sir William Petre, one of the sixteenth-century's great political survivors, managing to keep his head and reputation while serving Henry VIII and the very different regimes of his three children. He had also refounded Exeter College, Oxford, which was noted for its crypto-Catholicism in the early part of Elizabeth's reign. The Petre household famously employed the composer William Byrd and the martyr St John Paine.

Two of Benjamin's brothers also became priests, including Francis, later to become Vice-President of the English College, Lisbon. Benjamin himself entered Douai in 1690. He was ordained as deacon at Arras on 24 September 1695 and was a priest by 14 May 1697, when he left the college for England. His course through seminary was briefer than most, including just three-and-a-half years of theology. Years later, when he tried to resign as coadjutor bishop, he wrote that his training had made him

> entirely Ignorant not only of all Church Government and History, but of its Laws and the Decrees of Popes, of all Speculative and Positive Theology, so that thro my Ignorance I may very easily … hold controversial Propositions, and be a Jansenist or a Quenellist without knowing it.[3]

His first appointment was far from his native Essex – as chaplain to Edward Radcliffe, second Earl of Derwentwater, at Dilston, Northumberland. He gained this appointment through family connections, for the earl's sister had married a Petre. Throughout the seventeenth century, despite suffering persecution for their Catholicism, the Radcliffe family had acquired many valuable properties and estates through advantageous marriages. The jewel in the Radcliffe crown was undoubtedly the marriage of Edward to Lady Mary Tudor, natural daughter of Charles II and his mistress, the actress Moll Davies. Shortly after the marriage, the bridegroom's father, Sir Francis Radcliffe, was created Earl of Derwentwater. Lady Mary Tudor bore four children but the marriage ended in separation in 1700, partly on account of the countess' Anglican faith.

At Dilston, Petre acted as tutor to James, the eldest of the Radcliffe children, who succeeded his father as earl in 1705 and went on a tour of

---

[2] Anstruther, ii (1975), 348-349.
[3] AAW B39, Ep. Var. 7/137 (Petre to Mayes, 8 November 1722).

Europe, probably accompanied by Petre. As a grandson of Charles II, he became a zealous Jacobite and took part in the disastrous Jacobite expedition of 1708. Derwentwater was one of the heroes of the 1715 rising but, after surrendering at Preston, was impeached for treason and condemned to death. The young earl prepared himself to meet the headsman, despite petitions for his reprieve being presented by the House of Lords, individual members of the nobility and his pregnant wife, who approached the King directly. Petre was not allowed to visit the condemned man in the Tower but wrote a moving letter, assuring the earl that 'from the first moment of your imprisonment, [I] have had you constantly in my thoughts, and I have daily offered up the holy sacrifice for you.' He gave solid spiritual advice on imitating Christ not only in His life but also in His death and ended his meditation by saying:

> My Lord, these are the poor thoughts of me, that truly loves you; who is continually with you in his prayers, and who hopes to join with you for all eternity in a canticle of praise to the infinite mercies of our great God! *Misericordias, Domini in Aeternum cantabo.*[4]

Derwentwater was beheaded on Tower Hill on 24 February 1716 and quickly passed into legend. It seems that Petre continued as chaplain to the Dowager Countess at Dilston and Hatherop (Gloucestershire) until 1721, when he became a bishop and the countess moved with her family to Brussels, in order to avoid Lady Mary Tudor gaining the guardianship of her children. The fourth earl later left Petre an annual pension of £100, 'which my father intended to settle upon him.'[5] In 1732 Anne, Derwentwater's daughter, married the eighth Baron Petre. This union of the Petres and Radcliffes resulted in the translation of the bodies of the first three Earls of Derwentwater to Thorndon Hall, near Brentwood, a century and a half later in 1874.

As already mentioned, in 1721 Benjamin Petre was forced to leave his comparatively sheltered life in order to be coadjutor to Bonaventure Giffard. The appointment was the cause of considerable controversy. Giffard's Vicar General, John Talbot Stonor, had set his heart on the position before moving to the Midland District as bishop in 1715 and subsequently tried to secure the post for his great ally, the Abbé Strickland, or one of the regulars. In the process they discredited the venerable bishop, claiming that his age made him unfit and incapable to

[4] Major F.J.A. Skeet, *The Life of James Third Earl of Derwentwater and Charles Fifth Earl of Derwentwater* (1929), 104-106.
[5] Anstruther, iii (1976), 166.

continue, and a Brief of Inspection was even gained from Propaganda in March 1716, giving Stonor the right to govern should Giffard's age make him unable to carry on.

Giffard considered various names and first submitted that of Petre to Rome at the end of 1720. Petre seemed the ideal appointment since he came from relative obscurity (untarnished by political in-fighting) with a Douai training (which would make him acceptable to the seculars), membership of the Old Chapter (since 1710) and obvious connections to the Catholic nobility (the principal patrons of the clergy). Crucially, in view of Giffard's frequent debts, he had financial independence. Propaganda named Petre as coadjutor with right of succession (*cum jure successionis*) on 17 March 1721. Clement XI had no chance to confirm this, for he died two days later, but the short-lived Innocent XIII approved the appointment on 30 May, ignoring Stonor's claims that the Brief of Inspection had been compromised. Rumours were also spread, to no effect, that Petre had been the evil genius behind the rebellion of Lord Derwentwater.

Petre himself was unwilling to accept a mitre. He rightly suspected the political motives in his appointment and claimed that he was unworthy of so high an office – he even confessed to having too little theology and needing a dictionary to read Latin. However, he was duly consecrated Titular Bishop of Prusa by Giffard at Hammersmith on 11 November, exactly a year after the proposed consecration of Henry Howard. Petre remained a 'reluctant shepherd' and already by July 1722 was petitioning Propaganda and the nuncio in Brussels for a dispensation from his office. He told Mayes that 'if I am not soon freed from the obligation of exercising it by the Consent of [the pope] tis my opinion I shall soon be turned out of it for Mopishness or Madness.'[6]

The increasingly frail Giffard was keen for his coadjutor to continue, lest the resulting power vacuum was manipulated by Stonor and a regular appointed in his place. Petre's ability was widely regarded and in 1727, when it was believed that the 'Old Pretender' might be able to nominate an Englishman as Cardinal, many thought that Petre was the obvious candidate.

In 1728 Witham wrote to the Roman Agent Laurence Mayes:

> Though Bishop Petre makes great complaint of his heavy burden, and has writ strange letters of his own incapacity to the Nunce at Brussels and to

---

[6] AAW B39, Ep. Var. 7/137 (Petre to Mayes, 8 November 1722).

Propaganda, yet at the same time [he] acts with a great deal of fervour and firm zeal; instructs every Sunday to the satisfaction of all that hear him; keeps good order in all the Embassadors Chapels; keeps under him the Irish Priests and the Regulars, who thereupon make all the complaints they can about him, tho without reason.[7]

Petre continued in office but periodically threatened to resign and his lack of resolve began to irritate Giffard, who wrote to Mayes that:

Mr Prusensis [i.e. Petre], who should be a comfort to me in my old age, is often a great trouble to me, by his uneasiness and complaints and continual threats of laying all down. I have borne the burden much longer, and in much more difficult and dangerous times; I also was sufficiently sensible of the weight, yet would never think of casting it off, till I had provided for so important a concern.[8]

In London Petre resided in the house of George Jerningham, but he could often be found at his family estates in Essex, especially at his birthplace of Fidlers. Such was his retiring nature that no portrait of the bishop exists, although a painting exists of the large dog that saved the bishop's life in 1733 when he was attacked by robbers whilst saying his Office in the Lime Walk at Ingatestone Hall. Six years later, on 17 November 1739, he blessed the new chapel at Thorndon – a rare event at the time.

Petre became Vicar Apostolic on Giffard's death in 1734. He was anxious to appoint a coadjutor, to whom he could pass some of his burdens, and his choice fell on his able Vicar General, Richard Challoner. In 1738, however, Challoner was nominated President of Douai, in succession to Robert Witham. With uncharacteristic energy, Petre stepped in to block the appointment. Challoner was too important an asset for the London District to lose and if he did depart, then so too would Petre. He wrote to Mayes:

I cannot satisfy my duties without his help and counsel; nor will presume to do it. If he be forced from me by Superior Powers, for I will never give my consent to his leaving this metropolis whilst I continue in my post, in that case be pleased to send me the usual form of resignation of my duty.[9]

The bishop eventually won. Challoner was consecrated at Hammersmith on 29 January 1741. Anstruther declares this appointment as the 'one issue' on which Petre 'showed great wisdom and firmness with momentous

[7] Hemphill, 76.
[8] AAW B41, Ep. Var. 9/5.
[9] AAW B43, Ep. Var. 11/45 (Petre to Mayes, 15 May 1738).

consequences.'[10]

Petre had been a reluctant bishop for twenty years and he was now sixty-seven years old. It is perhaps understandable that he increasingly spent time in retirement in Essex and left Challoner to do the more arduous visitations. However, like his predecessors, Petre was long-lived and a number of important events occurred during his twilight years. Though Challoner did much of the work, it is unreasonable to think that Petre had no involvement in the actions of his celebrated coadjutor or the government of the District. His Pastorals, written jointly with Challoner, show a deep concern for the life of the clergy. In 1741 he wrote:

> For it is disgraceful that priests whose duty it is to lead the faithful and be shining lights in the narrow and toilsome paths of salvation, and to urge them both by word and example to care for Christian perfection, should lead a lazy life, indulge in sleep or waste their precious time in taverns, public houses, in evening drinking parties, in playing dice or cards, in profane plays, in public games, in hunting and such like things, all of which are forbidden to clerics as unbecoming of the ecclesiastical state.[11]

Indeed, when one of his London priests, John Verhuyck (alias Liddell), died in 1738, he left his estate to 'my dear wife Frances'.[12]

The Jacobite rebellion of 1745 led to renewed anti-Popery and Petre would have been saddened to witness the subsequent closing of the Catholic school at Twyford, near Winchester. It was refounded by Challoner at Standon Lordship four years later. Another challenge came in 1753, when Lord Hardwicke's Marriage Act was passed. This required all marriages to be conducted in the Church of England, with exceptions only being made for Quakers and Jews. Challoner opposed the Act, although it remained the law until 1837 and Catholics often organised a secret marriage ceremony before going to their local Anglican church.

Towards the end of Petre's rule, two important decisions were made in Rome about the English Church. The long-running question of the jurisdiction of the Vicars Apostolic over the regular clergy was resolved in 1753 with the Bull *Apostolicum Ministerium*, which favoured the authority of the Vicars Apostolic. Challoner had worked hard preparing for this document, together with Bishops Stonor and Dicconson.

Another important decision was made by Propaganda in 1757 regarding the British Colonies. In 1756 Challoner wrote to Propaganda:

---

[10] Anstruther, iii, 167.
[11] 1741 Pastoral.
[12] Anstruther, iii, 240.

All our settlements in America have been deemed subject in spirituals to the ecclesiastical Superiors here, and this has been time out of mind, even, I believe, from the time of the Archpriests. I know not the origin of this, nor have ever met with the original grant. I suppose they were looked upon as appurtenances or appendixes of the English Mission. And, after the division of this kingdom into four districts, the jurisdiction over the Catholicks in those settlements has followed the London district (as they are all reputed by the English as part of the London diocese); I suppose because London is the capital of the British Empire; and from hence are the most frequent opportunities of a proper correspondence with all those settlements. Whether the Holy See has ordered any thing in this regard, I cannot learn. But all the missioners in those settlements do now, and have, time out of mind, applied to the Vicar Apostolic here for their faculties, which is true of the padri also [the Jesuits] in Mariland and Pennsilvania; at least from the time of the Breve of Innocent XII in 1696, only that they used rather to ask for approbation, but now also for faculties.[13]

Rome replied that no formal approbation existed for this jurisdiction but granted it in 1757, and made good the acts up until that time. Thus, in name at least, Petre had jurisdiction over Maryland, Pennsylvania, Nova Scotia, New England, New York, New Jersey, Virginia, Carolina and Georgia, together with the British West Indies. Despite the vast area, Catholics were only present in large numbers in Maryland and Pennsylvania (where the Jesuits ran the missions), Montserrat and St Kitts.

Petre died at his London residence in King Street, Golden Square, on 22 December 1758, aged 86. He was buried in Old St Pancras churchyard on the Feast of the Holy Innocents (28 December), although his remains were later moved to St Edmund's, Ware (1908) to lie beside many of the other Vicars Apostolic of the London District.

Further Reading

S. Foster, 'The reluctant shepherd: the episcopal appointment of Bishop Benjamin Petre', in D. A. Bellenger, (ed.), *Opening the Scrolls* (1987),
D. Shanahan, 'Benjamin Petre, Bishop of Prusa and Vicar Apostolic of the London District, 1672–1758', *Essex Recusant*, 17 (1975), 39–41
W. V. Smith, 'Benjamin Petre and the Earl of Derwentwater', *Essex Recusant*, 18 (1976)

---

[13] Burton, ii, 126-127.

RICHARD CHALLONER

1691-1781
TITULAR BISHOP OF DEBRA (1741)
COADJUTOR TO BISHOP PETRE (1741-58)
VICAR APOSTOLIC OF THE LONDON DISTRICT (1758-81)

Petre's successor, Richard Challoner, has been called 'the greatest of the Vicars Apostolic',[1] chiefly remembered by posterity for his personal holiness and prolific production of books that served to form the English Catholic identity. Cardinal Wiseman wrote that Challoner 'has alone furnished us with a library of religious works, the privation of which would create a void, not easily to be filled up by many other men's writings … . He supplied, in fact, almost the entire range of necessary or useful religious literature for his Catholic fellow-countrymen; and that at a time when such a supply must have been truly as a boon from heaven.'[2] However, it would be misleading to distinguish Challoner the writer from Challoner the bishop for, as Richard Luckett has noted, 'to an extraordinary extent writing itself was the mode of his ministry, and … if it had not been he could never have accomplished what he achieved in his episcopate.'[3]

Richard Challoner was born at Chiddingly, seven miles outside Lewes, Sussex, on 29 September 1691. He was the only son of Richard Challoner, a wine cooper and 'a rigid Dissenter', and his wife Grace Willard. It seems that he only fully encountered the Catholic Faith after his father's death, when Mrs Challoner gained employment in the household of a local recusant landowner, Sir John Gage, at Firle. Employment in such a centre of popery suggests that Mrs Challoner was herself a Catholic. Mother and

---

[1] D. Mathew, *Catholicism in England 1535-1935* (1938), 133-134.
[2] Burton, ii, 280.
[3] E. Duffy (ed.), *Challoner and His Church* (1981), 78.

son later moved to another Catholic household, Warkworth Manor in Northamptonshire, which was the home of the widowed Lady Anastasia Holman, daughter of the martyred Viscount Stafford. The chaplain at Warkworth was John Gother, a highly respected priest and author of the popular *Papist Misrepresented and Represented* (1685) and other works. Gother is normally described as instructing and receiving Challoner into the Church in 1704, when he was aged thirteen, although given the possible Catholicism of Mrs Challoner he may have prepared the boy for his First Communion and Confirmation. Shortly afterwards Gother and Lady Anastasia recommended Challoner for a scholarship at the English College, Douai. In the same year Gother was appointed President of the English College, Lisbon, and also recommended as Bishop Ellis' successor in the Western District, but he died at sea on his way to Portugal. His memory continued to exert a strong influence on Challoner throughout his long life.

Challoner arrived at Douai on 29 July 1705, little realising that he would remain there for a quarter of a century. For reasons of security he used his mother's maiden name 'Willard' as an alias. The college was proud of its tradition and the last martyrs were still within living memory. However, at the beginning of the eighteenth century the college was in decline, affected by financial difficulties, decreasing numbers and the War of the Spanish Succession, which placed England against France. In 1708 Douai was besieged by the Allies and most of the English students moved to Lille for several months. The town was besieged by the French four years later, the students finding sanctuary this time in Arras. The President, Edward Paston, described as 'excessively grave, too starch'd and reserved,'[4] was a failed reformer who had tried to bring Douai into line with the Sulpician model but had encountered opposition on every side. His Presidency was dominated by accusations of Jansenism, directed in particular against the theologian, Edward Hawarden, although the college was cleared after careful investigation.

Little is known of the student Challoner, though his election as Professor of Poetry and Rhetoric (1710) and Professor of Philosophy (1712) testify to his academic abilities. On 16 July 1714 Challoner, together with the other professors, made a declaration in support of Clement XI's Bull *Unigenitus*, which condemned Jansenism. Dr Paston, who was keen to stress the college's orthodoxy, died a few days later and was eventually

---

[4] Ibid., 3.

succeeded by Robert Witham, under whom Douai's fortunes improved.

In 1716 Challoner was ordained priest by the Bishop of Tournai and continued teaching at the college. Already he stood out from his peers; in a letter to the Roman Agent, Witham declared that 'Mr Willard alias Challoner ye first Master of Philosophy is a man of extraordinary parts and I think of extraordinary virtue, and the other masters do's well enough'.[5] In 1718 Challoner became Prefect of Studies and the following year took the degree of Bachelor and Licentiate in Theology, defending the proposition 'that no Thomist could deny the Pope to be infallible.' This caused controversy with the Bishop of Arras and the *Rector Magnificus* of the university, since the topic offended Gallican sympathies. In 1720 Challoner was appointed Professor of Theology and Vice-President to Robert Witham. The following year he was unsuccessful in securing the chair of catechetics at the university. In 1727 he took his Doctorate.

In 1730 Challoner returned to the English Mission and worked among the poor in London, combining his pastoral work with the prolific production of books. By the end of his life he could claim a bibliography of over sixty titles. As already mentioned, writing was an important tool of his ministry and it was thus fitting that his nickname at Douai, in his younger days, was 'Book'. He was not a writer of great genius or originality, but always accessible and lucid; his writings were, in the words of Eamon Duffy, 'the work of a first-rate jobbing carpenter in command of his tools but disapproving of imaginative frills.'[6]

Challoner published two works while still at Douai, including *Think Well On't, or, Reflections on the Great Truths of the Christian Religion for Every Day in the Month* (1728). In the 1730s he produced a number of polemical works that appealed to Protestants from their own version of the Bible and their own authorities; these works included *The Unerring Authority of the Catholic Church* (1732), *A Short History of the First Beginning and Progress of the Protestant Religion* (1733) and *The Touchstone of the New Religion (1734)*. His debt to John Gother is revealed in a new edition Challoner prepared of *An Essay on the Change and Choice of Religion*, entitled *The Sincere Christian's Guide in the Choice of Religion* (1734). In 1736 he became 'controversial writer' to the Old Chapter. He also managed to translate into English Thomas à Kempis' *Imitation of Christ* (1737) and St Augustine's *Confessions* (1739).

---

[5] AAW B38, Ep. Var. 6/37 (Witham to Mayes, 8 May 1716).
[6] Duffy, op. cit., 11.

By 1737 Challoner was acting as Petre's Vicar General. Well-read in theology, fluent in Latin and able to deal with even the most difficult clergy, Challoner made up for some of Petre's weaknesses. The following year he was appointed President of Douai, but Petre resisted and asked that Challoner be appointed as his coadjutor. Ever true to character, Petre threatened to resign if his Vicar General was moved to Douai. The bishop got his way and on 29 January 1741, the Feast of St Francis de Sales, Challoner was consecrated Titular Bishop of Debra at the Hammersmith convent.

While Petre lived in obscurity at Fidlers in Essex, Challoner resided in the heart of London, cared for by Mrs Hanne, his housekeeper. He lived variously at Devonshire Street, Red Lion Street, Lamb's Conduit Street and finally Gloucester Street, Queen Square. Challoner's first biographer, James Barnard, recorded the regular pattern of his daily life as bishop for fifty years:

Summer and winter he rose at six; and giving his first thoughts to God, and employing them in pious ejaculatory prayers till he was dressed; he then employed a whole hour in Meditation, on one or other of the pious subjects set down in his Meditations ... And this was succeeded by his immediate preparation for, and celebration of the Eucharistic Sacrifice, which he always began at eight o clock ; but on Sundays and Holydays he began it at nine o clock, and always made it his practice on those days to preach on some Text contained in the Gospel of the day. This being finished and his usual prayers said, to return thanks to God for his having partaken of the precious body and blood of His Son in this divine Sacrament; if it was not a Fast day he took his breakfast at nine o clock; after which he recited with great recollection, attention and devotion, the little hours of the Divine Office ... After which he was ready to attend to any business concerning which any person might want to apply to him. But if no one wanted him, he then sat down to write something for the instruction and edification of his flock, or to answer Letters which he had received from different parts ... When tired with writing he would take a few turns backward and forward in his apartments; then take some pious book to read; say some prayers; or sitting in his chair contemplate on some pious subject; and then return again to his writing. At one o clock he used to say the evening part of the Divine Office; which finished, he used either to say some vocal prayers or else employ himself in Meditation till two; when, with his Chaplains, he sat down to dinner; at which time he unbent a little his mind from that close application; and was always very cheerful and agreeable; discoursing with them upon different subjects and endeavouring to inspire them likewise with a spirit of Christian cheerfulness.

Dinner being finished, and about half an hour's more conversation; if the weather was fine, or permitted it, he would usually take one of his Chaplains with him, either to go and visit some friend, or to take a walk in the fields for the benefit of the air. But he made it his invariable practice, before ever he quitted his house, to say a short prayer to beg that the protection and the blessing of God might attend him in his excursion. His time of returning home was between five and six o clock, when he was ready to attend those who wanted him: and from thence till supper-time, which was at nine o clock, he employed his time in giving spiritual advice to those who applied to him, in reading, Meditation, and saying the Divine Office, and in doing what other business he had in hand. After supper and a little conversation, he said his prayers, examined his conscience concerning the manner in which he had discharged the duties of that day; ... resigned himself into the hands of God, and then composed himself to rest under His divine protection.[7]

In London, the splendour of continental Catholicism could be tasted at the embassy chapels, many of which kept fine musical establishments. However, there were no other church buildings and Challoner found himself ministering in some unlikely places. Milner recalled hearing him preach in a cock-pit, possibly in Drury Lane. As part of the *cultus* of Challoner, the story was often told of how he could frequently be found at the Ship Tavern:

Bishop Challoner used to meet a few of his persecuted flock at a public-house in Gate Street, Lincoln's Inn Fields, hiring the apartment by the year as a club-room, and on the night of the meeting a sturdy Irishman at the door to admit none but the faithful, with the appointed watchword; how the same venerable prelate, pitifully bowed down by circumstances under cruel penal laws, came in coloured clothes, and preached a comfortable exhortation, much like his own series of meditations, and to save appearances, in case the Philistines should break in, with a pint of porter before him, which the good Bishop never tasted, but which was drunk reverently by one or other of the assembly as "the Bishop's beer."[8]

It was assumed that these meetings were of Freemasons and those concerned found it convenient not to deny the rumour. One of the employees of the 'Ship', James Archer, was impressed by the gatherings and came to the notice of Challoner, who duly sent him off to Douai to

---

[7] J. Barnard, *The Life of the Venerable and Right Reverend Richard Challoner, D.D.* (1784), 130-133.
[8] J. Dunford, *History of the Sardinian Chapel, Lincoln's Inn Fields* (1905), 41 (quoting Fr Price's *Sick Calls* of 1845).

study for the priesthood. He later became Vicar General of the London District and received an honorary Doctorate of Divinity from Gregory XVI. Such anecdotes of secret services in pubs and cockpits, however, can give a misleading impression of Georgian Catholicism. Eamon Duffy has noted that pub sermons, which were intended for poor Catholics, were 'dictated partly by the need to avoid embarrassing the Ambassadors, partly by lack of space in the chapels, partly by habit.'[9] These 'secret' activities were well-known to the authorities, who seldom acted against them.

In 1741 Challoner started an extensive Visitation of the London District and confirmed many hundreds of candidates. Over his long episcopate, he tried to encourage regularity in the life of clergy and criticised the laxity of the seminaries, especially the colleges at Lisbon and Rome. Drunkenness and worldliness were common problems and part of Challoner's solution was the introduction of weekly conferences for his clergy, which he hoped would 'cultivate in their Souls an Ecclesiastical Spirit.' He drew up a number of 'Regulations', stressing the importance of mental prayer, an annual retreat and the staying at home in the evening so that 'we may be found by those who shall want us for the sick; or be in the way for such as shall come for Instructions etc.' He recommended love for the poor and the avoidance of 'all unbecoming levity, and all familiarity with persons of the other sex.'[10]

In the aftermath of the 1745 Jacobite rebellion there was an eruption of 'No Popery' and one of the most notable casualties was the Catholic school at Twyford, near Winchester, which was dissolved. However, in 1749, this was refounded by Challoner at Standon Lordship, Hertfordshire. This moved to Hare Street in 1767 and then to Old Hall Green two years later, where it formed the base for St Edmund's after the collegians were expelled from Douai in 1794. Challoner realised the great need for schools in England and supported the founding of one at Betley in Shropshire in 1761, which moved to Sedgley Park, near Wolverhampton, in 1763. By 1771 there were a hundred pupils. In London he founded schools for boys and girls and in 1764 set up the 'Society for Educating Poor Catholic Children'.

Challoner tried to spend time every day writing pamphlets and books for the instruction of his flock and for all persons of good will. There were further works of controversy, such as *The Grounds of the Old Religion*

---

[9] Duffy, op. cit., 8.
[10] Ibid., 17.

(1742), which attacked Anglican orders, *A Letter to a Friend Concerning the Infallibility of the Church of Christ (1743)* and *A Caveat Against the Methodists, showing how unsafe it is for any Christian to join himself to their Society, or to adhere to their Teachers* (1760).

In 1740 Challoner first published a collection of English prayers and devotions in *The Garden of the Soul*. Seven editions were brought out in seventeen years. Many have used the term '*Garden of the Soul* Catholic' to distinguish the 'Old Catholics' from the less restrained, Ultramontane Catholics of the 'Second Spring'. However, despite this confusing nomenclature, the *Garden of the Soul* remained a favourite with the English Catholic community until the early twentieth century, although later editions were significantly different from Challoner's original. Many of the elegant prayers found in the *Garden of the Soul* were used in the official *Manual of Prayers for Congregational Use*, first prescribed by the English and Welsh Hierarchy in 1886.

A short book of 35 pages, *An Abridgement of Christian Doctrine* (1759), proved to be one of Challoner's most widely used. It consisted of short questions and answers regarding the essentials of the Catholic Faith and was intended for the instruction of children. Challoner drew upon Henry Turberville's *Abridgement of Christian Doctrine* (c. 1649), sometimes known as the *Douai Catechism*, and the earlier catechisms of St Peter Canisius and St Robert Bellarmine. Though hardly original in concept, Challoner's *Abridgement* went through many editions and eventually formed the basis of the celebrated *Penny Catechism*, first produced by the Catholic Truth Society in 1889 and still in print. Another highly popular book was *Meditations for every Day in the Year* (1754), an extended version of *Think Well On't*.

Challoner produced some important hagiographical works. His *Wonders of God in the Wilderness* (1755) set forth the lives of the Desert Fathers and was heavily based on the scholarship of the Bollandists, the group of ecclesiastical historians who produced the great series of hagiography, the *Acta Sanctorum*. Bishop Ullathorne later revealed that this was one of his favourite books while at Downside, feeding 'my still romantic imagination as well as my moral sense.'[11] However, Challoner was particularly concerned with local models of sanctity. His most famous collection was *Memoirs of Missionary Priests* (1741-42), largely drawn from the transcripts made by Alban Butler of the papers kept at Douai. The work remains

---

[11] W. B. Ullathorne, *The Devil is a Jackass*, ed. L. Madigan (1995), 37.

an indispensable source for the Elizabethan and Stuart periods and was crucial in raising the profile of the English Martyrs. Challoner was careful to avoid a polemical style and stated in the Preface:

> The following sheets are presented to the reader as a supplement to English history, which appeared to the publisher, by so much the more wanting, by how much the less, the trials and executions of catholics, on religious accounts, have been taken notice of by the generality of English historians: and which, he flattered himself, would not be disagreeable to the lovers of history, of what persuasion soever they might be in matters of religion: for if men of all persuasions read with pleasure the history of the lives and deaths, even of the most notorious malefactors; not that they are delighted with their crimes, but because they there meet with an agreeable scene of stories unknown before and often discover a surprizing boldness and bravery in their enterprizes; how much more may it be expected, that every generous English soul should be pleased to find in the following memoirs, so much fortitude and courage, joined with so much meekness, modesty and humility, in the lives and deaths of so many of his countrymen, who have died for no other crime but their conscience.[12]

He was keen to revive the memory of the pre-Reformation British saints. *Britannia Sancta* (1745) presented some four hundred of these, although the expense of the two-volume edition meant that it never caught the popular imagination. A more accessible British martyrology, *A Memorial of Ancient British Piety*, was published in 1761. Challoner also petitioned Rome to establish a local Calendar of English saints for use in the liturgy. In 1749, with the help of the Cardinal Duke of York, the Congregation of Rites restored the feast of St Edmund, King and Martyr, and elevated certain feasts already observed in the Universal Calendar (Ss Augustine of Canterbury, Edward the Confessor, George, Thomas of Canterbury and Ursula) to a higher rank. Further English feasts were restored by the Congregation in 1754 and 1774.

Challoner's all-consuming work was his revision of the original Douai-Rheims Bible, completed in 1750 with the help of the Carmelite, Francis Blyth. This modernized translation of the Clementine Vulgate would alone have made Challoner famous and became the standard English edition of the Bible for Catholics up until the mid-twentieth century.

Shortly before Petre's death in 1758, Propaganda had formally granted the jurisdiction of the British colonies to the London Vicar Apostolic. It was a duty that could hardly be carried out, since personnel and money

---

[12] R. Challoner, *Memoirs of the Missionary Priests* (1843), i, 1.

were limited and a pastoral visit was impractical. Moreover, the Empire was quickly growing: the Seven Years' War increased the number of colonies, which now included Canada. On 20 May 1763 Challoner wrote to Bishop Stonor:

> Under whose jurisdiction as to spirituals are these new acquisitions to be? I suppose the diocese of Quebec is out of the question, because it has its own chapter, and capitular vicars. But the difficulty is chiefly about the islands of Grenados and Grenadillos, Dominica etc where the French had divers priests, who, tis supposed, will continue there for the assistance of the inhabitants, and must have a succession kept up, for the keeping up the Catholic religion which by the Articles they are allowed to maintain. We are not ambitious of any new burden in this kind; being so little able to discharge that we have already: but we expect that some will be soon applying to us for faculties in those parts and therefore should be glad to be directed what we are to do.[13]

It was a confused situation with a frequent overlapping of jurisdictions: regular clergy would look to their own Superior while priests working in Barbados and St Kitts looked to the Apostolic Prefect of the Danish Islands, who was formally given jurisdiction in March 1776. Another inconsistency was that Challoner's nominal jurisdiction over the (former) American colonies continued after the Declaration of Independence. Burton points out that 'this feeble old man, living his retired life in an obscure London street' exercised a jurisdiction that 'remained the only remnant of authority in the hands of an Englishman that was still recognized in America.'[14]

On 24 August 1759 Challoner consecrated as his coadjutor James Robert Talbot, an alumnus of Twyford and Douai and the brother both of a future Earl of Shrewsbury and a Vicar Apostolic of the Midland District. Challoner, now in his late sixties and weakening in health, was glad to have a young energetic assistant, who could make visitations in the more remote corners of the London District.

Although, thanks to the Enlightenment and the demise of Jacobitism, conditions grew increasingly favourable for the repeal of the penal laws, the second half of Challoner's episcopate saw a final outburst of persecution. Barnard wrote that between 1765 and 1772

> scarce a week passed but Dr. Challoner had some fresh account brought to him, either of some Priest being arrested, some steps that were taken by the Informer, in carrying on his Persecution against some one or other

---

[13] Burton, ii, 132.
[14] Ibid., 148.

of those whom he had under Bail: some appearance to be put in and new Bail given, or some trial to come on: or else of his endeavouring to steal incog, into some of the Chapels, that he might lay a new information against the priests, or of his going accompanied with a number of others of his crew, and some constables, to the chapel doors, and endeavouring to force his way in; which frequently obliged those who were there present, to keep the doors close shut, and thereby hindered several Catholics from attending the Divine Worship on those days.[15]

The London clergy were particularly victimized by the informer, William Payne, known as the 'Protestant Carpenter'. Since, according to the 1699 'Act for further preventing the growth of Popery', such characters were rewarded with £100 for their information, it could be a lucrative business. In 1767 Payne succeeded in taking an Irish priest, John Baptist Maloney, to court on account of his priesthood; the sentence of life imprisonment was later commuted to banishment. Challoner himself was Payne's next target, together with four priests and a schoolmaster, although charges were dropped when it was discovered that Payne had forged several documents. He was more successful in bringing another group of four priests to court in 1767. However the judge, Lord Mansfield, had several important Catholic friends and interpreted the 1699 Act to the disadvantage of the informer – proof had to be given both of the defendant's ordination and of the fact that he had acted as a priest. In 1771 Payne indicted Bishop Talbot for 'exercising part of the office or function of a Popish bishop,' together with Richard Dillon and John Fuller, priests of Moorfields. They were acquitted due to the inconsistency of the evidence brought against them, although this result was by no means guaranteed.

Seven years after the trial of Challoner's coadjutor, the first Catholic Relief Act (1778) was passed. This was brought about by political expediency: the need to raise Catholic troops for the American War of Independence. When Sir John Dalrymple visited Challoner to discuss a possible Relief Bill, he found him 'old and timid and using twenty difficulties.' Prominent laymen such as the ninth Lord Petre led the negotiations, and the Catholic Committee was formed, which prepared an *Address* to the King. The Vicars Apostolic were hardly involved; the lawyer, William Sheldon, opposed 'any application to the clergy in temporal matters, the English Roman Catholic Gentlemen being quite able to judge and act for themselves in these affairs,' approving an oath of loyalty that seemed to deny the temporal jurisdiction of the Pope. But

---

[15] Barnard, op. cit., 160.

Challoner was confident it contained no error.

The 1778 Relief Act allowed Catholics to join the Army and own and inherit property. It also abolished the £100 reward for informers against Catholic priests and schoolmasters. Despite its limited nature, there was much opposition to the Act. At the beginning of 1780 John Wesley wrote of 'chains forging at the anvil of Rome for the rising generation' and the 'purple power of Rome advancing by hasty strides to overspread this once happy nation.'[16] The Protestant Association campaigned for the repeal of the new law and, in June, the most serious English riots of the century broke out, led by Lord George Gordon. These 'Gordon Riots' were one of the most agressive displays of English anti-popery and were described a hundred years later by the Jesuit historian, William Amhurst, as 'the most violent and destructive eruption of a volcano which is not yet extinct.'[17]

Challoner himself became the target of the mob's fury. Milner later testified that 'it is known to have been their intention to have chaired him in derision, and thus to carry about, in a kind of mock triumph, this peaceable and venerable old man upon their frantic expeditions. How this barbarous ceremony would have ended God only knows.'[18] Luckily for the bishop, the crowd could not find his lodging in Gloucester Street and shortly afterwards he moved to the safety of rural Finchley, where he was the guest of his friend, the woollen merchant William Mawhood. In the meantime 285 people lost their lives; the chapels at Moorfields and Lincoln's Inn Fields were destroyed; Newgate prison was set alight and over a thousand prisoners freed, and London illumined by the fire at Mr Langdale's distillery on Holborn Hill. Even Challoner's refuge at Finchley was twice searched, although the presence of a Book of Common Prayer misled the hunters and the household was left untouched.

Challoner returned to 25 Gloucester Street once the rioters' blue cockades and flags had disappeared from the streets, but he was badly shaken by the experience and saddened to see so much of Catholic London in tatters. He suffered a stroke on 10 January 1781 at his home. Four days later James Peter Coughlan, publisher of the *Laity's Directory*, wrote to George Hay, Vicar Apostolic of the Scottish Lowland District:

> You will have heard of our great loss in the death of the venerable Bishop Challoner, an event indeed to be expected by the course of years (now in his ninetieth year) but from his being perfect in his faculties to the last

---

[16] Burton, ii, 217 (quoting Wesley's *Defence of the Protestant Association*).
[17] W. Amhurst, *The History of Catholic Emancipation* (1886) i, 136.
[18] Burton, ii, 242-243.

might have given us hopes of having him much longer with us. At dinner on Wednesday he was first struck in his right arm which fell back. He had scarce time to say the words "I am struck" when his head fell also on his right shoulder and faintly uttered the word: palsy. Mr Bolton [one of his chaplains], rising, said Lord bless me, Sir, you are very bad. To which he assented by a small noise and very little motion of his head ... He remained till the last sensible and perfect tho' speechless and expired 'tween 12 and one o'clock last Friday morning [12 January 1781]. He is much regretted and Bishop Talbot scarce could say mass for him on Friday morning. He is left executor, but has not yet determined when or where he is to be buried.[19]

His last word had been 'Charity', as he indicated to Bolton some money in his pocket given to him that morning for the benefit of the poor.

Challoner was buried at Milton, Berkshire, in the vault of the Catholic Barrett family, with whom he was friendly. The Anglican vicar wrote in his register: 'Anno Domini 1781, January 22. Buried the Reverend Richard Challoner, a Popish Priest and Titular Bishop of London and Salisbury [sic], a very pious and good man, of great learning and extensive abilities.'[20] Just over seventy years later, a new Catholic church was built in nearby Abingdon and space was reserved for the body of Challoner, where it might receive the greater veneration of the faithful. However, the Barretts were reluctant to permit the translation of the bishop's remains. Eventually in 1940 an agreement was made with Cardinal Hinsley to move the body to Westminster Cathedral in order to encourage the cause for Challoner's beatification. War intervened and it was only on 1 May 1946 that the 'greatest of the Vicars Apostolic' returned to London, with typical discretion, and was buried in the chapel of Ss Gregory and Augustine at Westminster Cathedral. It was Low Week and most of the Hierarchy were present at the identification of his body and subsequent Requiem. Cardinal Griffin approved a prayer for Challoner's beatification:

O God who made your servant Richard a true and faithful pastor of your little flock in England, raise him, we beseech you, to the altars of thy Church, that we who have been taught by his word and example may invoke his name in heaven, for the return of our country to belief in the Gospel, and to the unity of all Christians in the one Church of Jesus Christ. We ask this through the same Christ our Lord.

---

[19] F. Blom et al. (eds), *The Correspondence of James Peter Coghlan (1731-1800)* (CRS Records Series vol. 80, 2007), 102.
[20] Burton, ii, 279.

The cause for Challoner's beatification, despite much initial enthusiasm, never fully got off the ground and was overshadowed by the on-going cause of the English Martyrs. However, when Pope John Paul II celebrated Mass at Westminster Cathedral on 28 May 1982, Challoner received, to the applause of the congregation, an honoured mention at the end of the homily:

> In this England of fair and generous minds, no one will begrudge the Catholic community pride in its own history. So I speak last of another Christian name, less famous but no less deserving honour. Bishop Richard Challoner guided the Catholics of this London District in the eighteenth century, at what seemed the lowest point of their fortunes. They were few. It seemed they might well not survive. Yet Bishop Challoner bravely raised his voice to prophesy a better future for his people. And now, two centuries later, I am privileged to stand here and to speak to you, in no triumphal spirit, but as a friend, grateful for your kind welcome and full of love for all of you. Bishop Challoner's courage may remind all of us where the seeds of courage lie, where the confidence of renewal comes from. It is through water and the Holy Spirit that a New People is born, whatever the darkness of the time.

Further Reading

J. Barnard, *Life of the Venerable and Right Reverend Richard Challoner, D.D., bishop of Debra* (1784)

E. H. Burton, *The Life and Times of Bishop Challoner, 1691–1781*, 2 vols (1909)

E. Duffy, (ed.), *Challoner and his Church: a Catholic bishop in Georgian England* (1981)

D. Gwynn, *Bishop Challoner* (1946)

M. Trappes-Lomax, *Bishop Challoner* (1947)

L. E. Whatmore, 'The Birthplace and Parentage of Bishop Challoner: an Enquiry', *Recusant History*, 12 (1973–4), 254–60

JAMES ROBERT TALBOT

1726-90
TITULAR BISHOP OF BIRTHA (1759)
COADJUTOR TO BISHOP CHALLONER (1759-81)
VICAR APOSTOLIC OF THE LONDON DISTRICT (1781-90)

Bishop Challoner died at a time of crisis for the Catholic community and his successor, Bishop Talbot, had to face many troublesome issues, including the aftermath of the Gordon Riots and the rise of Cisalpinism. It is no surprise that the new Vicar Apostolic referred to his new burden as one that 'would weigh down the shoulders even of an angel, which we feel ourselves to be wholly incapable of bearing.'[1] These were not empty words for, as Bernard Ward noted, 'notwithstanding the holiness of his private life, Dr Talbot was never qualified either by temperament or by natural gifts to hold a position which involved taking the lead in public action, still less so at a time of difficulty, when vigorous measures were called for.'[2]

James Robert Talbot was born on 28 June 1726 at Shrewsbury House, Isleworth, Middlesex, the fourth son of the Honourable George Talbot and Mary, the daughter of the fourth Viscount FitzWilliam of Merrion. The future bishop had three sisters and five brothers, including George, who became fourteenth Earl of Shrewsbury, and Thomas, the future Vicar Apostolic of the Midland District. He was also related to Bishop Stonor of the Midland District.

Talbot was educated at the Catholic school of Twyford, near Winchester, from which he entered the English College, Douai on 1 June 1738. Before beginning the study of theology, he left Douai to make the Grand Tour

---

[1] *Dawn*, i, 21.
[2] Ibid., 187.

together with his brother, Thomas, and their mentor, Alban Butler, author of the famous *Lives of the Saints*. Returning to the college in November 1748, James was ordained priest at Cambrai on 19 December 1750. He lingered on at Douai teaching philosophy and theology, and briefly acted as founding President of the new preparatory school at nearby Esquerchin. The house had been bought by Talbot as a gift for the college and was used also as a summer residence by Douai students.

In 1755, after completing his licentiate in theology, Talbot returned to England. Despite his youth and lack of pastoral experience, he was already tipped to be a bishop, partly due to his family background, and efforts were made to appoint him as coadjutor to the Western and Midland Districts. However it was Challoner who eventually gained his assistance in 1759. Talbot was consecrated as Titular Bishop of Birtha at Hammersmith on 24 August 1759. Given the difficulty of having several bishops under one roof due to the penal laws, new bishops were normally consecrated by a bishop assisted by two priests but Talbot's consecration was unusual in that Challoner was assisted by one other bishop, Francis Petre of the Northern District.

The new coadjutor was only 33 but his youthful energy was badly needed by Challoner, who had recently been taken seriously ill and increasingly focussed his concerns on his London flock and his many literary projects. Talbot, meanwhile, travelled around the District and tried to visit each mission once a year. He became known as an able preacher although unwilling to have too high a profile, which perhaps explains why there is no known portrait of him.

Such discretion was appropriate, for the days of persecution were not yet over. The clergy of the London District had for some years been harassed by an anti-Catholic informer, William Payne, who specialised in bringing priests to court and closing down Mass centres. In 1768 Talbot himself was indicted for saying Mass but was acquitted on a technicality. In 1771 Talbot was brought to trial at the Old Bailey, together with two priests, Richard Dillon and John Fuller. The three clerics were saved by Payne's clumsiness, especially in getting their names wrong on three occasions and in the inconsistency of the witnesses, but the threat was very real. The accused were acquitted by the Lord Chief Justice, William Murray, later first Earl of Mansfield, since no evidence was presented concerning their Ordination. Shortly afterwards, John Baptist Maloney, an Irish priest who had already suffered four years imprisonment, had his sentence commuted to banishment. Recusant hagiography remembers Talbot as the last Confessor of the Faith in Penal England.

Talbot was highly interested in the education of Catholics. Just as he had enabled the foundation of the school at Esquerchin as a young professor, so as coadjutor he was instrumental in the establishment of the Old Hall Green Academy (1769). This was a continuation of the Catholic school run by the secular clergy and secretly opened in 1662 at Silkstead, Hampshire. It was subsequently moved to Twyford (1685), where it had been attended by Talbot himself, and then Standon Lordship, Hertfordshire (1749). After a brief time at Hare Street, near what is now the Archbishop of Westminster's country residence, the school moved to Old Hall Green, where Talbot rented and then bought a house in 1771.

Care still had to be exercised; in March 1775 Talbot received an anonymous letter, stating that 'a Friend to the Roman Catholicks begs to inform your Lordship that the number of Roman Catholick Schools which of late have been set up in this nation have given cause of complaint.' It went on to recommend that the Bishop 'would take care of yourself not only in the country, but also in London where diligent search will soon be made for you.'[3]

Talbot succeeded Challoner as Vicar Apostolic of the London District in January 1781. In addition to the Embassies, Talbot inherited just three Catholic chapels in London – Moorfields, Virginia Street (now Commercial Road) and Bermondsey. He would witness the building of two important new churches, directly under the control of the Vicar Apostolic: Warwick Street (which had originated as the chapel of the Bavarian Embassy) and St George's Fields (now St George's Cathedral, Southwark). He continued his concern with education, enlarging the school at Old Hall Green and keeping an eye on his *alma mater*, the English College, Douai, viewing with especial concern the financial imprudence and modernizing policies of the President, William Gibson.

For the first four years of his rule, Talbot lived in Little James Street, Bedford Square, before moving to the peace of the Hammersmith convent in 1785. He was popularly known as 'Good Bishop Talbot' on account of his love for the poor. After the death of his brother, the Earl, in 1787, much of the money he inherited was given to charity. In his funeral oration, Milner said:

When have you observed in him the least symptom of vanity or self-

---

[3] *The Edmundian*, July 1901, 182.

importance on the score of his high descent and illustrious connections? When have you heard a word escape him to remind you that you were speaking to the brother of the first Earl of the land? ... At no time did he affect to pass for anything beyond a poor ecclesiastic. Every one knows that his delight was to be surrounded by his clergy and the poor, and that he more readily and more frequently would stoop into the sordid dwellings of the necessitous to administer to them comfort and assistance, corporal and spiritual, than enter into palaces of the great to taste their dainties and participate of their distinctions. With shame to myself must I add that on different occasions of my attending him on his journeys and elsewhere, I have seen him cheerfully and without complaint put up with inconveniences that to me appeared intolerable.[4]

Talbot's greatest challenge was the Catholic Committee, founded in 1782 and consisting of prominent laymen, such as Lord Petre, Sir John Throckmorton and Charles Butler, who campaigned for further liberties following the Catholic Relief Act of 1778. The Committee's key concern was to prove that English Catholics were loyal as citizens and to repudiate the charges of treason and superstition historically brought against them. They recognised the spiritual supremacy of the Pope but jealously guarded the rights and privileges of the local Church and clergy; they also denied that Rome had any temporal authority over governments. The Committee was prepared to compromise if it meant that Catholicism was recognised as 'mainstream'. Their chief mastermind was Joseph Berington, who had been dismissed from his professorship at Douai in 1771 for attacking scholasticism. His writings in the closing years of the eighteenth century repeated the key Cisalpine themes: he minimised those aspects of Catholicism that Protestants found most objectionable and presented the Pope merely as head of the executive. Clerical celibacy was attacked, ecumenical schools proposed and the vernacular liturgy suggested. Furthermore, the Committee advocated the replacement of the Vicars Apostolic by Bishops-in-Ordinary, thereby lessening anti-Catholic prejudice since diocesan bishops would rule in their own name and not in the name of the Pope.

In 1788 Talbot was elected onto the Catholic Committee (together with Bishop Berington) and hoped that his presence would be one of moderation. Negotiations were being held with the Prime Minister, William Pitt, for a Relief Bill that would benefit both Protestant Dissenters and Catholics. The waters were tested when Pitt consulted

---

[4] *Dawn*, i, 187.

the leading Catholic universities on the continent over the deposing and dispensing powers of the Pope. The Anglican Lord Stanhope suggested that the Catholics should produce an exposition of their principles, as the Dissenters had done, and himself quickly produced the infamous *Declaration and Protestation of the English Catholics*. The purpose of this document was conciliation, but it contained the assertion that 'we acknowledge no infallibility in the Pope, and we neither apprehend nor believe that our disobedience to any such orders or decrees (should any be given or made) could subject us to any punishment whatever.'

Despite misgivings, Talbot signed the *Protestation* and encouraged the clergy to follow his lead at a meeting held at Old Slaughter's Coffee House. However, in June 1789 an oath was proposed for inclusion in the Relief Bill, which introduced elements not contained in the earlier *Protestation*. It limited the temporal power of the Pope, denying him 'any spiritual power or jurisdiction ... that can directly or indirectly interfere ... with the constitution of the kingdom.' The oath went on to describe as 'impious and heretical' that 'damnable Doctrine and Position that Princes excommunicated by the Pope or by Authority of the see of Rome, may be deposed or murdered by their subjects or any other persons whomsoever'. Most controversially, Catholics taking the oath were referred to as 'Protesting Catholic Dissenters,' to distinguish them from the 'Papists' who refused to take it.

On 21 October 1789 the Vicars Apostolic met at Hammersmith and signed a joint Encyclical Letter condemning the oath, without meeting with the Committee or explaining their opposition. The closing words of the document expressed a new confidence amongst the bishops: 'to these determinations, therefore, we require your submission.' The Committee feared this would endanger negotiations with the Government and asked for a delay in the letter's publication. The indecisive Talbot brothers hesitated and the letter was never issued in the London and Midland Districts. Meanwhile, the Committee produced the first of the *Blue Books* justifying their actions.

By this time, Talbot was visibly ailing. He suffered failing memory and his speech had become indistinct after the loss of many of his teeth. He died at Hammersmith on 26 January 1790, aged 64, declaring on his deathbed that if he recovered he would take more decisive measures against the Catholic Committee. He was buried in the Baynard vault in the parish church of St Paul at Hammersmith. Although the burial service itself was performed by a clergyman of the Established Church, the Catholic rites had been read beforehand. A Solemn Requiem was celebrated at each of the Embassy chapels and the bishop left £1 to each priest of the London District so that Masses could be offered for the suffrage of his soul.

Following the translation of the bodies of three of the Vicars Apostolic from Moorfields to St Edmund's, it was thought appropriate that Talbot, the founder of the Old Hall Green Academy, should also join them. Thus, on 24 April 1901, Bishop Talbot's body was brought from Hammersmith and re-interred at St Edmund's College, in the presence of one of the last descendants of the Catholic Talbots, Lady Gwendolen Petre.

John Douglass

1743-1812

Titular Bishop of Centuria (1790)
Vicar Apostolic of the London District (1790-1812)

Unusually for the Vicars Apostolic of the London District, Bishop Talbot died without a coadjutor. The Northern District was also vacant and the resulting 'succession crisis' revealed the divisions tearing apart the Catholic community. Charles Berington, the coadjutor of the Midland District, was the Catholic Committee's favoured candidate for the London District and he also received the backing of many priests. Sir John Throckmorton wrote an anonymous letter to the clergy, proposing that canonical election, with the consent of the laity, was the most correct way of appointing a new bishop – indeed, confirmation or nomination by the Pope was undesirable and unnecessary. Once again, the system of governance by Vicars Apostolic was attacked and a hierarchy of diocesan bishops called for. Such demands for ecclesiastical democracy suggested parallels with events on the continent – the reforms of Joseph II, the Synod of Pistoia (1787) and even the Revolution then breaking out in France.

The Holy See unsurprisingly chose safe candidates for the two vacancies. The President of Douai, William Gibson, went to the Northern District, while John Douglass was named as Talbot's successor in London. In fact, he had nearly been appointed as Talbot's coadjutor in 1788. The Committee complained that Douglass had been imposed by a foreign power and continued to promote Berington, until he sensibly resigned his claims. Douglass was consecrated Titular Bishop of Centuria on 19 December 1790 by Dr Gibson in the Welds' chapel at Lulworth Castle, Dorset. For many, 1790 proved to be a year of triumph for orthodoxy in England.

John Douglass was born in December 1743, the son of John Douglass (a Scot) and Bridget Semson, in the north Yorkshire town of Yarm, situated on the River Tees and soon to become a favourite haunt of John Wesley, the founder of Methodism. Douglass' early education was at the hands of a secular priest, Simon Bordley, at Salwick Hall over the Pennines in Lancashire.

In October 1757 Douglass followed the well-trodden path to the English College, Douai, where he remained for eleven years. The date of his priestly ordination is uncertain, but by May 1768 he was both a priest and a Doctor of Divinity. Shortly afterwards, he reluctantly agreed to act as Professor of Humanities at the Royal English College, Valladolid. This seminary had recently been vacated by the Society of Jesus, which had directed the house since its foundation but which was suppressed in Spain in 1767. The college's management passed to the English secular clergy and Douglass arrived in Spain as part of a new vanguard, together with eight students from Douai. Robert Bannister, a teacher at Douai, described the young Douglass' character in a letter to his friend, Joseph Shepherd, the new Professor of Theology at Valladolid:

> He is young and has a great narrowness of mind and thinking, as yet: such persons stick close to their own few ideas, and to try to dissuade them directly not to cleave to their own preconceived and narrow notions, is the way to throw them entirely off their hinges and to get their ill will for one's pains.[1]

Douglass returned to England on 30 July 1773, due to a breakdown in health, and worked at Linton upon Ouse, Newton upon Ouse and York, where he remained until his elevation to the episcopate.

As bishop, Douglass moved to 4 Castle Street (now Furnival Street), Holborn, popularly known as 'the Castle', and made the bold move of openly wearing his pectoral cross and amethyst ring when at home, though he dared not wear a cassock. Henry Digby Beste, a Fellow of Magdalen College, Oxford who was received into the Church by Douglass in 1798, remembered arriving at 'the Castle' and being welcomed by 'an elderly, rather pompous, duenna-looking woman.' He was eventually taken upstairs to the bishop's room:

> We seated ourselves on each side of the fire in an old-fashioned wainscoted room, with corresponding furniture, the floor half-covered by a well-worn Turkey carpet. On the walls, yellow with smoke, hung portraits

---

[1] M. E. Williams, *St Alban's College, Valladolid* (1986), 79.

which, through the soot which encrusted them, I hardly discerned to be ecclesiastical worthies: Cardinal Allen, perhaps, founder of the College of Douay – a Campion or Arrowsmith, or other martyrs of the Reformation. A crucifix was in a conspicuous place. Over the chimney a little engraving of Pius VI, then a prisoner. The Bishop was a tall, thin man, between sixty and seventy, of a healthy look, with a lively and good-natured countenance. He wore a suit of black, not very fresh, with a little close white wig.[2]

As Vicar Apostolic, Douglass inherited the heated negotiations with the Government and Catholic laity over the new Relief Bill. In January 1791 he issued a pastoral, together with Bishops Walmesley and Gibson, confirming the earlier condemnation of the Oath of Allegiance to the Crown and stating that

> the assembly of the Catholic Committee has no right or authority to determine on the lawfulness of Oaths, Declarations or other Instruments whatsoever containing Doctrinal matters, but that this authority resides in the Bishops, they being, by Divine institution, the spiritual Governors in the Church of Christ, and the Guardians of Religion.[3]

This was an important principle and was quickly attacked by the Committee's *Second Blue Book*. Meanwhile the Catholic Relief Bill came before the House of Commons and the controversial reference in the oath to 'Protesting Catholic Dissenters' was replaced by 'persons professing the Roman Catholic religion'. Douglass proved to be more conciliatory than Walmesley and Gibson, who opposed the Bill outright, and supported the substitution of the Oath of Allegiance from the 1774 Irish Catholic Relief Act. This was achieved through an alliance with sympathetic High Churchmen of the likes of Samuel Horsley, Bishop of St David's, who made a decisive intervention in the House of Lords and suggested this amendment.

The Catholic Relief Act became law on 24 June 1791, admitting Catholics to the legal profession, permitting the exercise of their religion in registered places of worship and the existence of their schools. Douglass issued a Pastoral referring to the 'benignity of Government' and imploring Catholics to pray for King and Country. He encouraged his flock to 'hasten to give our gracious Sovereign that test of loyalty which the legislature calls for, and to disclaim every principle dangerous to society and civil liberty which has been erroneously imputed to you.'[4] Douglass personally

---

[2] B. Ward, *Catholic London A Century Ago* (1905), 66-67.
[3] *Dawn*, i, 242-243.
[4] Ibid., i, 297-298.

led a body of forty clergy to Westminster in early July to take the oath.

The disputes with the Catholic Committee did not end with the passing of the 1791 Relief Act. The following year the Committee became the Cisalpine Club and a *Third Blue Book* was issued. Further controversy was caused when, in May 1793, Sir John Throckmorton invited Joseph Berington to be his chaplain at Buckland in Berkshire and thus enter the London District. Douglass half-heartedly refused him faculties and the resulting struggles continued for nearly a decade. In 1799 Berington wrote to the *Gentleman's Magazine* in support of Dr Sturges' *Reflections on the Principles and Institutions of Popery*, which attacked Milner's *History of Winchester*. Berington's letter minimised the Pope's temporal power, attacked infallibility and advocated the abolition of priestly celibacy. Shortly afterwards, Douglass publicly denounced his writings and suspended him. It was only in 1801 that Berington signed a retraction and was rehabilitated.

On 12 November 1793 Mgr Charles Erskine landed at Margate; he was a protégé of the Cardinal Duke of York and, though not yet in Holy Orders, would later be elevated to the Sacred College. His arrival was largely independent of the Vicars Apostolic – he came as papal envoy at a time when the Papacy and the British Government were seeking closer relations in the face of European revolution. Erskine's visit was disguised as that of a British subject to his family and friends and he spent much time with the leading Catholic laity. Douglass was opposed to Erskine's presence, since the visit had been arranged behind his back, and suggested himself as a more appropriate papal representative. Erskine's mission ultimately pleased no one: he tried to walk a *via media* between the Cisalpines and the Ultramontanes, both of whom expected his support, and received only a nervous welcome from the authorities.

The London District saw much development under Douglass. Reporting to Rome in 1796, Douglass wrote that 'the Church is beginning to flourish in our metropolis, and the number of Catholics is daily increasing.'[5] Thanks to the Relief Act, the 1790s saw a succession of churches being built, including St Patrick's, Soho Square, and a new church at Spanish Place.

The French Revolution (1789 onwards) resulted in a flood of over 5,000 French clergy to England, many of whom settled in London. Douglass reported the presence of five archbishops, twenty-seven bishops and

[5] Ibid., i, 300.

thirteen Vicars General in his District. This influx of Catholic clergy could only have a positive effect on English Catholicism: society at large treated them with respect as refugees and a number of chapels were opened. When Pius VI died in captivity in August 1799, a Requiem was organised at St Patrick's, Soho Square. The Absolutions were carried out by Douglass together with the Bishops of Lombez, Rodez, Montpellier and Waterford; also present were the Archbishop of Narbonne and the Bishops of Nantes, Angoulême, Arras, Uzès, Comminges, Troyes, St Pol de Léon, Lescar and Moulins. Such an international gathering of Catholic bishops in Protestant London would have been unthinkable a few years previously.

Faced by the loss of English institutions overseas as a result of the political turmoil, Douglass spent much energy and money in providing continuity in Catholic education. Most notably, in November 1793 he transformed the Old Hall Green Academy, set up by Talbot, into a college dedicated to St Edmund of Abingdon (a patron of students) that would be a 'New Douai'. John Daniel, the last President of Douai, declined to take charge of the new college and so Gregory Stapleton, the last President of St Omer, was appointed as President, assisted by William Poynter. The latter succeeded as President following Stapleton's death in 1801 and, two years later, became Douglass' coadjutor. Douglass took great interest in St Edmund's, opening the new building and visiting regularly. An anecdote concerning Douglass' examination of a candidate for priestly ordination reveals that clerical formation in England was still in need of development:

> Bishop D: Did I not examine you a twelvemonth ago for deacon's orders, Mr L?
> Mr L: Yes, my lord, you examined me yourself in this room.
> Bishop D: Then I'll not trouble you any further.[6]

The French émigré clergy soon posed the authorities with a problem. In 1801 Napoleon and the new Pope, Pius VII, signed a Concordat, which included provision for a reorganisation of the French dioceses. All existing bishops were expected to offer their resignations so that new appointments could be made by the French Government, with the blessing of the Pope. Not surprisingly, many bishops saw the Concordat as a betrayal and thirty-eight of the ninety-three refractory prelates refused to obey, including fourteen of the bishops living in the London District. They were deprived

---

[6] E. Waylen, *Ecclesiastical Reminiscences of the United States* (1846), 306.

by the Pope, but their supporters initiated the *petite église* schism, which lingered on until around 1830, especially in the west of France.

The so-called 'Blanchardists' could be seen as the English branch of this schism, led by the Abbé Blanchard who believed that the Pope himself was in schism by signing the Concordat. Douglass initially dismissed these nineteenth-century sedevacantists as being an internal French matter and hoped the problem would gradually solve itself, especially as the deposed bishops grew older and died. However, Bishop Milner of the Midland District pushed for a strong denunciation of the Blanchardists and attacked them in a Pastoral of June 1808. Douglass saw Milner as interfering in the affairs of his District but brought out a Pastoral in August of that year, suspending Blanchard and his accomplice, Gaschet.

Douglass was willing to seek reconciliation, but Milner thought him too mild since he had made a distinction between schismatic works (such as those of Gaschet) and those only tending towards schism (Blanchard). He continued to issue strongly-worded statements, implying Douglass' lack of leadership and orthodoxy, and tried to arrange a joint condemnation from the Vicars Apostolic. He also enlisted the help of the Irish bishops in the matter.

Blanchard, in the meantime, wrote to Douglass defending the condemned works and attached seven supporting signatures of émigré priests. These individuals were quickly suspended, although the faculties of one of the number, Mgr Trevaux, were restored in 1811. This caused further controversy and Archbishop Troy of Dublin wrote to Douglass, demanding an explanation so that the Irish bishops 'may determine … whether we continue in Catholic communion with your Lordship.' Schism seemed to threaten the British and Irish Church and an emergency meeting of the Vicars Apostolic was called at Durham, to which Milner was not invited. They affirmed that they held their jurisdiction from the Holy Father alone and were not responsible to each other, judging that Milner had unjustifiably interfered in the affairs of the London District, especially in getting the Irish bishops involved. Blanchardism eventually died a natural death, as Douglass hoped, but for many years the *Laity's Directory* contained a 'List of the French Clergymen who have signed the Form of Declaration of Catholic Communion.' Any French priest not included on the list was not allowed 'to officiate in any public Chapel' or private dwelling.[7]

---

[7] *The Laity's Directory for the Year 1830*, 5.

Douglass was mild-mannered and the strong measures that his high office required of him cost dearly. By 1808 the Cisalpine Club, which had became more a social organisation for the Catholic lay elite, was replaced by the Catholic Board as the main body to promote Catholic Relief. This was comprised of a balanced membership of senior clergy and laity and all of the Vicars Apostolic were members. However, tensions remained. Douglass vigorously opposed the proposal that the Crown would exercise a veto over the appointments of Catholic bishops – as exercised by many Catholic sovereigns overseas. Other heated points of controversy were the right of the State to check and approve Roman documents arriving in the country (the *Exequatur*) or the idea of introducing State stipends for clergy. These securities were hardly unusual and could be found in many Catholic countries, but to the likes of Douglass they appeared a step too far.

In 1811 a number of charities existing in the London District were incorporated in 'The Associated Catholic Charities'. These included 'The Society for Educating Poor Catholic Children' (founded 1764), 'The Beneficent Society for Apprenticing the Children of Poor Catholic Parents' (1784) and 'The Laudable Association for Raising a Fund for the Maintenance and Education of Poor Catholic Children' (1797). Joined together, they were able to pool their resources and run five schools – two near Moorfields, two in Marylebone and one in Lincoln's Inn Fields.

Douglass died after a long illness at 'The Castle' on 8 May 1812. A Requiem was held at Lincoln's Inn Fields and he was buried at Old St Pancras Churchyard, although his name was not entered into the register and so his final resting place was only 'confirmed' for posterity when the Giffard Vault was opened in 1907 to remove the bodies of Bishops Giffard and Petre to St Edmund's. Permission to translate Douglass was subsequently gained and he was re-interred at Old Hall Green on 13 March 1908.

Further Reading

E. Duffy, 'Doctor Douglass and Mister Berington: an eighteenth-century retraction', *Downside Review*, 292 (1970), 246-70

WILLIAM POYNTER

1762-1827
TITULAR BISHOP OF HALIA (1803)
COADJUTOR TO BISHOP DOUGLASS (1803-12)
VICAR APOSTOLIC OF THE LONDON DISTRICT (1812-27)

Bishop Douglass was succeeded by William Poynter, his coadjutor and former President of St Edmund's. Born in Petersfield, Hampshire, on 20 May 1762, the new Vicar Apostolic was the eldest son of John Poynter, a coachbuilder, and Mary Todd. He was baptised four days later at his home by Ralph Faulkner, a priest born in Maryland and ordained from the English College, Rome.

Poynter attended the grammar school at Petersfield, where he was the only 'papist', and learnt his catechism at the nearby chapel in Brockhampton. In 1775, aged thirteen, he was sent to the English College, Douai, by Bishop Challoner. He was a good student, as is revealed in a note written by the President, William Gibson, to Bishop Douglass in 1784:

> We have one Poynter here. He has one or two brothers, one of which if not both would gladly come. If they be like him, we need not care how many we have of them.[1]

He was ordained priest in 1786 and stayed on at the college to teach logic and theology and act as Prefect of Studies. Three years later the storms of revolution broke out. At first, Douai seemed relatively peaceful and the college community assumed that they could claim exemption from revolutionary decrees on account of their British nationality.

One evening in 1793, shortly after the execution of Louis XVI, Poynter responded to some angry knocks and opened the main door of the college.

---

[1] Anstruther, iv, 222.

According to Thomas Gillow:

> Immediately four or five of the soldiers in a state of intoxication entered, and pushed forward through the porch and inner door into the corridor. They called out for the young men to be led out into the streets to go along with them. Dr Poynter attempted to remonstrate, saying that the students were many of them in bed, and the rest were now retiring, and begged that they would not disturb them. "Where are your prisons? Open your prisons," they exclaimed. "We have no prisons," replied Dr Poynter, and would have added that the young men were free and happy, but the soldiers grew furious. One drew his sword, and the consequences threatened to become serious, when, in an instant, Messrs Gillow, Silvertop, Riddell, and one or two more, as if moved by a common influence, rushed forward, and taking each of the soldiers by the arm, cried out *Vive la nation*! And so drew them out into the streets. The doors were closed, and the crowd moved away to the cry of *Vive la nation*! *Vive la liberté*! The students were carried in a sort of triumphal procession through the streets of Douay; and were out most of the night; and in this manner the College was temporarily saved.[2]

Later that year the collegians were moved by the authorities to the Scots College and, shortly afterwards, to the castle at Doullens. The prisoners numbered twenty-six from the English College, Douai, and six English Benedictines, also from Douai – the so-called '*Trente-Deux*'. The stories later told by the 'Confessors of Doullens' quickly passed into the lore of Ushaw and Old Hall Green, the twin successors of Douai. There were, for instance, heroic escapes. Since Doullens lay in a different diocese to Douai, Poynter and the other priests lacked faculties to hear confessions. In November 1793 a party of four students climbed down a rope fixed at the top of the castle wall and disappeared into the night to apply for the appropriate faculties from the Bishop of Amiens.

A letter of John Penswick (the brother of the future bishop) reveals Poynter's strength of character – or even rashness - during captivity:

> When our restrictions in matters of space and recreation ground, which had been imposed on account of the escape of so many of our companions, and to prevent the flight of more, had been somewhat relaxed, and a wider circuit had been conceded for air and exercise, Mr Poynter, profiting by this indulgence, ascended the walled ramparts which separated the two citadels, and in full view of both, calmly, quietly, and composedly recited there for a time, almost daily, the Divine Office. His purpose appeared to us to be twofold, viz. to testify by this noble demonstration his obedience to God in almost the worst times, his adherence to his own personal duties,

---

[2] *St Edmund's*, 71.

irrespective of consequences to himself, and to console and reanimate the faltering courage of so many French captives, to whom hope had become almost an entire stranger. If such were his object, he succeeded. When better times followed, they often expressed to us their great admiration of his noble conduct, and their grateful thanks for the well-timed edification he had given them.[3]

On 24 November 1794 the English prisoners were released. After a stay at the Irish College, Douai, they crossed to Dover in an American ship and landed on 2 March 1795. Poynter was asked by Bishop Douglass to find an alternative home for the students of Douai and St Omer. The school founded by Bishop Talbot at Old Hall Green seemed an obvious location and a new chapel had recently been opened there (1792). Poynter was quickly appointed first Vice-President of St Edmund's, with Stapleton as President. When the latter became Vicar Apostolic of the Midland District in 1801, Poynter succeeded as President and was also Stapleton's choice as Vicar General. After the bishop's untimely death the following May, Poynter acted as administrator of the Midland District and even issued a Lenten Pastoral at the time of Milner's appointment as the new Vicar Apostolic, though his jurisdiction was questioned by Bishop Gibson.

On 3 March 1803 Poynter was appointed coadjutor to Bishop Douglass and on 29 May was consecrated Titular Bishop of Halia at St Edmund's. Despite his onerous new duties, he remained President of the College for a further ten years and only reluctantly resigned in 1813 so that he could devote his energies to the issues that faced him as Vicar Apostolic. His long periods of absence from the college led to a breakdown in management and discipline and a 'rebellion' by the students in 1809.

As Vicar Apostolic in his own right (from 1812) Poynter was a gifted, prudent and conciliatory leader; well-read in theology and canon law, on good terms with many of the leading Catholic families and conversant in Latin, French and Italian, which gave him an obvious advantage in his dealings with the Holy See.

Above all, Poynter is remembered as Milner's chief opponent over the issues of the day. Tensions rose so high that Milner even accused Poynter on one occasion of financial irregularity. Poynter was Milner's opposite in temperament – Bramston compared him to a bee, 'with a sting to use only when necessity requires, but constantly productive of much honey,' while

---

[3] Ibid., 92-93.

Milner and his allies, the Irish bishops, were 'Mitred Wasps'.[4] Milner would hear of no compromise; Poynter took a more conciliatory approach.

It seemed that Milner opposed almost everything that Poynter did. The Blanchardist Schism, which had emerged during the governance of Douglass, continued to be a contentious issue under Poynter, Milner accusing him of acting too softly. Poynter's support of the new 'Catholic Bible Society' was interpreted as a dangerous concession to liberal, Protestantizing ideals. When Poynter disciplined Peter Gandolphy, a chaplain at the Spanish Embassy, for an apologetical work that he thought dubious despite having a Roman *imprimatur*, Milner came vigorously to the priest's defence.

Milner opposed the attempts of the Catholic laity to negotiate over Catholic Emancipation and discuss various concessions to the Government. Poynter, though keen to preserve the authority of the bishops, realised the dependence of the clergy on the laity (especially financially) and was willing to co-operate with their schemes. He signed the Fifth Resolution in 1810, which stated that the Catholic community 'are firmly persuaded that adequate provision for the maintenance of the civil and religious establishments of this kingdom may be made consistently with the strict adherence on their part to the tenets and discipline of the Roman Catholic religion.'[5] In 1813 a new Catholic Relief Bill contained an oath of allegiance that downplayed papal powers and spoke of a commission that would advise the King on the election of bishops and deans and inspect papal bulls and dispensations. Poynter was largely in favour and was backed up by Rome, who did not wish to offend the British Government and was used to reaching agreements with States over such matters. Milner opposed the measures vigorously and the Bill was dropped, the Speaker even declaring that the legislation, designed to put an end to strife, was creating additional strife within the Catholic body. Poynter was angry at Milner's lack of flexibility and excluded him from a meeting of the Vicars Apostolic at Durham in October 1813. The following year Poynter travelled to Rome with James Yorke Bramston (soon to be his coadjutor) to respond to accusations made against him by Milner and to try and reach some settlement. Though disrupted by political events (viz. the return of Napoleon from Elba), Poynter managed to return with Cardinal Litta's so-called 'Genoese Letter' in which Rome stated it was prepared

---

[4] *Eve*, ii, 6.
[5] Ibid., ii, 6.

to consider the veto, giving the Crown the power to remove names of candidates for the episcopate.

Poynter, like many of the Vicars Apostolic, was suspicious of the regular clergy and this antagonism won him enemies both at home and in Rome – including, of course, Milner. When the Jesuits were restored by Pius VII's bull *Sollicitudo omnium Ecclesiarum* in 1814, Poynter opposed its enactment in his District, fearful that it would add new fuel to old tensions within the clergy, increase anti-Catholicism and hinder the journey to Catholic Emancipation. Poynter was unwilling to recognise the restored Jesuits without the approval of the Government and the Society was not officially reinstated in England until 1829. In 1818 Poynter succeeded in gaining the appointment of his nominee, Robert Gradwell, as Roman Agent, a man who shared his prejudices, in particular, against Milner and the Jesuits and who would later become coadjutor in London.

Another key concern for Poynter was the recovery of the debt owed to the English Catholics after the confiscation of the colleges in France during the Revolution. The 1814 Treaty of Paris offered compensation to all British subjects who had suffered from French confiscatory decrees since 1793. Poynter crossed the Channel four times to appeal to the French Government and even secured the support of Louis XVIII and the Duke of Wellington. It was eventually settled that £120,000 should be paid in compensation and Poynter hoped to use this money for the education of priests in England. However, in November 1825 the English Government decided to stop the money from reaching the Catholic community since it would be used for 'superstitious purposes'. Different theories abound as to the eventual fate of the confiscated money: it may have been variously spent on furnishing Windsor Castle or the construction of Marble Arch and the Royal Pavillion at Brighton. Meanwhile, an arrangement was made with the French Government for the administration of the *fondations anglaises*. By 1826 it seems that three English students were using surviving bursaries from the old English colleges to study at the Paris seminary of St-Nicolas-du-Chardonnet. The bishops continued to be pre-occupied by the issue into the twentieth century; a 1907 Memorandum declared that 'the claims of the English Bishops at the present day are the same as those of their predecessors at the beginning of the last century.'[6]

---

[6] *Memorandum Respecting the English Foundations in France for the Education of English Catholics* (1907).

Poynter inherited the responsibility of overseeing the Catholic community in the British Colonies and was the first of the Vicars Apostolic to exercise jurisdiction in Australia – indeed, his image in stained glass can be found in St Mary's Cathedral, Sydney. Poynter enjoyed warm relations with Lord Bathurst, Secretary of State for War and the Colonies, and often consulted him over ecclesiastical affairs and appointments overseas. Aware that a better system of governance was needed, Poynter suggested to Propaganda the erection of separate Apostolic Vicariates. In March 1818 a priest of the Northern District, Thomas Gillow, was appointed 'Vicar Apostolic of the English, Dutch and Danish islands in the West Indies'. However, poor health necessitated his resignation before he was even consecrated and he was replaced by James Buckley, who had recently stepped down as President of the English College, Lisbon. Buckley was consecrated bishop at St Edmund's on 29 June 1819 and reached Trinidad the following year. Also in 1818 an English Benedictine, Dom Edward Bede Slater, was appointed first Vicar Apostolic of Mauritius, Madagascar, the Cape of Good Hope, New Holland and Van Diemen's Land, a vast jurisdiction based in Port Elizabeth.

A number of churches were opened in the London District by Poynter and in 1815 he set up the London Mission Fund to provide for the building of chapels and the education of priests. In 1809 a German Catholic chapel was opened in Bow Lane, Cheapside. A new chapel was opened in Holly Place, Hampstead, in 1816, replacing the room over a stable used since 1796. Poynter supported Joseph Hunt's efforts to build a larger church of St Mary Moorfields. The chapel had been destroyed in the Gordon Riots and, since then, a house in White Street had been used, purchased with the help of government compensation. Poynter laid the foundation stone in 1817 and opened the church three years later. A Requiem for Pius VII was held there in 1823 and was impressive for the splendour of the funereal decorations and for the length of proceedings – the clergy processed in at quarter past ten and Bramston only concluded his eulogy five hours later.

Poynter introduced clergy retreats into the London District. The first of these was held in July 1826 and consisted of the recitation of the Divine Office, Mass, a sermon preached by Poynter and meditations read from Challoner and Bourdaloue. It was one of the bishop's final acts, for he was fast ailing with a stomach tumour. He died on 26 November 1827, aged 66, at his home in Castle Street, Holborn, where his predecessor also had died. On 11 December he was buried in the newly constructed vault at

St Mary Moorfields. This vault had become one of the main burial sites for Catholics in London, and one of the most famous interments there was that of the German romantic composer, Carl von Weber, who died in London in 1826, though his body was later transferred to Dresden. Poynter's body was also later moved, to St Edmund's at the end of 1899, when the old Moorfields was being demolished, and now rests in the chapel cloister. It thus rejoined his heart for, according to his instructions, the bishop's heart was placed in a velvet heart-shaped box and buried under the sanctuary of St Edmund's, around the spot where the priest began Mass.

Further Reading

P. Philips (ed.), *The Diaries of William Poynter, V.A. 1815-1824*, CRS (Records Series) Vol. 79, (2006)

JAMES YORKE BRAMSTON

1763-1836
TITULAR BISHOP OF USULAE (1823)
COADJUTOR TO BISHOP POYNTER (1823-27)
VICAR APOSTOLIC OF THE LONDON DISTRICT (1827-36)

James Yorke Bramston is one of the most attractive Vicars Apostolic, 'his genial face', as Bernard Ward put it, 'and portly figure being welcome at every gathering.'[1] A trained lawyer and convert to Catholicism, Bramston was a mature vocation and he himself jested that 'a Popish priest grafted on a Protestant lawyer should be a switch for the devil himself.'[2]

The future bishop was born on 18 March 1763 to John Bramston, a solicitor, and Elizabeth Yorke, the daughter of the Vicar of Oundle, Northamptonshire. He was raised as an Anglican and attended Oundle School, where one of the houses is still named after his grandfather, Stephen Bramston, who had given the institution a fine Queen Anne town house.

Like his father and grandfather, James decided to follow family tradition and pursue a career in the law, turning down positions in the Indian Civil Service or the Navy – the latter being highly unsuitable because of his propensity to violent sea-sickness. He was admitted to Lincoln's Inn in April 1785. Bramston spent four years studying under Charles Butler, a Catholic lawyer who was also Secretary of the Catholic Committee. Brought under such distinguished Catholic influence, Bramston became interested in the Faith and started accompanying his teacher to the Sardinian Chapel in nearby Lincoln's Inn Fields. He was eventually received into the Church in 1790 by the charismatic Irish Franciscan,

---

[1] *Eve*, ii, 7.
[2] Ibid., 8.

John Leyburn

Bonaventure Giffard

The dog that saved Benjamin Petre

Richard Challoner

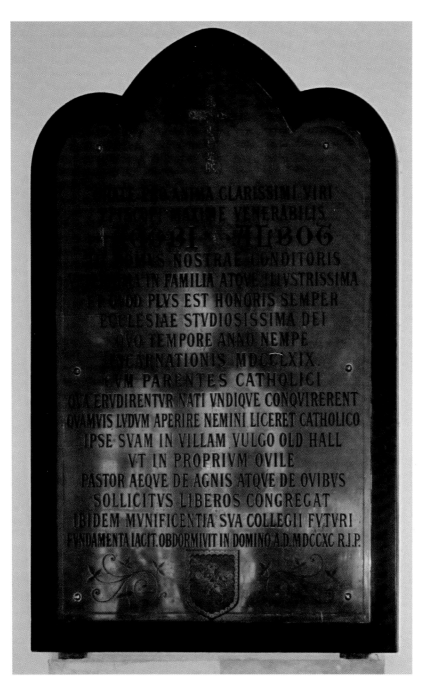

Memorial of James Robert Talbot

John Douglass

William Poynter

James Yorke Bramston

Robert Gradwell

Thomas Griffiths

Thomas Walsh

Nicholas Wiseman

George Witham

John Talbot Stonor

Gregory Stapleton

John Milner

Arthur O'Leary. As his memorialist piously noted:

> The name of Catholic was then in this country a name of infamy and reproach ... but Bishop Bramston was deaf to the whisperings of human prudence: he heard the dictates of his conscience, and determined generously to obey ... He was thus separated in religion from the whole of his numerous family; but not an angry word nor an angry feeling followed this sudden separation. His father (his mother had been some years dead) continued to love him as he had ever loved him: his friends ceased not to respect him, nor frequent his society; they could only praise the noble spirit, that could sacrifice early principles and future hopes upon that altar, to which he felt assured that truth had conducted him.[3]

Bramston wished to start his studies for the priesthood immediately, but waited out of respect for his father who advised him to remain in England for at least twelve months to test his vocation. Meanwhile, he continued to acquaint himself with the London Catholics. Thomas Doyle, who was for many years his curate at Southwark, wrote that 'Dr Bramston used to describe with much effect the Tenebrae in Castle Street, Holborn, where he, a limb of the law, and Charles Butler, another limb, and the Rev. Mr Lindow, and Bishop Douglass, met in the "Episcopal palace" in an upper chamber, at the fourth house on the right hand – and a dirty, dingy, shabby-genteel house it was – for the purpose of reciting the Divine Office. They met and separated, too thankful that even that much was done, and hoped for better days.'[4]

After a year of discernment Bramston's mind was unchanged and so, at the mature age of thirty, he entered the English College, Lisbon, in December 1792. Unsure of his credentials, he was conditionally baptised by the President and confirmed by the Protector. The College *Register* records that Bramston was never treated as a student, always eating with the Superiors – indeed, 'his arrival led to improvements in the Superiors' food.'[5] Bramston could also go out as he pleased, and his memoir in the 1837 *Laity's Directory* records that 'his friendship was sought and valued by many among the most noble of the Portuguese families, with several of which his connexion continued until the time of his death.'

The memoir also states that after ordination, at Christmas 1799, Bramston remained in Lisbon for a further 18 months: 'he was laboriously employed in the duties of the holy ministry, chiefly among the British

---

[3] *Laity's Directory for the Year 1837*, 2-3.

[4] Ward, *Catholic London*, 69.

[5] M. Sharratt (ed.), *Lisbon College Register, 1628-1813*, CRS (Records Series) Vol. 72, (1991), 19.

troops that were in garrison.' The obituarist had 'heard himself relate that for six weeks, when an epidemic raged among the soldiers, he did not once put off his dress to retire to rest.'[6] The College's President, William Fryer, considered appointing the new priest to the Chair of Theology, but this was opposed by many of the staff, who 'thought him more suitable for mission since he had never lived under College rule and had not learned methods of scholasticism; they feared he might erode the College's constitutions.'[7]

In July 1801 Bramston returned to England and was duly appointed by Bishop Douglass to the mission of St George-in-the-Fields, Southwark. This had been established in 1788 and the first church was built five years later in the London Road, in a style similar to Milner's church in Winchester. Bramston is unique among the Vicars Apostolic for spending a long period – nearly twenty-three years – labouring in a poor, urban mission, with a large debt. There were around four thousand Catholics in the area and the priests also looked after four prisons, two hospitals and several workhouses, as well as the mission schools. According to the memoir in the *Laity's Directory*:

> His laborious zeal is still visible in the fruits that it has left there. He spared no exertions of body or of mind, to save the souls of those whom God had consigned to his care. The day and the night were the same to him, when the welfare of his flock, or the honour of the Almighty, called for his labours. It was his delight to visit poverty in its miserable dwellings, that he might present relief to its sufferings; to stand at the bed of sickness to afford consolation, the consolation of religion, to the dying-man, and to minister to him those graces that should bear his soul to heaven. The poor and the infirm were the cherished object of his guardian care, and while he ceased not to watch over them with all the zeal of a vigilant pastor, he continued ever to love them as a father. His powerful exhortations and admonitions from the pulpit, shewed their fruits in the numbers who crowded around him in the tribunal of penance. While at St George's Fields, he lost a sincere friend and a beloved relative by the death of his elder brother. The poor were the chief gainers by the increase of fortune which this event, of which he could never speak without a sigh, placed at his disposal.[8]

In 1808 Bramston became a founder member of the Board of British Catholics, which entered into negotiations with the Government for

---

[6] *Laity's Directory for the Year 1837*, 3-4. The memoir mistakenly dates his ordination to 'about four years after his arrival in Lisbon.'

[7] Sharratt, op. cit., 19.

[8] *Laity's Directory for the Year 1837*, 4.

further liberties. Like other similar ventures in which compromises were seen to be made and the Catholic laity took a leading role, it was strongly opposed by Milner.

In 1812 Bishop Poynter appointed Bramston as one of his Vicars General, which saw him make regular journeys across the river to 4 Castle (now Furnival) Street, Holborn. Bramston was elected a member of the Old Brotherhood in 1813 and seven years later became Dean.

Bramston was greatly trusted by Poynter. He attended the Bishops' Meeting at Durham in 1812 and travelled with Poynter to Rome in 1814. They left the Eternal City just as Pius VII fled the city in the aftermath of Napoleon's escape from Elba and Murat's march through the Papal States. They met the Pope at Genoa on 5 April 1815 and Poynter, amongst other things, asked for Bramston as his coadjutor. This was soon blocked by Milner, on account of Bramston's friendship with Charles Butler and his connection with the Board of British Catholics. Milner also stated that Bramston had once been under restraint in a lunatic asylum and had spent time in prison. Both these events, Bramston admitted, had related to the period before his conversion – though never in an asylum, he had been afflicted with an 'illness of the brain' for several weeks in 1787, and the other incident 'he declared himself able to explain if called upon to do so.'[9]

A further eight years were to elapse before the appointment was secured. His legal background and long pastoral experience made him a most suitable candidate. However, as he was in poor health and already aged sixty, he hardly expected to outlive Poynter, who was twelve years younger. Poynter wrote to Collingridge that:

> He has never led me wrong. He has by his caution kept me right in cases where from my less experience I might have run wrong. We have not his equal for such business as the situation in London requires. He is equally zealous and prudent, strictly conscientious, and a man of solid and tender piety. He is indeed sometimes jocular; but he knows when to be serious. I have heard him say when he has made one with me that it would never do for the Bishop (alluding to me) to crack jokes as he did.[10]

On one occasion Bramston fell off his horse and lost consciousness for a few minutes. His companions gathered around him and he eventually came to life and gasped: 'If you see any brains about – they are – mine!'

Bramston was consecrated as Titular Bishop of Usulae on 29 June 1823

---

[9] *Eve*, ii, 8-9.
[10] Ibid., iii, 96.

at St Edmund's College by Poynter, assisted by Collingridge and Baines. He left St George's Fields shortly afterwards and lived separately from Poynter at 15 Tavistock Street, Bedford Square.

After Poynter's death in 1827, Bramston became Vicar Apostolic of the London District, aged sixty-four. Despite his infirmities, he lived for a further nine years. Like his predecessors, he looked for the appointment of a coadjutor bishop and recommended Griffiths of St Edmund's College, and Kimball of Moorfields. However the Holy See instead appointed the Rector of the Venerable English College, Rome, and English Agent, Mgr Robert Gradwell, who was duly consecrated on 24 June 1828.

The following year, the Catholic Emancipation Bill was passed. After decades of division amongst the Catholic body, the key cataclyst turned out to be events in Ireland, when thanks to the efforts of the Catholic Association, Daniel O'Connell was elected as MP for Clare, although he could not take his seat as a Catholic – Emancipation followed from the resulting crisis. The Vicars Apostolic reacted cautiously. Bramston's *Pastoral* of New Year's Day 1830 urged Catholics who might now take public office 'to remember that you are by the blessing of Almighty God *Roman Catholics*, and that your first and highest ambition should be to show forth in your lives and conversation every Christian virtue.' He urged the faithful not to be corrupted by mixing with 'persons unhappily impressed with the false philosophy, or rather irreligion and infidelity, with which the world is in these our days so lamentably infected' but to nurture their Faith, especially by being 'diligent and devout frequenters of the Holy Sacraments of Penance and the Eucharist.'[11] The reaction to Emancipation was more colourful at the English College, Rome, where a solemn *Te Deum* was sung and the words *Emancipazione Cattolica* were emblazoned in lamps on the front of the building, with an orchestra opposite providing suitably festive music.

Bramston moved out of his residence in Tavistock Square and, together with Gradwell, occupied a larger house at 35 Golden Square, which was in the vicinity of the Warwick Street chapel. However, that is not to say that the neighbouring chapel became a 'pro-Cathedral', even though it housed an 'episcopal pew', ornamented with a carved mitre. St Edmund's College continued to be used for great feasts, episcopal consecrations and the blessing of the Holy Oils on Maundy Thursday. Even the bishop's private chapel at Golden Square witnessed the occasional red letter day, such as

---

[11] Ibid., iii, 272-273.

the episcopal consecration of John Bede Polding, a monk of Downside, on 29 June 1834. Polding was the first and only Vicar Apostolic of New Holland, Van Diemen's Land and the adjoining islands, and in 1842 became the first Archbishop of Sydney. On the day of his consecration, Bishop Polding wrote that

> the solemn rite was performed [by Bramston] in the private chapel – much too small for the proper display of the ceremonies, yet on the whole I infinitely preferred this comparative absence of pomp and bustle to the convenience of a public chapel accompanied as it would have been with pomp and bustle.[12]

Due to the small size of the oratory there were only four people in the congregation for this momentous occasion, which proved to be the birth of the Australian hierarchy. One of the co-consecrators was the Vicar Apostolic of Oceania Orientalis (including New Zealand and the Sandwich and Friendly Isles), who happened to be visiting London at the time. During his episcopate Bramston also consecrated Daniel Macdonnell as second Vicar Apostolic of Trinidad and Tobago (25 March 1829), and William Placid Morris as Vicar Apostolic of the Cape of Good Hope (5 February 1832). On 18 March 1833 Gradwell died at Golden Square and, later that year, was replaced as coadjutor by Thomas Griffiths.

In 1833 two wealthy sisters, the Misses Gallini, approached Bramston about the building of a church in the fashionable country district of St John's Wood. However, the two patrons hoped that the mission would be staffed by the recently-restored Jesuits, who had run a small day school nearby and were thus well-known in the area. The age-old tension between seculars and regulars re-emerged, as Bramston maintained that his priests were quite able to look after this important assignment and the Society meanwhile brought the matter to the attention of Cardinal Weld in Rome. Propaganda gave a response that seemed to favour the Jesuits and stressed that the church should be opened as soon as possible for the good of the faithful, but Bramston persisted that he could not give the mission to the Jesuits 'without inflicting a grievous wound on his conscience.'[13] The matter was dropped, however, after all the Vicars Apostolic of England and Scotland (except Walsh) sent a joint letter of protest to the Holy See, which referred to St John's Wood and other disputes between the bishops

---

[12] H. N. Birt, *Benedictine Pioneers in Australia* (1911), i, 238.
[13] *Sequel*, i, 62.

and the regulars. On 9 February 1836 Bramston opened the new church at St John's Wood, where he appointed Cardinal Manning's future Vicar General, James O'Neal, as rector.

This was one of Bramston's last solemn acts before his health failed after Easter of that year. He was already affected by his debilitating corpulence and he now suffered loss of appetite and erysipelas in the right foot, which greatly reduced his mobility. As summer approached he sought a change of air and travelled to Southampton. However, the journey proved too much for the old man and, after seven days of suffering, he died in Southampton at three in the morning on 11 July 1836, aged 84.

His body was transported back to London for the Requiem at Moorfields. According to *The Gentleman's Magazine*:

> On the 27th of July a solemn dirge was performed at the Roman Catholic Chapel in Moorfields. The altar and the prominent parts were hung with black, including the Bishop's throne in the sanctuary, over which an escutcheon was placed with the armorial bearings of the deceased. The coffin, containing the body, was elevated in the centre, surmounted with the mitre and crozier, and surrounded by wax lights. The service consisted of the office and mass for the dead, celebrated by Dr Griffiths, successor to the deceased Bishop, to whom he was coadjutor, another Bishop, Dr Kyle, of Scotland, and between seventy and eighty priests disposed about the bier, by whom the choral portions of the service were chaunted in the plain Gregorian style. The funeral sermon was preached by the Rev. Mr. Hearne. At the conclusion of the service, the body was deposited beside the late Bishop Poynter, in a vault beneath the chapel, with the following inscription on the coffin: *Illustrissimus et Reverendissimus Dominus, Jacobus York Bramston, Episcopus Usulensis, et in hoc districtu Londinensi Vicarius Apostolicus. Obiit die xi Julii, 1836. Requiescat in pace.* The heart had been extracted from the body and inurned, and shortly after the funeral was conveyed by Bishop Griffiths to the Catholic College in Hertfordshire, to be placed beside the heart of Bishop Poynter, who was President of that College.[14]

With the demolition of the old Moorfields church, Bramston's body was moved to the chapel cloister at St Edmund's at the end of 1899.

---

[14] *The Gentleman's Magazine*, October 1836, 429.

Robert Gradwell

1777-1833
Titular Bishop of Lydda (1828)
Coadjutor to Bishop Bramston (1828-33)

Robert Gradwell, who died as coadjutor to Bramston, could be considered the 'lost leader' of London Catholics in the approach to the restoration of the Hierarchy. He was born at Clifton-cum-Salwick in the Fylde, the heart of Catholic Lancashire, and belonged to the junior branch of an old Catholic family whose home had been at Barbies Moor. He was the son of John Gradwell and his wife Margaret Gregson, and had a twin brother, John, to whom he remained close throughout his life and who later became a JP in Preston.

The future bishop entered Douai on 30 September 1791, just as the storm clouds of Revolution were about to end the college's existence in France.

In August 1793 the college community were ordered to go to Esquerchin, although the President, Daniel, was permitted to stay at Douai with two sick students, including Gradwell, whose health was never robust. The young man made good use of his time for he managed to save one of the precious Douai Diaries.

In 1795 he returned to England. A French *laissez-passer* described him at this time as 5 feet 2 inches tall, with chestnut hair, grey eyes, an oval face with two small warts, a high forehead and a large nose. Gradwell joined the community of students at Crook Hall, near Durham, and completed his formation there. On 4 December 1802 he was ordained priest and for a time taught poetry and rhetoric at Crook Hall and its successor Ushaw. In July 1809 he returned to his native Lancashire to assist at Claughton as chaplain to the Fitzherbert-Brockholes. William Fitzherbert-Brockholes was a somewhat eccentric character, a devoted cock fighter known as

'Pink William' on account of the colour of his coats. The head chaplain at Claughton, John Barrow, had in early life been conscripted into the Navy but, after five unhappy years, escaped by diving through a porthole. He came ashore at Dunkirk and was soon arrested, but avoided harsh punishment by pretending to be an Italian who spoke no English – a part he was able to play well since he had spent some time at the English College, Rome. After this dramatic experience, he entered Douai and spent most of his priestly life at Claughton. However, by the time of Gradwell's arrival he was an old and ailing man and he died two years later, leaving his assistant in charge. Alongside his missionary labours and the enlargement of the priest's house, Gradwell continued to study and produced articles for the *Catholicon* journal and a controversial *Dissertation on the Fable of Papal Antichrists* (1816). This increased his reputation and the authorities soon felt that his talents were not being fully used in a country mission.

Gradwell's great work began in 1817, when he was sent to Rome with a deputation from the Vicars Apostolic (with the exception of Milner) to be their Agent at the Holy See, and with a recommendation to Cardinal Consalvi that he be installed as Rector of the Venerable English College in Rome, which had formerly been in the hands of the Jesuits and had been closed after the French occupation of 1798. Gradwell had been considered in relation to the post as early as 1813 and his friend, John Lingard, warmly encouraged the appointment. He sailed for the Eternal City in November 1817, enduring a nerve-racking voyage in which 'after being tossed about for three days, in querulous impatience and helpless misery, we were almost miraculously saved from shipwreck. During the storm my bed was so drenched with water that for the last six days of our voyage I never durst undress.'[1] Claughton, meanwhile, was to be served by members of the Gradwell family until 1906 – the new Roman Agent handed the reigns over to his younger brother, Henry Odo Gradwell, who many years later (1860) was succeeded by his nephew, Mgr Robert Gradwell.

In Rome, Gradwell based himself at the Scots College and combined business with enthusiastically touring the sites of ancient and Christian Rome. On 22 December he was presented to Pius VII as the English Agent; 'passing through the files of guards and the splendid Halls and rooms of the Quirinal Palace,' he noted, 'I was almost confused: and greatly awed when I came into the presence of the Pope.'[2] It took Gradwell time

[1] *Eve*, iii, 6-7.
[2] AAW E7, 22/12/1817.

to settle in, learn the workings of the Curia and deal with the competing factions within the English Catholic community, present even in Rome – particularly Milner's 'party' and the Jesuits, who he suspected were trying to regain governance of the English College. On New Year's Eve 1817 he reflected melancholically in his *Journal*: 'I am determined to defend myself and the public interest of the Mission. But how shall I proceed not able to speak Italian, and studying Italian having now spoiled my speaking French? The agency is becoming a formidable and difficult business.'[3] A few months later, he wrote of

> reports of the Jesuits being very active against me. I am sorry for it. I wish to be at peace. They are forcing me to take an active and decisive part against them. If I oppose myself to them, they will decry me as an enemy. If I do not resist, I abandon my duty. I will keep peace if I can. If I cannot, I will not trim. I will take decidedly the side of the true interests of the Mission sincerely and honestly and leave the event to God.[4]

It took time also to negotiate the opening of the English College and secure its control by the English secular clergy. This had been on the cards ever since the Pope returned to Rome in 1800 and, at one stage, Milner was offered the Rectorship as a means of giving him an honourable position far away from the English scene, where he was considered a controversial firebrand. None of the bishops were alumni of the college (very different from the situation a century later) but they saw its re-opening under English seculars as a strengthening of their own position in Rome and also as a defeat for the Jesuits. Gradwell had to face the members of the Society who tried to out-manoeuvre him as well as a fraudulent attempt by an Irish Augustinian, Fr O'Handley, to open a Venerable British College at Sant' Eusebio. However, on 8 March 1818 Gradwell was formerly appointed Rector and entered the college on 1 April.

Ten students arrived from Ushaw and Old Hall just before Christmas, including two future bishops (Nicholas Wiseman and James Sharples) and a noted antiquarian (Daniel Rock). Soon after their arrival, a group was presented to the Pope and a splendid celebration was organised for the feast of St Thomas, at which nine cardinals were present. The papal choir sang at the High Mass and, given the semi-ruinous state of the college, the altar furniture was borrowed from the Lateran's Corsini chapel.

When Gradwell first visited the Via di Monserrato the previous November he noted that the college was 'empty and in a bad state in some

3 AAW E7, 31/12/1817.
4 AAW E7, 1/2/1818.

parts, dirty and neglected. Valuable papers lying in heaps on the library floor.'[5] Indeed, Gradwell had not lost his love for archives, previously shown in his saving of the Douai Diary, and used his spare time in Rome to organise the college's papers and conduct research for his friend and mentor, Dr Lingard. Gradwell wrote that he had 'selected all the valuable papers and carried them carefully to my own room, where I filled three drawers with them. I read them with curiosity ... Unfortunately two of my drawers did not lock. A superannuated servant had used these valuable papers as waste paper before I found out.'[6]

The first students did exceptionally well at the Roman College and won prizes at the end of their first year of lectures. Indeed, Leo XII awarded Gradwell with the Doctorate in Divinity in recognition of his achievements in a very short time. However, questions arose about whether a Roman education was the best way of preparing future English priests. Gradwell wrote to Consalvi presenting the advantages for in-house teaching, as practised at Douai and many of the other English colleges overseas: 'there are no journeys to schools, no attachments to tedious and obsolete forms, no spending disproportionate time to minor questions, no reducing of all scholars to one uniform standard and pace.'[7]

During the *villeggiatura* of 1827, Leo XII visited the college's summer residence at Monte Porzio, and commented, as he sat down to lunch, that 'it is seldom that a poor Pope can enjoy the pleasure of sitting down to dinner with such a fine set of young men.' It was an occasion remembered fondly by Wiseman in his *Recollections of the Last Four Popes* and a mark of the success of Gradwell's Rectorship.[8]

On 19 May 1828 Propaganda appointed Gradwell coadjutor to the ageing Bishop Bramston and he was consecrated Titular Bishop of Lydda by Cardinal Zurla at the English College on 24 June. He resigned the Rectorship of the college and was replaced by the young Nicholas Wiseman. On returning to England, he was soon immersed in the round of meetings, visitations and confirmations. There were lighter moments too, as his *Diary* reveals. On visiting the Berkshire area in January 1830 he recorded: 'At Windsor Castle. Saw all the old staterooms, hall, chapel. Viewed the paintings with Mr O'Reilly the surgeon. The Marquis of Cunningham who had seen me at Rome came and permitted us to see

[5] AAW E7, 14/11/1817.
[6] M. E. Williams, *The Venerable English College Rome. A History 1579-1979* (1979), 108.
[7] Ibid., 111.
[8] N. Wiseman, *Recollections of the Last Four Popes* (1856), 200.

the new State apartments. Very fine and costly.' That September he was in Hampshire and combined his visitations with a trip to the 'regatta at Poole' and a happy day spent 'with Mr Robinson in a yacht to see Portsmouth and ships in harbour.'[9]

However, his health was declining for, as Ward argues, 'his eleven years' residence in Rome had enfeebled his constitution, at no time strong, and the return to the cold, damp English climate was more than he was able to stand.'[10] At the beginning of January 1833 he was diagnosed with dropsy and the following month he 'ceased to attend meals in dining room' at Golden Square and his medication included 'Rhenish wine'. One of his final diary entries, on 28 February, noted that he had 'revived with fine weather,'[11] but there was a relapse shortly afterwards and his sister and twin brother were summoned to the sick room. On 18 March he unexpectedly passed away, aged 57, seated in his chair, for he was unable to lie down, and, according to Bramston, 'to his last breath was endeavouring to pronounce the Holy Name.'[12] David Mathew noted 'a pause in ecclesiastical affairs' after Gradwell's premature death, such had been his 'great energy of character'.[13] He was buried at Moorfields but in 1900, when the old church was demolished, his remains were removed to St Edmund's. He is still remembered at the English College, where a 'Gradwell Room' was opened before the Millennium.

Further Reading

D. J. Leahy, 'Robert Gradwell', *The Venerabile*, VI, 123-140

[9] AAW B3.

[10] *Sequel*, i, 51.

[11] AAW B3.

[12] *Sequel*, i, 52.

[13] D. Mathew, *Catholicism in England 1535-1935* (1938), 175.

THOMAS GRIFFITHS

1791-1847
TITULAR BISHOP OF OLENA (1833)
COADJUTOR TO BISHOP BRAMSTON (1833-36)
VICAR APOSTOLIC OF THE LONDON DISTRICT (1836-47)

Thomas Griffiths was born in Southwark on 2 June 1791 and brought up in the Church of England. His mother was a Catholic and at the age of fourteen he was received into the Church at St George-in-the-Fields, where the priest-in-charge was James Yorke Bramston. Like many converts, Griffiths showed great enthusiasm in his new faith and walked to church early each morning to serve Mass. The tradition was passed down that this so displeased his Protestant father that his boots were often hidden, although this did not stop the boy walking through the London streets barefoot.

Bramston arranged for the young Griffiths to enter St Edmund's College on 5 January 1805. He thus became the first English bishop since the Reformation to receive all his formation on home soil. It was at St Edmund's that Griffiths spent the next 28 years: after ordination in July 1814, he served as Master of the Preparatory School and looked after the mission of Old Hall Green. In 1816 he was named Vice-President and the following year took care of the 'ecclesiastical seminary' formed by the new President, John Bew, after the church and lay students were separated. Griffiths introduced monthly half-day retreats and the wearing of cassocks, with removable skirts, though without the Roman collar (a later development). This was quite an innovation, for hitherto cassocks had only been used in choir. Poynter, who himself liked to wear a brown suit, represented the established view when he used to remark: 'Church dress for Church use, Sir.'

Dr Bew did not stay at St Edmund's long and, disillusioned by the poor state of college finances and declining student numbers, tendered his resignation. Poynter took the bold step of appointing Griffiths as the new President, despite the fact the twenty-seven year old had only been ordained four years. In order to save money, Poynter directed that henceforth St Edmund's would be a solely ecclesiastical college and up to thirty lay boys were reluctantly dismissed, though the Preparatory School continued as a lay establishment.

One student, William Bower, later recalled entering the college in September 1827:

> A servant met us and led us up to the President's room. There I was introduced to Dr Griffiths, whose kind greeting, "I am to be your father now," made an impression on me which still lasts. In appearance Dr Griffiths was the very picture of neatness; his hair cut quite short and powdered white, gave a contrast to his closely-shaven face. He wore spectacles, and had on a University gown; and while showing us round the house, wore a mortar-board cap.[1]

After the unexpected death of Bishop Gradwell in March 1833, the ageing Bramston needed a new coadjutor and Griffiths was quickly appointed. His association with St Edmund's meant that he was highly respected by many of the clergy, but it was feared that he lacked experience of the ways of the world since he had spent his entire adult life in the seminary.

He was consecrated by Bramston during a five-hour ceremony at St Edmund's on 28 October and remained President until the following April, when Bramston's decline in health necessitated the constant presence of his coadjutor. Bramston finally died on 11 July 1836 and was succeeded automatically by Griffiths.

Griffiths was a striking figure. Canon Oakeley remembered seeing him at St Edmund's in 1846 and noting his 'truly paternal manner of administering the Ordination rite,' which made up for 'the want of external accessories to its celebration.'[2] An Anglican clergyman famously wrote of him:

> I just now saw the R.C. Bishop of London get out of an omnibus in Piccadilly, seize his carpet bag, and trudge straight home with it to Golden Square. He had a blue cloak, but it hung below the skirts, and on he went. A very pleasing, venerable, episcopal-looking man, very like any other

---

[1] *St Edmund's*, 232.
[2] Ibid., 248.

Bishop, save that none of ours would touch a carpet bag with his little finger.'[3]

In May 1837 Griffiths went to Rome with Bishop Walsh to discuss the creation of more Districts and to sound the Holy See out on the possible restoration of the Hierarchy, though they had not been authorised by their brother bishops formally to petition for it. They were met affectionately by the Pope and were created Assistants at the Pontifical Throne at the Solemn Mass on Trinity Sunday. They found the mechanics of the Roman Curia frustrating and had to wait until 12 June before gaining another audience. Pope Gregory XVI expressed his fears that the Government should interfere in the nomination of the bishops, if the Hierarchy was restored, but approved of the further division of the country into Districts and also proposed the creation of Chapters for the selection of new bishops. The Apostolic Vicariates were thus increased from four to eight in 1840, although the London District itself remained substantially unchanged and only lost the counties of Bedfordshire and Buckinghamshire.

Ullathorne considered Griffiths to be 'a holy and industrious Prelate' but 'he had long run in a groove, and wanted that expansion of mind and elasticity of character requisite for taking the leading position in the development and guidance of a new order of things.'[4] Ward likewise referred to 'the unconscious damping spirit which he almost naturally applied to any work at all off the beaten track.'[5]

In May 1840 Frederick Lucas started *The Tablet*, a Catholic weekly printed in London, which became noted for its ultramontane and strongly pro-Irish views. However, it soon brought down the censure of Griffiths due to its strongly-worded criticisms of the bishops. If changes were not made, Griffiths warned, 'it will be necessary for the Bishop in the London District where it is printed, and whose spiritual subject the editor is, to make known to his flock that this paper is not to be considered Catholic in principle or in feeling.'[6]

Griffiths was suspicious of the foreign missionaries. He allowed the Rosminian Luigi Gentili to preach missions in the London District but told him to shorten his exhortations and to refrain from openly criticising the clergy. Gentili seems to have obeyed, although he later wrote in a report to Propaganda that 'Griffiths cannot preach without

---

[3] *Sequel,* i, 171, quoting the Reverend W. H. Brookfield.
[4] Ibid., i, 169.
[5] Ibid., ii, 27.
[6] Ibid., ii, 48.

reading his sermons, and when he reads them they are so poor that they say almost nothing.'[7] The bishop was also suspicious of those who promoted Italianate devotions. In Newman's *Letter to Dr Pusey* (1865) Griffiths is mentioned as having warned the eminent convert 'against books of devotion of the Italian school,' which were 'excellent in its place, not suited to England.'[8] Griffiths was generally unsure what to do with the converts. When William George Ward arrived at Old Hall in 1846, he was welcomed by Griffiths with the words: 'We are glad to welcome you, Mr Ward. Of course we have no work for you.'[9]

Unsurprisingly, he was cautious of Wiseman, whom he saw as something of a dreamer, and poured cold water on his hope for the 'conversion of England'. The bishop's views are well expressed in a letter, dated 4 May 1842, to James Jaunch, the priest of London's German Church:

> We have sufficient reason to thank Almighty God for the removal of prejudices in some quarters, and for the recovery of many lost sheep; but when we look at the whole population, and consider the progress of conversion, we cannot say there is a reasonable prospect of England's reunion to the Church of Christ. The population of Great Britain is nearly nineteen million; of this number about 900,000 are Catholics. The annual number of conversions is about 2,000 or 3,000; many years, therefore, without the especial interposition of Divine Providence, must elapse before any great progress is made in the conversion of our country: particularly as we lose many Catholics from neglect, from allowing their children through worldly motives to be educated in error, etc.[10]

Elements in Rome viewed Griffiths with suspicion, including Pope Gregory XVI. When Griffiths attacked the idea of England's conversion in the 1841 *Catholic Directory*, the Pope wrote a letter to the London clergy: 'if, therefore, this Bishop of yours, where everything is so clear, is the only man who cannot see the sky brightening in England, all the more must you and we take care, Beloved Sons, that you and the laity of England may not have your eyes darkened by the clouds that overshadow his.'[11] Wiseman later recalled that in an audience, the Pope had looked forward to the day when there would be an English Hierarchy but, referring to Griffiths, 'never during the lifetime of that man, because he

---

[7] C. Leetham, *Luigi Gentili, A Sower for the Second Spring* (1965), 293.

[8] J. H. Newman, *A Letter to E. B. Pusey, D.D. on his Recent Eirenicon* (1866), 21.

[9] W. Ward, *William George Ward and the Catholic Revival* (1893), 8.

[10] *Sequel*, ii, 97.

[11] Ibid., ii, 103.

is a Gallican for life.'[12]

Despite his caution, Griffiths saw substantial growth in the London District. Money, of course, was a problem, although he was able to use several legacies – including a large bequest of £200,000 from Charles Blundell of Ince Hall, Lancashire, which was disputed both by the family and by Bishop Walsh. Griffiths oversaw the establishment of eighteen new missions and the completion of nine new churches. Twelve others were under construction at the time of his death, including the Jesuit church at Farm Street. Griffiths had actually opposed this foundation since he thought it would inevitably compete with the secular clergy at Warwick Street, and suggested alternative sites in Hackney and Saffron Hill, where missions were badly needed. The Society was anxious to have a central location, where the Fathers could minister to the wealthy and educated Catholics of the capital, and appealed to Rome. By this time the property on Farm Street had already been purchased. Griffiths visited Rome to discuss the matter and the Pope decided in the Jesuits' favour, on the condition that the church did not act as a 'quasi-parish' (meaning that all sacraments other than the Eucharist and Confession were to be administered by Warwick Street), that the Society paid an annual contribution to the bishop and parish, and provided a priest for any poor district that the Vicar Apostolic should name. By the time the church was opened, Wiseman was Vicar Apostolic and a new agreement was arranged, including the stipulation that the Jesuits should serve the poor mission of Horseferry Road, Westminster.

In 1841 Griffiths inaugurated regular 'Golden Square Conferences' for the clergy. The group first listened to a theological reading and then offered their observations, starting with the oldest priest. Then a case of conscience was presented and a solution offered, this time starting with the youngest priest. One of the first cases considered was: 'The husband of Susan is transported for life – nothing is heard of him for 15 years – can Susan marry again?'[13]

Griffiths continued to take a keen interest in St Edmund's and often spent Sunday there, where he could be refreshed by the country air and attend High Mass. Ward speaks of the preservation of French traditions from Douai in the college's ceremonies, so that Griffiths 'used neither throne or faldstool, but knelt at a *prie-dieu* in the middle of the choir,'

---

[12] Schiefen, 178.
[13] AAW 142, *Golden Square Conference Book.*

where he could 'bless the incense and perform other episcopal rites as if he had been in the sanctuary.'[14] Griffiths' great dream was the building of a larger, more appropriate chapel at St Edmund's and throughout his episcopate laid aside funds for this purpose. In 1845 he was finally able to commission Pugin to draw up designs. The foundation stone was laid on 28 October 1845 and the building was roofed by autumn 1846. Sadly, Griffiths never lived to see the chapel completed.

The bishop's health was failing, despite his comparatively young age, and he lost sight in one eye. He now needed a painful cataract operation in the other eye, to which he looked forward since 'his being shut up in a dark room would give him more time to pray and meditate.'[15] His final illness was the result, it was said, of several months of overwork in order to deal with pending matters before the operation. He died on 12 August 1847 from a form of tuberculosis. Shortly before his death he had the personal consolation of receiving his 84 year-old father into the Church. Bishop Griffiths was temporarily buried at Moorfields and two years later moved to the splendid Griffiths Chantry at St Edmund's.

---

[14] *St Edmund's*, 248.
[15] Ibid., 262.

Thomas Walsh

1777-1849
Titular Bishop of Cambysopolis (1825)
Coadjutor to Bishop Milner (1825-26)
Vicar Apostolic of the Midland District (1826-48)
Vicar Apostolic of the London District (1848-49)

For Walsh's life up until 1848, see pp. 129-132

For the second time in fifty years, a Vicar Apostolic of the London District died without a coadjutor. In actual fact, a few days before his death Griffiths had written to Propaganda nominating three priests as coadjutor: Edward Cox, William Hunt and John Rolfe. The letter had still not been sent off on the day of the bishop's demise and a postscript was added recording the sad news.

Wiseman briefly acted as 'Pro-Vicar' of the London District, until it became clear that Propaganda desired Walsh, the senior Vicar Apostolic, to transfer to London and become, in due course, the first Archbishop of Westminster. The bishop had spent over twenty years shepherding the Midland District and was, by 1848, an ailing septuagenarian. It was thus understandable that he showed great reluctance in transferring to the London District, with the further prospect of becoming the Metropolitan of a restored Hierarchy. Rome was adamant that Walsh, with his wealth of experience, was the best candidate. He tried to refuse the honour and memorials circulated round the London clergy supporting Wiseman as a candidate or even asking for a canonical election. However on 28 July 1848 Walsh found himself appointed Vicar Apostolic of the London District, with Wiseman as coadjutor. He told Lord Shrewsbury that the Pope 'had impressed on me *sacratissimum preceptum* to accede to the appointment ... Thus in my old age am I banished from the midst of many dear kind

friends and as it were into a strange country! God's holy will be done! ...
The Holy See, aware of my infirmities, required from me to take no more
of church government than I feel disposed to do.'[1]

Revolution in Rome and the Pope's subsequent flight to Gaeta meant
that the restoration of the Hierarchy was delayed. Wiseman effectively
continued to govern the District, as his master's health declined. Walsh
survived in London less than a year. On the evening of 18 February 1849
he died at 35 Golden Square and the funeral took place ten days later at St
Mary Moorfields, on which occasion Dr Weedall delivered the oration. It
was only appropriate that the bishop's body should then be taken back to
Birmingham, the scene of his greatest achievements. His mortal remains
rest in the crypt of St Chad's Cathedral and Pugin designed a monument
with the late bishop's reclining effigy in the style of the fourteenth
century.

[1] Schiefen, 161.

NICHOLAS PATRICK STEPHEN WISEMAN
1802-65
TITULAR BISHOP OF MELIPOTAMUS (1840)
COADJUTOR TO BISHOP WALSH – CENTRAL DISTRICT (1840-47)
PRO-VICAR APOSTOLIC OF THE LONDON DISTRICT (1847-48)
COADJUTOR TO BISHOP WALSH – LONDON DISTRICT (1848-49)
VICAR APOSTOLIC OF THE LONDON DISTRICT (1849-50)
ARCHBISHOP OF WESTMINSTER (1850-65)
CARDINAL PRIEST OF SANTA PUDENTIANA (1850)

For Wiseman's early years and period as Coadjutor in the Central District,
see pp. 133–6

Walsh was succeeded by his coadjutor, Nicholas Wiseman, who would soon become the first Archbishop of Westminster. Wiseman had actually been named 'Pro-Vicar' of London after Griffiths' death in 1847. He had been in Rome with Sharples discussing the restoration of the Hierarchy and was entrusted with a diplomatic mission to seek from the British Government support for the Pope against any potential Austrian aggression in Italy. Thus Wiseman returned to England on Griffiths' death and, as Pro-Vicar, took nominal command of the London District. On this occasion, Walsh wrote to Lord Shrewbury from Birmingham, complaining that he had lost his coadjutor at a period when 'my health is not so good' and fully expecting Wiseman to become 'Bishop of the London District'.[1]

As Pro-Vicar Wiseman wrote to Propaganda that the churches were too small, that the poor were turned away because they could not afford pew rents and that the older priests were 'Gallican' and opposed reform, though the young priests were on the whole more reliable and orthodox.

---

[1] Ibid., 156.

In his first circular to the clergy Wiseman made himself available to priests on Tuesdays, Thursdays and Fridays, between eleven and three, as well as an open evening every Tuesday.

On 28 July 1848, after the circulation of various memorials and a period of procrastination in Rome, Propaganda finally decided to transfer Bishop Walsh from the Central District to London, where – despite his age and infirmities – it was assumed he would eventually become first Archbishop of Westminster. Wiseman continued as his coadjutor but in effect administered the District. On Walsh's death in February 1849, Wiseman succeeded as Vicar Apostolic in his own right.

Wiseman's brief time in the London District as successively 'Pro-Vicar,' Coadjutor and Vicar Apostolic were important years of preparation for the soon-to-be-created Archdiocese of Westminster. In 1848 he opened the Jesuit church of Farm Street (against which Griffiths had fought so hard) and welcomed the Passionists. The following year a contingent of Oratorians arrived under the leadership of Fr Faber and the Redemptorists set up house across the river in Clapham. By January 1850 Wiseman could report that within two years three communities of men had been set up in his District and seven houses of religious women.

The restoration of the Hierarchy had been delayed by the 1848 revolution in Rome and the Pope's subsequent flight to Gaeta. It was only in September 1850 that the long-awaited plan could be actualised. Full of emotion at his appointment as Cardinal Archbishop, Wiseman wrote his famously triumphal Pastoral Letter, *Out of the Flaminian Gate*, proclaiming that, by Papal Brief, 'we govern and shall continue to govern, the counties of Middlesex, Hertford and Essex, as Ordinary thereof.' This caused uproar back home – Queen Victoria, perhaps somewhat understandably, asked: 'Am I Queen of England or am I not?'

Wiseman's years at Westminster, which lie beyond the scope of this volume and have been well described elsewhere, were marked by numerous disputes with the other bishops and even his own Coadjutor, Vicar General and Chapter. It seemed to his brother bishops that Wiseman acted as if he was Primate of England. Many of the 'old' English Catholics mistrusted his zeal and the introduction of Italian customs and devotions. Despite his weaknesses, Wiseman presided over a Church growing in self-confidence – in London alone, the number of churches increased from 24 in 1826 to 102 in 1863, and priests from 113 to 215. He died at his residence at 8 York Place (where he had moved to from 35 Golden Square) on 15 February 1865 and was buried initially at St Mary's Cemetery, Kensal Green. In 1909 his body was moved to the crypt of the new Cathedral at Westminster.

Further Reading

B. Fothergill, *Nicholas Wiseman* (1963)

D. Gwynn, *Cardinal Wiseman* (1950)

E. E. Reynold, *Three Cardinals* (1958)

R. J. Schiefen, *Nicholas Wiseman and the Transformation of English Catholicism* (1984)

W. Ward, *Life and Times of Cardinal Wiseman*, 2 vols (1897)

N. Wiseman, *Recollections of the Last Four Popes* (1856)

The Midland District (1688-1840)

and

the Central District (1840-50)

The Midland District consisted of the counties of Cambridgeshire, Derbyshire, Huntingdonshire, Leicestershire, Lincolnshire, Norfolk, Northamptonshire, Nottinghamshire, Oxfordshire, Rutland, Shropshire, Staffordshire, Suffolk, Warwickshire, Worcestershire and the Isle of Ely. This area corresponds to the modern dioceses of Birmingham, East Anglia, Northampton (in part), Shrewsbury (in part), and Nottingham. In 1840 it was renamed the Central District and lost the counties of Cambridgeshire, Huntingdonshire, Lincolnshire, Norfolk, Northamptonshire, Rutland and Suffolk, which went to form the new Eastern District. By the end of the period covered by this book, the District witnessed a dynamic Catholic revival and was home to many important institutions and religious houses and some of Pugin's finest creations.

BONAVENTURE GIFFARD

1642-1734
TITULAR BISHOP OF MADAURA (1688)
VICAR APOSTOLIC OF THE MIDLAND DISTRICT (1688-1703)
VICAR APOSTOLIC OF THE LONDON DISTRICT (1703-34)

Bonaventure Giffard has been called 'one of the most outstanding of all the long line of Vicars Apostolic between 1685 and 1850.'[1] He was also the longest lived, seeing twelve Popes and eight monarchs. Bonaventure Giffard – known as Joseph in his youth – was born in 1642 into one of the leading Catholic families in Staffordshire, the third son of Andrew Giffard and Catherine Leveson. Two of his brothers became secular priests: Augustine was for many years chaplain at the main family seat, Chillington Hall, and Andrew was only prevented from becoming Vicar Apostolic of the Western District by death. Many other relations entered the priesthood or religious life, and the Giffard property at Longbirch later became the headquarters of the Vicar Apostolic of the Midland District. However, many Catholic families had mixed histories of religious allegiance and the black sheep of the Giffard family was the bishop's great-uncle, Gilbert, an Elizabethan spy who kept a close eye on Catholics and uncovered the Babington Plot.

Bonaventure Giffard was born in the first year of the English Civil War. The Giffards were resolute Royalists: Chillington Hall, garrisoned by his uncle Peter, fell briefly into Parliamentarian hands in August 1643 and his father was killed in action near Wolverhampton shortly afterwards. Writing many years later, Bishop Giffard told his mother 'you have told me that God Almighty moved my infant tongue to give some ease to your

---

[1] Hemphill, 18.

sorrowful apprehensions as to my Father.'[2]

Giffard was educated at the English College, Douai, and was ordained priest around 1667. The 1660s were unsettling times to be at Douai, due to the ongoing dispute between the President, George Leyburn, and the Old Chapter of the English Secular Clergy. A small group of Douai priests, Giffard, John Betham and Edward Paston went to Paris in October 1667 and the following February moved into a property on the Rue des Boulangers, with the support of Thomas Carre, confessor to English Austin Canonesses who lived nearby. This house became St Gregory's, a house of further studies for English priests completing the prestigious Sorbonne doctorate. After a brief time teaching divinity at Douai, under a new President, Giffard returned to St Gregory's and was awarded the doctor's cap in June 1678, making him one of the most highly qualified of the English secular clergy.

Dr Giffard was back in England in July 1678 and probably worked as chaplain to the Arundell family of Lanherne. However, he was soon driven overseas in the aftermath of the Titus Oates Plot. On 16 April 1679

> Dr Giffard came to live at St Gregories being forced soon after the beginning of Oats [sic] his plot to quit England, from whence he came first to ye English Monastery of poor Clares in Roan [sic], and after having livd there for some months, he came to Paris where he Dr Godden and Dr Betham were employd in preaching to the English Catholicks who were then very many in Paris.[3]

As can be seen, Giffard maintained close relations with the Poor Clares of Rouen, where his cousin, Winefride Giffard, was Abbess.

Giffard was only able to set foot again in England in July 1681, working as Secretary to the Old Chapter. Three years later he was named capitular archdeacon of Essex and involved in discussions over the appointment of a new bishop, who, it was hoped, would be a Bishop-in-Ordinary rather than a Vicar Apostolic. However, it was a Vicar Apostolic that was appointed over England in 1685 (Bishop John Leyburn), who was quick to appoint Giffard as his Vicar General in the Eastern District. He was also highly esteemed by James II, despite the fact that Giffard had tried to persuade him to break relations with a mistress, Catherine Sedley, the Countess of Dorchester.

Giffard was appointed one of his preachers-in-ordinary at the end of

---

[2] J. A. Williams, '"Our Patriarch": Bishop Bonaventure Giffard, 1642-1734', *Recusant History*, May 2003, 426.
[3] AAW A81, *Register of St Gregory's, Paris.*

1685 and in November 1686 he was chosen as one of two priests to defend the Real Presence in a debate with a pair of leading Anglican divines, in the King's presence. The conference lasted nearly four hours and was later published. Giffard briefly served as a royal chaplain and court preacher. He was involved in an abortive attempt to secure St Winefride's Well for the secular clergy and in furnishing the new Chapel Royal at Whitehall. He also continued to act as Secretary to the Old Chapter, which still proved to be an influential body of clergy despite its loss of authority under the Vicar Apostolic.

1688 was a momentous and fast-changing year for Giffard. In January he was appointed Vicar Apostolic of the newly-erected Midland District, consecrated Titular Bishop of Madaura at Whitehall on 22 April and granted an annual income of £1000. He was also elected President of Magdalen College, Oxford. From the beginning of his reign, James had attempted to re-Catholicise the universities. In Oxford he found a key ally in Obadiah Walker, a convert to Catholicism and popular Master of University College. He opened a Catholic oratory in the college, beside the Master's Lodgings, where the King himself attended Vespers during his State Visit of 1687. Walker's Catholic 'disciples' at the university included John Barnard of Brasenose, who was elected Professor of Moral Philosophy, and John Massey of Merton, who became Dean of Christ Church much to the canons' disgust and who erected a chapel in Canterbury Quad.

When Magdalen's President, Henry Clerke, died on 24 March 1687, Walker advised the King to secure the election of a Catholic, Anthony Farmer. There was nothing extraordinary in the monarch involving himself in this way; as a modern fellow, Gerald Harriss, has noted, 'the tradition of royal intervention in the affairs of the college, and notably in the choice of the president, was almost as old as the college itself.'[4] However, Farmer was a Catholic and neither a fellow of Magdalen or New College, as the statutes required. Moreover, he seems not to have enjoyed a high reputation. Macauley later wrote that 'he generally reeled into his college at night speechless with liquour' and was 'a constant frequenter of noted haunts of libertines,' such as *The Lobster* in Abingdon, where he was seen kissing the landlady.[5]

---

[4] Gerald Harriss, 'A Loyal but Troublesome College 1458-1672', in Laurence Brockliss et al., *Magdalen College and the Crown: Essays for the Tercentenary of the Restoration of the College 1688* (1988), 28.

[5] T. B. Macauley, *History of England from the Accession of James II* (1931), ii, 248.

It is little surprise that the fellows objected to the King's candidate and, on the day of the election, chose one of their own number, John Hough. In due course, Hough was expelled by the Ecclesiastical Commissioners, who also decided against Farmer, and the ailing Bishop Parker of Oxford was put in his place. The new President died in March 1688 but during his brief government a number of Catholic fellows were admitted by order of the King, including the Jesuit Thomas Fairfax, the secular priest George Plowden and John Dryden, son of the poet.

On 31 March Giffard succeeded Parker as President, a move that was criticised by moderate Catholics, including Bishop Leyburn. The *Diary* of the Oxford antiquary, Anthony Wood, describes the events of his brief Presidency. Life was not easy for Giffard and the Catholic fellows, who were repeatedly taunted, even 'in their groves and water-walks.'[6] When Giffard preached in his chapel on 8 July, 'many flocked downe to here [*sic*] him; some admired, the generallity laughed and scorned.'[7] At University College, a boy attended Mass on 4 August with a cat deliberately concealed in his coat, 'which he sometimes pinching and at other times pulling by the tayle made her make such an untunable noise that it put them to some disorder.'[8]

Despite this, a celebration was held to mark the birth of the Prince of Wales on Sunday 1 July 1688:

> Peckham, a Sorbonist and stranger, preached at Magdalen College before the new president, society, popish officers and soldiers of Oxon, and all papists in and neare Oxford, where besides was verie solemn service. Gaudies at some colleges! At Magdalen College in the hall, where the bishop-president dined and all the officers, were the chief doings. When the president and officers went into the hall, the trumpets and kettledrums sounded at the hall staire foot; and when each health at the table was dranke they sounded and beat againe in the same place. The bishop all the while he was in the hall had his purple cassock on, downe to the foot, girt about.[9]

Illuminations were displayed at University College, but elsewhere the rejoicing was muted. According to Wood, people realised that 'if he [the Prince] lives he is to be bred up a papist and so consequently the crowne of England and popish religion will never part.'[10]

---

[6] *The Life and Times of Antony Wood*, vol. 3 (Oxford Historical Society, vol. 26, 1894), 257.
[7] Ibid., 272.
[8] Ibid., 274.
[9] Ibid., 271.
[10] Ibid., 268.

Giffard was also highly conscious of his duties beyond the dreaming spires to the flock of the Midland District. On 10 July 1688 the great bell of Magdalen rang between nine and ten to mark that day's Confirmation ceremony of Catholic children. The bishop also travelled further afield and consecrated the new Franciscan chapels at Warwick and Birmingham. On visiting Worcester in September 1688, the bishop was met outside the town 'by the High Sheriff and about 100 on horseback and conducted to his lodging in the City.'[11]

The idyll came to a dramatic end in October 1688. Giffard tried to flee overseas at the so-called 'Glorious Revolution' but was intercepted at Faversham and sent to Newgate, where he also found Bishop Ellis of the Western District. Obadiah Walker was imprisoned in the Tower, though Dean Massey managed to escape to France dressed as a trooper in a red cloak. Giffard was kept at Newgate until July 1690. His period of captivity proved to be fruitful since he managed to receive into the Church a disillusioned Anglican clergyman, who went on to study at Lisbon and, as John Vane, became a leading secular priest.

. On his release, Giffard exercised a discreet ministry, despite official orders that he leave the country, and was most likely based in a family property at Cock Street, Wolverhampton. He visited his vast District and used the funds of an unsuccessful Institute of Secular Priests, founded with the support of Cardinal Howard, for the relief of destitute clergy. In the absence of Ellis, Giffard also kept an eye on the Western District and in the summer of 1699 administered Confirmations in Wales. He visited London whenever he could and maintained close connections with the convent and school at Hammersmith, where he would later reside as Vicar Apostolic. These visits became more frequent during Leyburn's last years. Giffard is recorded as celebrating a Confirmation at Hammersmith in April 1700 and dealing with Propaganda on the ailing Leyburn's behalf.

For his subsequent life as Vicar Apostolic of the London District, see pp. 19-23

Further Reading

J. A. Williams, 'Bishops Giffard and Ellis and the Western Vicariate, 1688–1715', *Journal of Ecclesiastical History*, 15 (1964), 218–28
J. A. Williams, '"Our Patriarch": Bishop Bonaventure Giffard, 1642–1734:

---

[11] J. A. Williams, op. cit., 436.

an introductory sketch', *Recusant History*, Vol. 26, no. 3 (May 2003)

B. C. Foley, *Some People of the Penal times* (1991), chap. 8

L. Brockliss, G. Harriss, and A. Macintyre, *Magdalen College and the Crown: Essays for the Tercentenary of the Restoration of the College, 1688* (1988)

George Witham

1655-1725

Titular Bishop of Marcopolis (1703)
Vicar Apostolic of the Midland District (1703-16)
Vicar Apostolic of the Northern District (1716-25)

Giffard was succeeded by George Witham, who was originally intended to act as Leyburn's coadjutor in the London District. Born at the Withams' home of Cliffe Hall, near Darlington, on 16 May 1655, George had six brothers, three of whom also became priests, including Robert, later President of the English College at Douai, and Thomas, Superior of the English Seminary in Paris. George entered the English College, Douai, in 1666, taking the missionary oath on 26 May 1674 in the name of 'Wyvill' (his mother's maiden name). In 1678 he moved to St Gregory's, Paris to complete his theological studies and was ordained in 1688. The same year he was awarded the doctorate in Divinity and returned to Douai to teach theology for four years.

A period as missioner at Newcastle-on-Tyne and Vicar General to Bishop Smith followed. In 1694 he was entrusted by the English bishops with a mission to Rome to deal with problems that had arisen between the secular clergy and the Benedictines. Witham stayed on in Rome as the English bishops' Agent for nine years.

In 1703 Witham learned of his nomination as coadjutor to Bishop John Leyburn of London. He did not seek such preferment and would have been happy to remain in the life of a simple clergyman. Mary of Modena, the widow of James II, had suggested his name for the English episcopate, with the idea that he should become coadjutor to Bishop Leyburn. Witham was consecrated Titular Bishop of Marcopolis on 15 April 1703 in the chapel of the seminary of Montefiascone. The consecrating bishop on that occasion was the seminary's founder, Cardinal Marcantonio Barbarigo, whose cause for beatification was later opened and who was in his own turn ordained a bishop by his uncle, St Gregory Barbarigo. Witham wrote that the Cardinal 'made a sumptuous dinner after the consecration which might be fit to entertain a Prince, and this upon the occasion of the consecration only of a poor Missionary Priest.'[1]

Although Witham had originally been appointed as coadjutor to the London District, by the time of his return Giffard had been transferred to London. Thus Witham was appointed to the Midland District in Giffard's place, living at St Thomas' Priory, Stafford, the home of the Fowler family, and assuming the name 'Markham'. He shepherded the Midland Catholics for thirteen years, though towards the end of the period was limited by poor health. He considered applying for a coadjutor, but was afraid a petition to Rome would lead to an unsuitable appointment, particularly that of Thomas Strickland, a controversial figure who was highly critical of the Vicars Apostolic and who accused Witham of being scrupulous and incapable of business.

For his subsequent years in the Northern District, see pp. 147–8

---

[1] Hemphill, 32-33.

John Talbot Stonor

1678-1756
Titular Bishop of Thespiae (1716)
Vicar Apostolic of the Midland District (1716-56)

John Talbot Stonor, Vicar Apostolic of the Midland District for over forty years, has been surprisingly neglected by historians. Yet J. C. H. Aveling called him 'the most effective Catholic clerical leader of the eighteenth century':

> Stonor was no textbook bishop. He was almost aggressively unecclesiastical in his manner of living. As a red-faced, bucolic country squire, residing habitually in his own or his family's mansions …, he shot and hunted with his Protestant neighbours, hob-nobbed with Protestant peers, and experimented with enclosures and root crops … In his eccentric, aristocratic way, using the "pull" of his class on inferiors, equals and superiors alike, he laid the foundations of the reforms that were mostly achieved, or in train, in 1830 … Through his two agents in Rome, one of whom was his priest nephew, he devised ways of by-passing the Curia or pushing it into courses it distrusted. Though he never questioned the Papal primacy, he was clearly working towards the practical independence of English Catholics. Without ever laying down principles of Episcopal authority, he much increased the prestige and weight in the community of the Vicars Apostolic as a body.[1]

The future bishop was born in 1678, the second son of John Stonor and his wife, Lady Mary Talbot, the daughter of the eleventh Earl of Shrewsbury. The family had lived at Stonor in the Chilterns since at least 1204 and the attached chapel of the Most Blessed Trinity was one of the few in the country that could boast uninterrupted Catholic use across the centuries.

John Talbot Stonor, together with his brothers Thomas and Charles,

---

[1] J. C. H. Aveling, *The Handle and the Axe* (1976), 325.

obtained the licence to travel overseas to Douai. By the age of fourteen both the future bishop's parents had died. His two sisters soon married into well-established Catholic families: Mary married Colonel William Plowden, a Jacobite exile in France who had commanded James II's 2nd Regiment of Foot Guards at the Battle of the Boyne; and Anne married Charles Bodenham of Rotherwas, Herefordshire.

Meanwhile, John moved to Paris to the elite St Gregory's, where the best English students completed the doctorate at the Sorbonne. A glimpse of his conduct in Paris is afforded by the *College Register*:

> Mr Stonor having given offence to some particular persons in ye house by his frequent not rising in due time, and by his having taken too much liberty in defending some opinions which though not condemned yet sounded a little harsh particularly in matters of Grace: He being within a few days to receive Tonsure, upon that occasion to remove the offence given, he voluntarily acknowledged in the presence of all the house, first his shameful negligence in not rising in due time in ye morning, which he said, he always condemned in himself, etc at that time resolved by God's grace to amend for the future. Secondly his indiscretion in maintaining some particular opinions in private disputes at home, which though he did not defend as his own judgement but only problematically, yet he promised that he would not take so much liberty for the future, and that he would defend nothing which sounded more harsh than ye ordinary Thomisticall Doctrine.[2]

Seminaries down the ages have always included such characters and perhaps it was little surprise that he decided to leave the college in February 1698, discerning that he was not called to the priesthood. The next seven years were spent living at Stonor, with his elder brother, Thomas. It was a comfortable existence but also one marked by tragedy. Thomas married Isabella, daughter of the great Royalist, the First Lord Bellasis of Worlaby, but she died prematurely at the age of twenty-five, without giving him children. By this time John had lost not only his sister-in-law but also his younger brother and two sisters. At this juncture, he himself was about to enter the married state but, at the last minute, pulled out and returned to St Gregory's in October 1705. His brother, meanwhile, married Winifred Roper, a descendant of St Thomas More and his beloved daughter Margaret Roper. It is thought that this Winifred may have been the bride originally intended for John.

---

[2] 'The Register Book of St Gregory's College, Paris, 1667-1786', in *Miscellanea* (Catholic Records Series 19), 113-114.

Stonor was ordained priest in Paris in March 1711, at the relatively mature age of thirty-three, and gained his doctorate in May 1714. Several months later he returned to Stonor Park and was soon acting as Vicar General to Bishop Giffard of the London District.

Dom Basil Hemphill, the historian of the Vicars Apostolic, divided Stonor's ecclesiastical career into two: 'in his youthful days he was a storm-centre, and an object of dislike to both bishops and clergy alike' while as time went by 'he gradually won his way to a position of great influence in the Catholic affairs of the country, and was held in the highest respect by all.'[3] As a young priest and bishop, Stonor's great ally was a friend from St Gregory's, Thomas Strickland. Both men were confident and well-connected. Both dreamed of becoming a Vicar Apostolic, despite the obvious perils and hardships involved – Stonor having his eye on the London District and Strickland the Northern. Both had 'Whig' sympathies and, in contrast to many Catholics, supported the Hanoverian Succession. Stonor was thus in sympathy with his Protestant uncle, the Duke of Shrewsbury, who had taken a leading role in negotiating the accession of George I, but differed from his Catholic relatives. Another uncle, William Stonor, had gone into exile with James II and named his first son after the King. 'Bonnie Prince Charlie' was even known to use the alias 'Mr Stonor' in homage to that family's loyalty.

Stonor hoped that King George would improve the conditions of English Catholics, especially since relative toleration existed in his native Hanover. Indeed, his German territories included the English Benedictine Abbey of Lambspring. The King realised the advantage of having the support of a Catholic priest from a distinguished Jacobite family and tried to reward Stonor with a red hat, for as an Elector of the Holy Roman Empire he was able to access the patronage of the Emperor and ultimately the Roman Pontiff. Stonor was never raised to the Sacred Purple, but he did gain the title of Abbot and Baron of Lieu Dieu at Jard-sur-Mer in the Vendée (western France), providing him with a personal income.

In order to fulfil these hopes and secure Catholic allegiance to the new King, Stonor and Strickland publicly atttacked Bishop Giffard, alleging that the octogenarian was approaching senility and not fit to rule. In 1716, having been ordained five years and with limited pastoral experience, Stonor was named Vicar Apostolic of the Midland District. He was consecrated Titular Bishop of Thespiae in Paris that summer by the nuncio, Cardinal

---

[3] Hemphill, 50.

di Bissi. Included in his Briefs were additional faculties to administer the London District in case of Giffard's absence or incapacity.

As a new bishop, Stonor was 'a constant source of trouble and was deeply distrusted by his fellow-clergy ... partly because of his Hanoverian sympathies, but chiefly because of his undisguised ambitions and pushing, intriguing ways which earned him many opponents.'[4] Realizing that the friendship was harming his cause, Stonor distanced himself from Strickland, to the latter's great disappointment. The Treasurer of the Chapter reported with some glee that Strickland's 'own Uncle at Rouen and Mr Meynel [chaplain to the Rouen Poor Clares] do assure us that in all the time he has been there (which was several months) he never said Mass nor even heard Mass but upon holydays, nor even went to the Sacraments.'[5] However, Strickland used his impressive network of contacts to gain from the Government an improvement in the condition of Catholics in return for the taking of an oath of allegiance to the new King. When these negotiations failed, partly due to the lack of support of his co-religionists, he launched a vendetta against the likes of Giffard and Stonor's Jesuit cousin, Gilbert Talbot, Earl of Shrewsbury. Despite his blackened reputation in some circles, he gained the revenues of the abbey of St Pierre de Préaux in Normandy in 1718 and nine years later became Bishop of Namur, seemingly through the influence of George I and the Emperor Charles VI.

Initially Stonor spent most of his time in London, where his interests clearly lay, but in time focussed increasingly on the vast Midland District. Based in Oxfordshire, hardly the most central location from which to govern, he resided variously at Watlington Park, Old Heythrop and Stonor itself, writing his letters to Rome *'ex castello Stonorio in Comitatu Oxoniensi'*. From 1750 he took over the management of the Stonor estates after his nephew, Thomas, moved to Cambrai.

For much of his episcopate Stonor was heavily involved in clarifying the relationship between Vicars Apostolic and the regular clergy, who had up until that time claimed several immunities. In 1723 he complained that it was hard to get a response from his brother bishops: Giffard 'will not act', Petre 'dare not', Witham was 'afraid of every shadow' and Prichard was deemed to be 'waspish and intractable'.[6] A memorial presented to Propaganda in 1745 mentioned a dispute between Stonor and a Franciscan

---

[4] Ibid., 50.
[5] AAW B38, Ep. Var. 6/42 (21 May 1716).
[6] AAW B40, Ep. Var. 8/119.

Recollect by the name of Hall who looked after a mission in Warwickshire but ventured into Derbyshire 'speaking disadvantageously of the clergy missioners, and gathering up contributions that were designed for them.' Stonor wrote to the Provincial complaining of this and 'empowering him at the same time to curtail his faculties.' According to the document, Fr Cantrill replied 'I know not what is meant [by Bishop Stonor] when he talks of suspending Mr Hall and taking away his faculties.'[7] This highlighted the need for a clarification of episcopal jurisdiction with regard to the regular clergy in England. Stonor's campaign led to Benedict XIV's Brief of 1745 and the Bull *Apostolicum Ministerium* of 1753, much to the disgust of the regular Bishops Prichard and York in the Western District.

Stonor was also much-concerned with the quality of teaching at the English College, Rome, which was controlled by the Italian Jesuits. The bishop argued that the college should be given over to the English secular clergy, although he admitted that things would be even worse if the Jesuits were replaced by Italian seculars. He thought the three years of philosophy were useless and that pastoral training was lacking; indeed, students often returned with very poor English.

Stonor's aristocratic background and Whig leanings gave him security and an advantage over his fellow bishops – Giffard, for example, had become little more than a fugitive during the 1715 Jacobite rebellion. However, Stonor's pro-Hanoverian views and emphasis on obedience to civil government also attracted much criticism from fellow Catholics and his 'party' was derisively referred to as the 'Whig Catholics'.

Despite the bishop's stance, his nephew, Mgr Christopher Stonor, was closely allied to the Stuart Court in exile. Ordained in 1743, he had lived for a time at Stonor and, thanks to his uncle's patronage, became Roman Agent for the English bishops. Before moving into the Quirinale Palace, he lived with the Cardinal Duke of York and acted as his chaplain.

By the 1750s Stonor's physical powers were failing and he was no longer able to visit his flock. On 10 February 1752 he consecrated Dr Hornyold as his coadjutor at Stonor. Despite being able to arrange an episcopal consecration in his family chapel, the bishop still had to exercise a degree of caution and used coded language in describing the event to his nephew:

> We have lately had a transaction here, such a one as never was before, I mean the completely fitting out my helper for this business. The performance cost me some pains, but there were so many inconveniences in having it

---

[7] F. Edwards, *The Jesuits in England* (1985), 109.

done elsewhere that it seemed to me worth the while to venture upon it…
Now he is returned to his old Lady in Staffordshire, to take care of ye good
people there and to proceed in time to the work of the perambulation.[8]

Stonor encouraged his new assistant to continue residing at Longbirch,
Staffordshire, thus enabling him to look after the needs of the northern
part of the Midland District. The venerable bishop lasted several more years
and finally died on 29 March 1756, aged 76. He was buried at Stonor.

Further Reading

R. J. Stonor, *Stonor* (1952)

---

[8] R. J. Stonor, *Stonor* (1952), 290.

John Joseph Hornyold

1706-78
Titular Bishop of Philomalia (1752)
Coadjutor to Bishop Stonor (1752-56)
Vicar Apostolic to the Midland District (1756-78)

The Hornyolds of Blackmore Park and Hanley Castle were an old Worcestershire family that had suffered much for King and Faith. The bishop's great-great-grandfather had been killed at the first Battle of Worcester (1643), fighting for Charles I, and his great-grandfather, who helped Charles II escape the country in 1651, lost two-thirds of his estates on account of his royalist and Catholic sympathies, though these were partially reclaimed at the Restoration. A more recent Hornyold, Ralph, became a Jesuit priest and was convicted of recusancy at the Lancaster Sessions in January 1716. The family later built the Church of Our Blessed Lady and St Alphonsus at Blackmore Park and added the noble Italian name of 'Gandolfi' to their surname, thanks to an advantageous marriage.

John Joseph Hornyold himself was born on 19 February 1706, the eldest child of John Hornyold and his wife Mary, eldest daughter of Sir Piers Mostyn of Talacre, Flintshire. He was a late vocation, originally intending to pursue a secular career as the eldest son and heir. In the event, his brother, Thomas, inherited the Blackmore Park estate, married into the Lancashire Towneley family and became a leading Catholic layman and banker. A sister, Anne, became a Carmelite nun and eventually Prioress of the Convent at Lierre in Brabant. The future bishop, meanwhile, entered the English College, Douai, on 7 August 1728, aged twenty-two. Dr Challoner, who was Vice-President of the College, would become a close friend. Hornyold's progress towards ordination was threatened on one occasion when 'one of his companions uncautiously waving a fire-brand, in the hour of recreation, struck our Prelate's left eye with it, and, for some time, deprived him of his sight.'[1] Fortunately he regained full use of his right eye and was able to continue his studies.

Hornyold was ordained at Arras on 22 December 1736. On returning to England in 1737, he spent two years working as chaplain to a certain Mrs Robinson at Westgate, Grantham, in Lincolnshire. His time there was not without incident, as Milner's memoir in the 1818 *Laity's Directory* records:

> Hearing that one of his flock at a distance was in danger of death, he flew to his assistance in the midst of a terrible storm, and swam his horse through a river, swollen with a flood, with imminent danger of being drowned. On another occasion, the constables coming to seize upon him as a Catholic Priest, just when he was finishing mass, he could barely save himself by substituting a female cap for his flowing periwig and throwing a large woman's cloak over his vestments, and in this disguise, throwing himself in a corner of the room into the attitude of prayer.[2]

In 1739 Hornyold became chaplain to Mary, the widow of Thomas Giffard of Chillington, who lived at Longbirch, Staffordshire. After her death in 1753, the house was rented as the residence of the Vicars Apostolic of the Midland District, until Milner decided to move the seat of the Vicariate to Wolverhampton in 1804. As well as fulfilling his pastoral duties as chaplain, Hornyold managed to publish three works during his time with Mrs Giffard: *The Decalogue Explained* (1744), *The Sacraments Explained* (1747), and *The Real Principles of Catholics* (1749), which was based on the work of Rev. John Johnson, his predecessor at Longbirch. The first of these books was the most successful, going through many editions. According to Milner, 'this was so generally approved of, that he received something like official thanks from Oxford for the publication. It was not to be expected, however, that he should be thanked from that quarter for his other works.'[3]

In 1750 Bishop Stonor decided to ask Propaganda for the appointment of Hornyold as his coadjutor. He had already been working as his Vicar General, in succession to Thomas Brockholes of Chillington. The relevant Bull of Benedict XIV was received at the end of 1751 and the new bishop was consecrated at Stonor Park on 10 February 1752, with the titular see

---

[1] *Laity's Directory for the Year 1818*, pages unnumbered.
[2] Ibid.
[3] Ibid.

of Philomalia. The new coadjutor remained at Longbirch, which was a convenient headquarters for administering the northern part of the Vicariate.

On Bishop Stonor's death on 29 March 1756, Hornyold succeeded as Vicar Apostolic of the Midland District. Continuing to use Longbirch as his base, he was regular in visiting his extensive District and even supplying for priests during their absence. He gained the reputation of being a devout and hard-working pastor. Milner said that 'though he was most abstemious and mortified in his way of living, he was cheerful and good humoured, as his friends in general testify, and particularly those clergymen, who, in succession were his chaplains.' Milner also included in his memoir this edifying anecdote, which Hornyold himself liked to relate:

> Making one of his pastoral visitations, on a time, on horse-back, and coming to a division of the road where each path led to the same place, he could with all his force and management make his horse go the way he was desirous of travelling; he therefore let the beast go the other road. He had not proceeded far in this, when he found a poor traveller lying on a bank and near expiring. Approaching to him, and inquiring of the sick man what he could do to relieve him, the latter exclaimed: I want a Priest: for God's sake procure me a Catholic Priest. On this Bishop Hornyold assured the dying man that he himself was a Priest, and also a Bishop. It is needless to describe the joy of the penitent, or the charity and zeal of the confessor: let it suffice to say, that having received the sick man's confession, and administered the Holy Viaticum and Extreme Unction to him, ... he remained with the poor object of his pastoral care, until he witnessed his happy end.[4]

In 1765, with his health declining, Hornyold began actively seeking a coadjutor and Thomas Talbot, the brother of Challoner's coadjutor, was duly consecrated. Hornyold did not, however, step into the shadows, and remained heavily involved in the concerns of the Vicariate. After the death of William Errington in 1768, Hornyold took over the management of the recently established school at Sedgley Park. He also rebuilt the house and chapel at Old Oscott (later known as Maryvale) in 1752, seeing this as a possible residence for his successors.

Bishop Hornyold died at Longbirch on Boxing Day 1778 and was buried at Brewood. Although most of his estate was left to Bishop Talbot,

---

[4] Ibid.

a gold watch was reserved for his nephew, Rev. Anthony Clough, who was working as chaplain to the Giffards of Chillington.

Further Reading

Lillian Lascelles, 'The Hornyold Family of Blackmore Park', *Worcestershire Recusant*, no.22 (December 1973), 1-12

THOMAS JOSEPH TALBOT

1727-95
TITULAR BISHOP OF ACON (1766)
COADJUTOR OF THE MIDLAND DISTRICT (1766-78)
VICAR APOSTOLIC OF THE MIDLAND DISTRICT (1778-95)

Hornyold's successor was the brother of James Talbot, at that time coadjutor to Challoner. The Talbot brothers shared much in common and, according to Edwin Burton, 'their long disinterested service of the Church is among the brightest memories of our eighteenth century history.'[1]

Thomas Joseph Talbot was born on 17 July 1727 at Heythrop, Oxfordshire, the son of George Talbot and his wife Mary Fitzherbert. His eldest brother later became fourteenth Earl of Shrewsbury. He was educated at Twyford, a school in Hampshire run by the secular clergy, and entered the English College, Douai on 6 August 1740. He later took a year out of Douai to make the Grand Tour together with his brother, James, and their mentor, Alban Butler, author of the *Lives of the Saints*. This was considered essential formation for any respectable English gentleman. Talbot was ordained on 19 December 1752 and returned to the English Mission the following year. He spent nine years ministering at Brockhampton, Hampshire.

In 1762 the Society of Jesus was expelled from France and the English Jesuits thus had to leave the College at St Omer, which had been founded by Robert Persons in 1592. The College community found refuge in Bruges, where the school continued, and the buildings at St Omer were offered by the authorities to the English secular clergy. The Vicars Apostolic did not need another institution overseas and feared it would compromise the position of Douai. Challoner had, on this occasion, great sympathy with the Jesuits and saw their expulsion as an indirect attack on the Pope

---

[1] Burton, ii, 47.

himself. However, when they realised that the College would otherwise be lost to the English Church, they reluctantly accepted the offer of the French Government. Thomas Talbot was nominated President and eventually moved, with great reluctance, to St Omer. The preparatory school at Esquerchin (founded thanks to the Talbots) was moved to St Omer and the school continued until the Revolution, producing the likes of Daniel O'Connell, the great Irish patriot and statesman.

The Jesuits understandably resented the loss of St Omer and saw the takeover by the secular clergy as a betrayal; there followed a heated controversy that resurrected the age-old tensions between seculars and regulars, and resulted in numerous pamphlets being printed and petitions sent to Rome. The Jesuits even alleged that the seculars had persuaded the Parlement of Paris to expel them from St Omer.

Talbot, however, only remained at St Omer a short time. His distinguished pedigree and obvious abilities soon ear-marked him for promotion and in February 1766 he was nominated coadjutor to Bishop Hornyold of the Midland District. Despite expressing his reluctance to exercise such office, he was consecrated Titular Bishop of Acon later that year, possibly in France, and passed the reins at St Omer to Alban Butler, who had accompanied the Talbot brothers on their Grand Tour.

Talbot had many gifts and his business acumen is revealed in his enlargement of the farm at Longbirch and involvement in turnpike trusts and property around Wolverhampton. However, Burton described Talbot as 'a man of singularly retiring nature, mistrustful of himself and anxious to avoid notice.'[2] He resented the controversies that characterized the English Church at the time and his moderation, as Ward argued, produced 'a separation between his district and the other three which almost amounted to a schism.'[3]

In 1786 he chose as his coadjutor Charles Berington, a former chaplain to the Petre family at Ingatestone and cousin of Joseph Berington, the controversial Cisalpine writer. It would prove to be a divisive appointment, especially after Berington's election onto the Catholic Committee in 1788.

Talbot signed the encyclical of 21 October 1789 condemning the Oath of Allegiance proposed by the Catholic Committee, but held back its publication in his District. 'If a schism and division amongst ourselves

<hr />

[2] Ibid., ii, 46.
[3] *Dawn*, ii, 130-31.

could be avoided,' he wrote, 'it would be a most desirable thing.'[4] In November 1789 Bishop Berington publicly declared his support of the oath. In January 1790 all fifteen Staffordshire clergy signed an address to Talbot, composed by Joseph Berington and declaring support for the oath. This was widely circulated and became known as the 'Staffordshire Creed' and was eventually declared heretical by Bishop Walmesley, the Committee's main opponent.

Talbot was reluctant to put any further views in writing, but in February 1791 met a deputation of the 'Staffordshire Clergy' at Longbirch. They reported that the bishop 'approved of the oath in its present form' and lamented that 'the measures in the condemnation of the first Oath had been so precipitately conducted.' He also 'admired the temper and great moderation of the Gentlemen of the Committee, whose views he thought were most upright, and whose zeal to promote the cause of religion, and the interest of their Catholic brethren, merited the warmest commendation.'[5]

His brother, who had similar views, died at the beginning of 1790 and Talbot took his place as a member of the Committee. After the death of Bishop Gibson that May, Talbot showed his sympathy for the ideals of the Committee by suggesting that the clergy of the Northern District elect their next bishop. This view was seconded in a pamphlet signed by 'A Layman' (Sir John Throckmorton) who also used the opportunity to attack the institution of Vicars Apostolic. The war between the 'Orthodox' and the Cisalpines intensified.

When the Vicars Apostolic issued a second encyclical on 19 January 1791 condemning the oath, Talbot's signature was conspicuous by its absence. In a letter to Gibson, he stated his preference for a more 'conciliatory scheme' and explained that 'the Oath which it holds forth I have already condemned once, I cannot see any good end it can answer to condemn it a second time.'[6] Talbot was concerned to promote peace and conciliation. However, he prevented the Vicars Apostolic from acting jointly. Once again in 1792 a Pastoral was issued by all the Vicars Apostolic except Talbot, condemning fourteen propositions from Throckmorton's works and books by Berington and other Cisalpines. The following year Talbot opposed the suspension of Joseph Berington:

Without abetting any wrong opinion Mr Berington may have broached, and without pretending to exculpate him from censure when he deserves

[4] Ibid., i, 184.
[5] Ibid., i, 245.
[6] Ibid., i, 244.

it, I consider him as a man of learning, and as a person very regular and even exemplary in the exercise of his missionary functions. He is ready, as he declares, to explain or even to retract what may be deemed amiss in his writings. Why, then, must he be run down like a wild beast? and now that the conflagration seems to be over, why light up a new one?[7]

Encouraged by Berington and John Kirk, Talbot supported the establishment of a new college for both lay and ecclesiastical students at Old Oscott in 1794, the precursor of the seminary for the Archdiocese of Birmingham. The first President was John Bew, who had presided over the English seminary in Paris, and Talbot maintained control over religious matters. However, a lay board of governors took responsibility for the day-to-day running of the college, ensuring that the education was more extensive and up-to-date than that in the colleges of the English Catholic diaspora.

Talbot began to suffer poor health and on 14 April 1795 made the journey to Hotwells, outside Bristol, to take the waters at the spa, accompanied by his coadjutor. The bishop unexpectedly suffered an apoplectic fit during dinner on 23 April and died the following day, without regaining consciousness. He was buried in the 'Dead Vault' at St Joseph's, Trenchard Street, although such was the reputation of Berington in Walmesley's District that the local priest, Robert Plowden, did not allow him to celebrate the Requiem and did so himself. In 1906 Talbot's body was translated to Downside Abbey, since the old Trenchard Street church was being pulled down.

---

[7] Ibid., ii, 44-45.

CHARLES BERINGTON

1748-98

TITULAR BISHOP OF HIEROCAESAREA (1786)
COADJUTOR TO BISHOP TALBOT (1786-95)
VICAR APOSTOLIC OF THE MIDLAND DISTRICT (1795-98)

Bernard Ward summed Bishop Berington up as 'a man whose career disappointed his early promise.'[1] Born at Stock Hall (now Greenwoods) at Stock, near Chelmsford, Essex, he was the third child of Thomas Berington of Moat Hall, Pontesbury, Shropshire, and his wife, Anne Bates. He was highly esteemed by his teachers at the English College, Douai, where he studied between 1761 and 1765, and was then sent to St Gregory's College, Paris. Ordained a priest in 1775, he finished his DD the following year and returned to the English Mission. For eight years he served as chaplain at Ingatestone Hall, just a few miles from his birthplace, and then between 1784 and 1786 accompanied Thomas Joseph Giffard of Chillington on his Grand Tour.

On his return to England in 1786 Berington was appointed coadjutor to Bishop Thomas Talbot of the Midland District, aged thirty-eight. On 1 August he was consecrated Titular Bishop of Hierocaesarea in Talbot's private chapel at Longbirch.

In 1788 Berington was elected as a member of the Catholic Committee. His involvement with this controversial body, which later became the Cisalpine Club, dominated the rest of his life and attracted much criticism. Milner described him as 'an unambitious, sweet-tempered prelate, of strong natural parts, and qualified for the highest station in the Church, had he been resolved to support her necessary authority against

---

[1] Ibid., i, 122-23.

the prevailing encroachments and aberrations of powerful laymen.'[2]

After the death of Bishop James Talbot, the Catholic Committee vigorously campaigned for the translation of Berington to the London District. Unusually for the Vicars Apostolic of the London District, Talbot had died without a coadjutor and there was no fixed method for the selection of his successor. Berington had many supporters among the clergy, too, since he was a native of Essex and well-known in London. Indeed, at a clergy meeting in London following the late bishop's Requiem, Berington came out as the favourite for succession with 39 votes out of 60. Eventually the Holy See chose Dr John Douglass as the new Vicar Apostolic, much to the Committee's displeasure. The lay members even considered refusing to acknowledge Douglass as bishop and emphasised the need for the clergy and laity to choose their own bishops, even without reference to Rome. Berington quickly printed a Circular addressed to the London clergy resigning any pretension to the London Vicariate.

At the death of Bishop Thomas Talbot at Bristol on 24 February 1795, Berington automatically succeeded as Vicar Apostolic of the Midland District. Propaganda refused to grant him the extraordinary faculties usually conceded to Vicars Apostolic until he renounced the Committee's *Blue Books*. These volumes, so-called because of the blue binding, contained the documents issued by the Committee, including the controversial oath, which formed part of the proposed Relief Bill in which the members referred to themselves as 'protesting Catholic dissenters'. The result was a long correspondence between Berington and Propaganda. In the meantime, the Midland District was in the unusual position of being ruled by a bishop without full faculties. This meant, among other things, that he could not ordain seculars (only regulars) or consecrate the Holy Oils on Maundy Thursday, which had to be sent to him from one of the other Districts.

A suitable retraction was eventually signed on 11 October 1797. Berington did not live to receive the extraordinary faculties from Rome, which reached Bishop Douglass on 5 June 1798. Berington died suddenly three days later, having been taken ill as he was riding home from Sedgley Park. He expired by the roadside, about eight in the evening, in the arms of Dr Morrison of Wolverhampton, having been given absolution by his chaplain, Dr Kirk. He was buried in the

[2] Ibid., i, 123.

cemetery at Brewood, not far from the grave of Bishop Hornyold, and his brother later erected a memorial in his honour.

Further Reading

S. Foster, *The Catholic Church in Stock* (1991)

GREGORY STAPLETON

1748-1802

TITULAR BISHOP OF HIEROCAESAREA (1801)
VICAR APOSTOLIC OF THE MIDLAND DISTRICT (1801-02)

It took over two years to appoint Bishop Berington's successor, partly due to the French occupation of Rome. Dr Milner was the choice of the other Vicars Apostolic who promised to follow a path very different from Berington. Eventually Rome decided on a neutral candidate, Gregory Stapleton, who had had little to do with the Midland District. The Scotch Agent in Rome, Mr McPherson, revealed that Stapleton's appointment was a stop-gap to prevent Milner's nomination. As it happened, Stapleton ruled for little over a year and he is best remembered in the field of Catholic education, as the last President of St Omer and the first President of St Edmund's, Old Hall Green.

Gregory Stapleton was born on 7 December 1748 at Carlton Hall in Yorkshire, the seventh son of Nicholas Stapleton and his third wife, Winifred, the daughter of John White of Dover Street, London. His uncle, Thomas, was an alumnus of Douai and a priest based in London until his death in 1754. The young Gregory also entered the English College, Douai, after preparatory studies at Esquerchin. By the time of his diaconate he was acting as Professor of Music and, following his priestly ordination in 1773, remained at the college as Procurator. However, after twelve years in the post, he left Douai due to a disagreement with the new President, William Gibson.

In 1787 Stapleton accompanied two young Stonors on the Grand Tour. In Rome he met their ailing great-uncle, Mgr Stonor, and briefly considered replacing him as the English Agent in the Eternal City. However, on his return, Stapleton instead succeeded Dr Wilkinson as President of the

English College at St Omer, formerly run by the Jesuits but handed over to the English secular clergy in 1762 following the expulsion of the Society from France. It proved to be a difficult Presidency due to the Revolution. On 1 August 1793 two hundred soldiers 'invaded' the college, on the pretext of a forged letter supposedly written by one of the professors. Stapleton, several members of staff and some fifty-two students were imprisoned at the nearby French College. Conditions were tolerable and Stapleton managed to communicate with friends in England, as well as the imprisoned members of the English College, Douai.

In January 1794 they were transferred in wagons to Arras, where they remained for four months and were 'distressed for clothing, ill-fed, and had only straw to lie on.'[1] According to Thomas Cleghorn, a St Omer professor who had managed to avoid imprisonment, Stapleton and some of the other St Omerians were condemned to the guillotine and the customary red mark was painted on their doors.

However, at the end of May 1794 they were moved once again to Doullens, where they joined the *Trente-Deux* from Douai. Although kept in separate quarters, the two groups were allowed to see each other and, to the amazement of the guards, amuse themselves during the hours of recreation by playing Leap-frog and Prisoners' Base. Conditions improved, although one of Stapleton's professors, Richard Brettargh, died in captivity. Petitions were sent to the authorities and on 20 October the St Omerians were given leave to depart Doullens, singing the psalm *In exitu Israel de Ægypto* from their wagons. They returned to the French College at St Omer, where they were better treated. At the beginning of 1795 Stapleton received permission to travel to Paris to present further petitions for the two colleges. As Poynter recalled in the *Catholic Magazine and Review* (1831):

> After many repulses, he at length succeeded in his object. By remonstrance, by entreaty, and by the more powerful influence of money, he obtained from the Directory an order addressed to the magistrates of St Omer's and Douai, empowering them to release from imprisonment the citizens, ex-members of the two *ci-devant* English colleges, and to furnish them with passports to return to England.[2]

Stapleton brought the good news to the Irish College, Douai, where the *Trente-Deux* were under house arrest. Poynter wrote:

[1] *St Edmund's*, 91.
[2] Ibid., 94.

We shall never forget the impression made on our minds by the unexpected arrival of Mr Stapleton [President of St Omer] at the door of our prison at Douai, on his return from Paris. During the hesitation and delay of the turnkey to admit Mr Stapleton, we had nearly all heard of his arrival, and had assembled in the court to meet him. It was a moment of the most intense anxiety. He soon relieved us from our suspense. "Good news, my boys," said he; "thank God, we are going to England." I believe we never in the whole course of our lives experienced such lively emotions of joy; many of the collegians gave loud cheers of applause.[3]

Shortly afterwards, Stapleton travelled back to England with the remnant of the two colleges and arrived in Dover on 2 March 1795. It was decided to reconstitute the fledgling school at Old Hall Green into a college. Stapleton joined Bishop Douglass in meeting William Pitt and the Duke of Portland to gain their approval. Stapleton was already acquainted with the duke and the two statesmen encouraged the project, suggesting that a popular outcry might be avoided since it would be seen as an extension of the existing institution at Old Hall.

Thus the College of St Edmund was born, instituted, according to its *Rules*, 'for the purpose of promoting the good of religion and society by forming Catholic youth, particularly of the London District, to the duties of the sacred ministry, or of civil life, according to each one's respective vocation.'[4] On 15 August 1795 Stapleton began his role as the college's first President, with Poynter as his deputy. Matters were still unsettled – Propaganda tried to appoint John Daniel (formerly President of Douai) as President of St Edmund's and there were discussions to unite Old Hall with Crook Hall (the foundation that later became Ushaw). In 1798 there were rumours that Stapleton was to be named the new Rector of the Venerable English College, Rome, but the declining situation in the Eternal City made this impossible.

In the meantime, Stapleton concentrated on consolidating the reconstituted college at Old Hall Green. He oversaw a major extension of the buildings, which were opened and blessed by Bishop Douglass on 29 September 1799. He also enjoyed welcoming two nephews to the college, 'one of whom,' as Bernard Ward wrote, 'distinguished himself as an officer during the Peninsular War. He used in later life to talk about his days at St Edmund's, and of his uncle, the President, whom he would often try and

---

[3] Ibid., 95.
[4] Ibid., 138.

put out of temper, he said, in order to see him pull his wig on one side.'[5]

On 21 March 1799 'some sacrilegious Robbers broke into the Chapel through the window of the Sacristy, and carried away the Tabernacle with its Divine contents, plundering the Sacristy of everything that had the appearance of gold or silver.'[6] The Tabernacle was discovered at the bottom of a pond and an Act of Reparation was ordered to be recited every year on Maundy Thursday, after the Mandatum. This practice continued into the twentieth century.

In the autumn of 1800 Stapleton went to Rome on 'a deputation of equal secrecy and importance.'[7] This concerned the relationship between the Prince Regent and the Catholic Mrs Fitzherbert. They had secretly married in 1785 but separated nine years later, shortly before the marriage of the Prince to Caroline of Brunswick. However this marriage did not last long and the Prince soon turned back to Mrs Fitzherbert, who agreed to renew relations providing the Holy See decided favourably on the validity of their secret marriage. Stapleton accompanied the Rev. John Nassau, a priest of Warwick Street chapel and confessor to Mrs Fitzherbert. Rome eventually decided in favour of the marriage and Stapleton returned with Nassau via Ancona, Trieste, Linz, Dresden and Hamburg, thus avoiding France during hostilities. They landed at Great Yarmouth on 10 October 1800.

Having been noticed in Rome, Stapleton was appointed to succeed Bishop Berington as Vicar Apostolic of the Midland District on 7 November 1800. The long inter-regnum had proven to be chaotic since two parties claimed jurisdiction over the Vicariate: John Bew, the Vicar General, and Bishop Gibson, the senior Vicar Apostolic, who argued that Bew's appointment had not been valid due to Berington's lack of full faculties. It must have been a relief to all when Dr Stapleton was consecrated on 8 March 1801. The ceremony took place at St Edmund's, the consecrating bishops being Douglass, Sharrock and Moylan (Bishop of Cork). Bernard Ward noted that this was the first time for several centuries that three bishops took part in a consecration ceremony and that hitherto the English privilege was followed of the ordaining bishop using two priest assistants. Stapleton moved to Longbirch, near Wolverhampton, and appointed Thomas Walsh, then a deacon, as his private secretary. The young man was ordained priest shortly afterwards in the bishop's private

[5] Ibid., 164.
[6] Ibid., 172.
[7] Ibid., 178.

chapel and would, of course, later become Vicar Apostolic of the Midland District.

Stapleton's health failed soon after his consecration. According to Dr Kirk, 'for some years he had laboured under a confirmed asthma, which was much increased by the fatigue he underwent in giving confirmation in several places during the spring before he left Staffordshire.'[8] In May 1802 he seemed well enough to travel to the continent. The Treaty of Amiens (25 March 1802) had resulted in a decree declaring that the English colleges should be restored to their rightful owners. Stapleton joined a party consisting of John Daniel, Thomas Smith (a Douai professor), John Bew (President of Oscott) and Thomas Cleghorn (a professor at St Edmund's). The day before his departure, Stapleton spent a restful day at Shooter's Hill, near Greenwich. After arriving at his beloved St Omer on 19 May and taking a room in *l'auberge de Sainte Catherine*, he fell ill and required medical assistance. Having been bled by the doctors, as Bishop Douglass related, 'better symptoms then appeared, but the stupor continued, and at the half-past-ten at night [on 23 May 1802] he expired, without a groan.'[9]

Bishop Stapleton had always assumed he would one day return to St Omer and, during his Presidency at Old Hall, was referred to as 'President of St Omer's temporarily appointed over St Edmund's'. The church of Saint-Denis was crowded for the Requiem and included a deputation from the municipality. The bishop was then interred in the cemetery of St Martin-au-Laërt, about a mile outside the town.

---

[8] J. Kirk, *Biographies of English Catholics in the Eighteenth Century*, eds J. H. Pollen and E. Burton (1909), 218.
[9] *St Edmund's*, 182.

JOHN MILNER

1752-1826

TITULAR BISHOP OF CASTABALA (1803)
VICAR APOSTOLIC OF THE MIDLAND DISTRICT (1803-26)

Dubbed by Newman the 'English Athanasius',[1] Bishop Milner was one of the most forceful and influential of the Vicars Apostolic and even Pius VII referred to him as a firebrand (*un tizzone*). He offered a new model of what an English Catholic bishop could be – confident, unafraid of controversy, keen to uphold the primacy of ecclesiastical authority and defend orthodoxy, and also truly pastoral. Many of his fiery opinions could be found in the appropriately named *Orthodox Journal*. Milner moved the Church away from dependence on the great Catholic families and looked towards the victory of Ultramontanism later in the nineteenth century.

Unlike his predecessors in the Midland District, John Milner came from humble stock and this freedom from attachments to the Catholic nobility and gentry enabled him in later life to assert the authority of the Church against that of the leading laymen. He was born in London on 14 October 1752, the son of a tailor, Joseph Miller, and his wife Helen Marsland, both of whom had moved to the capital from the Catholic stronghold of Lancashire. At the age of seven John was sent to the school at Edgbaston run by the English Franciscans and five years later moved to Sedgley Park, thanks to the patronage of Bishop Challoner. His family name was entered at the Park as 'Milner' rather than 'Miller', a mistake often attributed to the poor state of his father's mental health.

The following year, in April 1766, Milner went to the English College, Douai, where he remained eleven years and earned the nicknames of 'Jupiter', on account of his physical and intellectual strength, and (for more

---

[1] W. Ward, *The Life of John Henry Cardinal Newman* (1907), i, 119.

obscure reasons) 'Apollo'. His contemporaries among the lay students included the future eleventh Duke of Norfolk and John Philip Kemble, who won fame as a Shakespearian actor and manager of Covent Garden.

After his priestly ordination in 1777, Milner returned to London where he lived in Gray's Inn, running the library of the Old Chapter and acting as a supply priest or 'jobber' at the various chapels and missions. In October 1779 he was appointed to Winchester, a rare instance of an urban mission not dependent on gentry patronage. Milner replaced an Irish priest, James Nolan, who had caught a fatal infection while ministering to some French prisoners of war.

Members of his new flock were at first taken aback by Milner's youthful appearance and complained to Challoner that they had been sent a mere boy. However, they quickly warmed to him and admired his energy and pastoral zeal. In 1782 Milner helped find one of the younger members of his congregation a place at Douai. The youth was John Lingard, who later became a great historian and an opponent of Milner in controversy.

Milner was often found visiting prisoners in Winchester. In 1788, for example, he became convinced of the innocence of a condemned man named Sainsbury. He wrote several letters to the press, though the poor man's innocence was only established after the execution. Milner later returned to the condemned cells to visit four seamen from Java who had been convicted of murder. The young priest succeeded in converting them through the use of signs and a picture of the Crucifixion. Sarak, Raboo, Rabone and Chumoo were subsequently baptized, taking the names of the four Evangelists. He accompanied them to the scaffold by riding behind the cart, but was so affected that he had to leave Winchester for a short period immediately afterwards.

Alongside his pastoral work, Milner managed to find the time to research and write works on antiquarian subjects. He became a Fellow of the Society of Antiquaries in 1790, producing many articles for the Society's *Archaelogia* and dedicating *An Historical and Critical Enquiry into the Existence and Character of St George* (1792) to the Society's President. He also wrote pieces for the *Gentleman's Magazine*.

His magnum opus was the two-volume *History, Civil and Ecclesiastical, and Survey of the Antiquities of Winchester* (1798), which was the result of a request from a local bookseller and completed within twelve months. Despite the narrow nature of the subject, Milner was able to touch upon many elements of historical and apologetic importance. To take one example, he defended the reputation of Mary Tudor, who had married Philip of Spain in Winchester Cathedral. 'If Mary was a persecutor,' he wrote, 'it was not in virtue of any tenet of her religion that she became so.'[2] Moreover, he pointed out that Mary was provoked to take a strict policy, that both Protestants and Catholics were guilty of much persecution in the period and that the Queen's black reputation had been exaggerated and misrepresented by the likes of John Foxe.

Milner criticized the widespread lack of respect for medieval buildings, which resulted in a great deal of destruction and vandalism, and built a new Gothic chapel dedicated to St Peter in 1792, designed by a fellow enthusiast, John Carter. Milner had first met Carter when he was copying some recently uncovered wall paintings in Winchester Cathedral. It should be remembered that the typical Catholic church at the end of the eighteenth century resembled a dissenting chapel, with a notable lack of religious iconography and even an absence of the reserved Blessed Sacrament. The chapel in Winchester expressed a new confidence, thanks to the Catholic Relief Act, and Milner's own ideas about what a church should look like. He wrote that

> instead of following the modern style of building churches and chapels, which are in general square chambers, with small sashed windows and fashionable decorations, hardly to be distinguished, when the altars and benches are removed, from common assembly rooms; it was concluded upon to imitate the models in this kind which have been left us by our religious ancestors, who applied themselves with such ardour and unrivalled success to the cultivation and perfection of ecclesiastical architecture.[3]

The Gothic altarpiece at St Peter's contained a tabernacle based on the West End of York Minster and a reproduction of Raphael's *Transfiguration*. The stained glass windows had depictions of the many saints connected to Winchester over the centuries. Throughout the chapel, the whole wealth of Catholic symbols could be found, especially in the roof bosses and on the shields under the arches.

Rosemary Hill has referred to Milner as 'Pugin's immediate intellectual predecessor'.[4] The two shared a belief that the Gothic style was a living symbol of the Faith and a clear sign of the continuity of Catholicism. Indeed, Milner transported the twelfth-century doorway of the Magdalen Hospital to St Peter's, to serve as the main street entrance, and arranged

---

[2] J. Milner, *History and Survey of the Antiquities of Winchester* (1798), ii, 296.
[3] Ibid., 251.
[4] Rosemary Hill, *God's Architect: Pugin and the Building of Romantic Britain* (2007), 141.

such artifacts as a 'druidical stone' and capitals and bosses rescued from Hyde Abbey in the grounds to illustrate the church's place in history. However, there was no mistaking St Peter's as a Georgian creation; there were none of the rood screens or chantry chapels that would become such a familiar feature of the nineteenth-century Gothic Revival.

Milner became a well-known figure not only in the field of ecclesiastical architecture and antiquities but also in that of controversy and apologetics. His study of the history and antiquities of Winchester had itself begotten a passionate debate in print with Dr Sturges, Prebendary and Chancellor of Winchester, and had eventually resulted in Milner's famous *End of Controversy*, written in 1802 but, on the advice of friends such as Bishop Horsley of Bangor, not published until 1818. It consisted of letters supposedly written by ministers of different denominations and was one of Milner's most enduring works – translated into French and Italian and inspiring Victorian converts such as Frederick Faber, Edward Caswall and William Lockhart.

It was at Winchester that Milner first championed the cause of orthodoxy not only against Protestants but against liberal Catholics, in particular the members of the ascendant Catholic Committee, and he acted as an adviser to the Vicars Apostolic in the struggles that he would eventually fight as a bishop. Milner preached the supremacy of ecclesiastical authority and resented lay interference in ecclesial matters. It was perhaps no accident that the priest's chair at Winchester was based on the coronation throne at Westminster Abbey. Milner violently opposed the inclusion of the phrase 'Protesting Catholic Dissenters' in the second Catholic Relief Bill and assisted Bishops Douglass and Walmesley in seeking the support of the Anglican bishops in defeating it in the House of Lords.

As a prominent churchman, it seemed only a matter of time before Milner gained a mitre. In 1797 the Prefect of Propaganda, Hyacinthe-Sigismond Cardinal Gerdil, considered making him coadjutor to the troubled Bishop Berington, the brother of Milner's nemesis, Joseph Berington. After the bishop's sudden death in 1798, Milner was considered the choice of the other Vicars Apostolic and, according to Robert Smelt, the Roman Agent, his Briefs had actually been drawn out. Then, at the last moment, Pius VII made a change, apparently because of Milner's controversy with Dr Sturges, which made him an unacceptable choice with the British Government – a not unimportant consideration given the Pope's reliance on British Forces in the face of French aggression.

After Stapleton's untimely death in 1802, the name of Milner was once more put forward by the other bishops to Propaganda and, once again, there was a long delay. In the meantime, Bishop Gibson, the senior Vicar Apostolic, tried to control the affairs of the District, claiming that Stapleton's Vicar General, Dr Poynter, had no right to jurisdiction since he was a priest of the London District. Poynter was, indeed, the late bishop's choice as successor but was instead appointed coadjutor to Bishop Douglass. Around the same time, Milner was finally confirmed as Vicar Apostolic of the Midland District, thanks to the influence in Rome of Cardinal Erskine. Though he had reservations about Milner, the cardinal also realized that his strength of character was required by the situation in the District. Milner was consecrated at his beloved Winchester on 22 May 1803, followed, a week later, by the consecration of Poynter at St Edmund's, on which occasion Milner preached. The two new bishops then spent the rest of their lives disagreeing with each other.

It took Milner some time to settle into his new role. He found Longbirch an unsuitable residence, not only remote but forcing him to live beyond his means as a gentleman farmer. In September 1804 he decided to move to Giffard House, in the centre of Wolverhampton, which had been built by Francis Smith of Warwick between 1727 and 1733. It included a public chapel, hidden behind the three storey façade, which became a sort of pro-cathedral for Midland Catholicism under Milner. This move to the 'Great House' was highly significant. It involved turning away from dependence on the Catholic families, based as they were in the countryside, and embracing the emerging urban Catholicism of the new industrial centres.

Wolverhampton was still a long way from London. Milner was an effective and pastorally-minded bishop, with a great sympathy for the poor and the middle classes, but initially saw his new life in the Midlands as something of an exile and he was seemingly surrounded by unorthodoxy, as represented by the liberal views of the 'Staffordshire Clergy'. Milner tried to engineer a move to London and asked Archbishop Troy of Dublin and Bishop Moylan of Cork to petition the Holy See for a transfer, either exchanging places with Poynter or ruling the Midland District from London through a coadjutor. This was vigorously opposed by Douglass and the other bishops and a Decree from Propaganda finally settled the matter in December 1806 – Milner was to stay where he was.

Milner was the first Vicar Apostolic to appreciate the close connection between Irish affairs and the English Catholic community, especially after the Union of Great Britain with Ireland in 1800. The story of Catholic Emancipation was, to a large extent, the story of Irish influence on English politics and from 1800 the Irish demand for the total emancipation of Catholics constantly rang in the ears of the Government. In 1807 Milner became the parliamentary agent in England for the Irish bishops, who were also great opponents of the Cisalpine spirit, and was given permission to reside in London whenever this new responsibility required it. Milner's confidence rose still further for he believed he had behind him the strength of Irish Catholicism.

It would be tedious to record in detail the numerous battles fought by the bishop against the various lay-led bodies campaigning for Emancipation: the Cisalpine Club and (from 1808) the Catholic Board. Throughout his life, Milner stuck to his principles and saw no middle way. In particular, he opposed any form of government interference in Catholic affairs and resisted all attempts to democratize the Church or usurp clerical authority, whereas the other bishops were generally willing to negotiate with the authorities in return for increased liberties. Milner's great fault was that his passion for orthodoxy led to sharpness in his words. Bernard Ward wrote that he had 'grievances against everyone, from the Holy Father downwards, with the inevitable result that he fell out one time or another with everyone with whom he came into contact.' Yet the clergy of the Midland District, whom he at first mistrusted, tended to stick by him and would even refuse 'a priest from the South permission to say Mass in their churches unless he would first promise to take no part in persecuting their bishop.'[5]

A particular focus of Milner's disdain was the question of the veto of episcopal appointments by the State. He had in fact initially consented to the veto as a reasonable security but changed his mind in 1808, taking the lead of the Irish bishops. Milner was a lone voice of opposition amongst the Vicars Apostolic and wrote that 'I shall be baited like a bull but I am ready to encounter the white bears of Hudson's Bay ... rather than yield.'[6] A new Bill including provision for a veto, was prepared by Henry Grattan in 1813 and introduced by Canning in the following year. The Bill was agreed upon by the Catholic Board but eventually dropped,

[5] *Eve*, ii, 181.
[6] F. C. Husenbeth, *The Life of the Right Rev. John Milner D.D.* (1862), 231.

thanks in part to Milner's persistent opposition. Milner was subsequently dismissed from the Catholic Board and he departed the meeting with the dramatic words: 'You may expel me from this Board, but I thank God, Gentlemen, that you cannot exclude me from the Kingdom of Heaven.'[7] Even Rome accepted the idea of a veto, through the celebrated rescript of Mgr Quarantotti, the Secretary of Propaganda. Government vetoes, after all, were common in Catholic Europe and the Papacy was in need of British help against Napoleon. However, the document was condemned by the Irish bishops and attacked by the populist Daniel O'Connell. When Milner visited Rome in 1814 the Pope agreed to refer the rescript to a special Congregation – seen as tantamount to a revocation.

Milner found an ally in Cardinal Litta, the Prefect of Propaganda, but when the latter died in 1820 and was replaced by Cardinal Fontana, Milner found himself more vulnerable to censure. He was asked to stop contributing to the *Orthodox Journal* or else be removed from his Vicariate. The new Cardinal Prefect wrote:

> Scarcely are we able to persuade ourselves how a Vicar Apostolic, bound by such close ties to the Holy See and the Sacred Congregation, can dare to forget his own ministry and spread abroad the seeds of discord, to trample upon the honour of high dignitaries who by their piety, learning and office shine pre-eminent among the clergy, and to incite the Catholic people against nobles of high birth, who not less for their rank than for the generosity with which they support the missions, deserve to be treated with all honour and respect.[8]

Milner had no choice but to submit, though not without complaint, and the journal that was for so long his mouthpiece soon ceased circulation. However, the bishop continued to defend orthodoxy. He opposed Plunkett's Relief Bill of 1821, which was the last one to include provision for a veto, and Sir Francis Burdett's relief measure four years later. He was pleased to support O'Connell's Catholic Association, which galvanized the Irish Catholic masses and eventually succeeded in electing O'Connell as MP for Clare in 1828, even though (as a Catholic) he was unable to take his seat in Parliament.

Milner also stood alone amongst his brother bishops in supporting the Jesuits (the 'Gentlemen of Stonyhurst') on their restoration by Pius VII in 1814, which Gibson and Poynter failed to acknowledge without the

---

[7] *Eve*, ii, 55.
[8] Ibid., 187.

recognition of the State. He distrusted the new Roman Agent appointed in 1817, Robert Gradwell, who was seen as an ally of Poynter and an enemy of the Jesuits and himself.

David Mathew argued that 'Emancipation was an Irish victory, fought out in Ireland and decided when O'Connell won his seat at the Clare election.'[9] It had not happened earlier because of factors such as the opposition of George III and the Duke of York, the long administration of Lord Liverpool and the great 'distraction' of the Reform Bill. Due credit should be given to Milner – though he did not live to see Emancipation, it was partly due to his principled stand that it was passed without the surrender of any major concession. At the same time, the vindictiveness and divisiveness of his polemic questions the heroic status often given to him.

In his own District, the bishop was deeply interested in the education of the clergy, thereby ensuring the quality and orthodoxy of future generations of priests. He was concerned by the Cisalpine tendencies at the combined school and seminary at Oscott, which had been established in 1794. Financial troubles led to the trustees offering Milner full control of the college in return for covering the debt of £600. This gave the bishop an opportunity to remodel Oscott. At the opening on 15 August 1808 Low Mass was celebrated, followed by a sermon preached by Milner. Such was the simplicity of Catholic ceremonial in those days that the music for this grand occasion, as Husenbeth notes, was 'chiefly the Litany of Loreto performed by the Jones family from Wolverhampton, accompanied by one of them on the pianoforte. The Litany was spun out and made the most of on this occasion, as little else was produced in the musical department.'[10] The so-called 'new government' of Oscott separated clerical students from lay ones. Much was now expected from the seminarians, especially in terms of piety and learning.

Old Oscott became the first English centre of devotion to the Sacred Heart. This devotion had first been preached in London in the 1670s by St Claude de la Colombière, the Jesuit chaplain to Mary of Modena and formerly confessor to St Margaret Mary Alacoque. However there is no evidence that this devotion continued after the Popish Plot of 1678, when St Claude was forced to return to France. Milner had noted the

---

[9] Mathew, op. cit., 173.
[10] Husenbeth, op. cit., 117.

important role played by devotion to the Sacred Heart in combating Jansenism and Gallicanism in France. The devotion had become the litmus test of loyalty to the Holy See and Milner hoped it would counter the liberal, Cisalpine tendencies he so vigorously opposed. During his visit to Rome in 1814, Milner obtained an Indult from Pius VII awarding a plenary indulgence for those who prayed before an image of the Sacred Heart on the First Friday or the Friday after the Octave of Corpus Christi. Milner also established the Sodality of the Sacred Heart in his District and built the first English shrine to the Sacred Heart in the sacristy at Oscott. This was simple enough, centred around a small painted panel of glass depicting the Sacred Heart, which Milner seems to have brought back from Rome (although it was broken during the journey). In 1820 Milner issued a Pastoral Letter, informing people of the indulgences granted by Pius VII and including a selection of prayers and pious exercises for public and private use. Preaching at Dr Weedall's Requiem in 1859, Newman pointed out that Milner 'set himself to soften and melt the frost which stiffened the Catholicism of his day, and to rear up, safe from our northern blasts, the tender and fervent aspirations of Continental piety.'[11]

In his personal life, Milner did not live as a prince bishop and had no qualms about staying in the sort of hotel room commonly used by a commercial traveller.

> He was remarkable for plainness of dress, and aversion to all finery. He never wore silk stockings. His dress in these days would appear strange and undignified; but it was quite clerical in his time. In company, his dress was always very becoming and respectable. He usually wore a black velvet waistcoat, double-breasted, a coat with a straight collar, and a white cravat or stock, which was fastened with a large steel buckle behind his neck. In those days cassocks were never worn, either by bishops or priests, except when officiating in their ministry; nor did Bishops venture to display their pectoral crosses.[12]

He spent much time on visitations and confirmations, and managed to cover the entire District every four or five years. His pontificals are preserved at Oscott, including a foldable mitre and a crosier that was 'so contrived as to be easily taken to pieces, and packed in his port manteau. It was in fact a straight walking stick, over which he drew a case of silver tissue, and then fitted on a head of the same, worked with gold, and

---

[11] J. H. Newman, *Sermons Preached on Various Occasions* (1908), 261.
[12] Husenbeth, op. cit., 532.

having a graceful crook, so that it then formed a small but good looking crosier.'[13]

Husenbeth vividly describes the subject of his biography in a section entitled 'Milneriana', which helps us discover something of the man beneath the mitre:

> His figure was dignified and imposing and it was pleasantly remarked of him, that when walking processionally in his episcopal vestments, he had a fine pontifical strut. His voice was loud, and his delivery impressive; but his speech was somewhat affected by a slight lisp. Thus, when intoning his part of the litany at an Ordination, he used to sing the words nearly thus: *Ut hoth electoth beneditliere dignerith.*[14]

Husenbeth takes delight in recording certain eccentricities. Milner had stained glass windows installed in his bedroom at Oscott, his favourite dish was boiled corned beef and he disliked both cheese and flies, considering the latter to be diabolical. We read that 'even in the chapel, he has been seen to leave his place, and chase a buzzing fly to the window in hopes of killing it.'[15] Moreover,

> he would always, when he preached on a Sunday, read the Epistle and Gospel in English from the large Latin altar Missal, which he held in his arms, with very bad effect. The consequence was that from his translating the Latin extempore, one heard considerable variations from the usual version. He was fond of smelling the smoke of wax candles when extinguished; and while saying St John's Gospel at the end of Mass, he often blew out the candle near him, on purpose to enjoy the smoke.[16]

In the mid-1820s Milner's health declined and he began looking for a coadjutor. His former Secretary and the third President of Oscott, Thomas Walsh, was eventually chosen and duly consecrated at Wolverhampton on 1 May 1825.

By March 1826 Milner was convinced that his death was near and undertook a retreat to prepare for the end. He died peacefully on 19 April and the funeral was held at Wolverhampton eight days later. In an attempt, perhaps, at reconciling past differences, Walsh asked Poynter to preach, although the offer was politely declined. Milner's mortal remains were first buried in the orchard behind Giffard House and later moved to the crypt of Ss Peter and Paul, Wolverhampton, which was

---

[13] Ibid., 551.
[14] Ibid., 531.
[15] Ibid., 555-556.
[16] Ibid., 555.

built in the Perpendicular style the following year. His late twentieth-century successor, Archbishop Couve de Murville, summed Milner up by writing that 'he had many faults, but there could be no doubt about his complete devotion to the Church's task of preaching the Gospel – not a bad obituary for a Catholic bishop.'[17]

Further Reading

M. N. L. Couve de Murville, *John Milner 1752-1826* (1986)

F. C. Husenbeth, *The Life of the Right Rev. John Milner D.D.* (1862)

---

[17] M. N. L. Couve de Murville, *John Milner 1752-1826* (1986), 33.

THOMAS WALSH

1777-1849

TITULAR BISHOP OF CAMBYSOPOLIS (1825)
COADJUTOR TO BISHOP MILNER (1825-26)
VICAR APOSTOLIC OF THE MIDLAND DISTRICT (1826-40)
VICAR APOSTOLIC OF THE CENTRAL DISTRICT (1840-48)
VICAR APOSTOLIC OF THE LONDON DISTRICT (1848-49)

On the death of Milner, the Midland District passed into the hands of the coadjutor, Bishop Thomas Walsh. Born in London on 3 October 1776, his father, Charles, an Irish Catholic merchant, died shortly after the birth, and so his widowed mother, Mary Brittle, raised the young Thomas according to her own Protestant beliefs and sent him to a grammar school at St Albans. However, his father's brother, also called Thomas, was a Catholic priest and he arranged for his nephew to be sent to St Omer in 1792, where his classmates included Daniel O'Connell, 'the Liberator'. The following August the college was seized by revolutionaries and the students were imprisoned at Arras and then Doullens. Such dramatic events had the advantage of concentrating Walsh's mind and he decided finally to embrace Catholicism. On his release he was enrolled at St Edmund's College, Old Hall Green, in August 1795 and received conditional baptism from Dr Poynter on 27 September.

On 20 December 1800 Bishop Douglass ordained him deacon. Shortly afterwards he was appointed chaplain to Dr Stapleton, the former President of Old Hall Green who had become Vicar Apostolic to the Midland District. Walsh was ordained priest on 19 September 1801 at Longbirch, Staffordshire, the bishop's residence, which boasted an attached mission over which Walsh was given pastoral oversight. When

Stapleton unexpectedly died during a visit to St Omer the following year, Walsh continued his secretarial duties for Bishop Milner.

In October 1804 Walsh moved to Sedgley Park as spiritual director and had a great effect on the boys. He assembled a catechism class each day either in the chapel or, if the weather was cold, around the fire in the playroom, and illustrated his lessons with pious stories, often returning to the miserable ends of the leading protagonists of the French Revolution. He often addressed his pupils with the words, 'Good Christian Gentleman'. His popularity with the boys was despite the fact that poor health and constant headaches made him unbusinesslike and slow. Nor was he a good speaker. A historian of Sedgley Park has noted that 'he had a style and a manner all his own; judged by the canons of elocution, his inflexions, his delivery and his pauses were all wrong; his voice was not good and his enunciation was thick; but his earnestness and his fervour stirred the hearts of his hearers.'[1]

In 1808 he was appointed Vice-President and spiritual director of the new college at Oscott. He was also given pastoral care of the local mission and was noted for his collecting of alms and unwanted clothing for the poor. In 1818 he became the third President of Oscott. Concentrating on the formation of the students, he passed much of the temporal administration of the college into the hands of the Vice-President, Henry Weedall.

As Milner's health declined, he became anxious to select a coadjutor and secure succession to the Midland District. Walsh was appointed and consecrated Titular Bishop of Cambysopolis at Wolverhampton on 1 May 1825. Eight bishops were present at the ceremony, thought to have been the largest episcopal gathering on English soil since the Reformation. Just under a year later Walsh succeeded Milner as Vicar Apostolic and left Oscott for Wolverhampton.

Walsh's episcopate, spanning over two decades, witnessed Catholic Emancipation, the continuing progress of the Industrial Revolution and the effects of the Oxford Movement. The position of Catholicism within the nation strengthened and the size of his flock increased, thanks to Irish immigration, conversions and urbanisation. Walsh, like the other Vicars Apostolic of the period, oversaw much expansion – 29 new missions were established in the Midland District and about 50 churches were built. In 1837 Walsh accompanied Griffiths to Rome to discuss the state of the Church

---

[1] W. Buscot, *The History of Cotton College At Sedgley Park, 1763-1873, At Cotton, 1873-* (1940), 138.

in England and Wales and the possibility of erecting additional Vicariates. He used the opportunity to request Nicholas Wiseman as his coadjutor, though he would have to wait several years before his request was granted. During the restructuring of the Vicariates in 1840, the Midland District became the Central District and lost the counties of Cambridgeshire, Huntingdonshire, Lincolnshire, Norfolk, Northamptonshire, Rutland and Suffolk, which went to form the new Eastern District.

What marked Walsh out was the grandeur of his vision and his openness towards new forces within the Catholic community. At his death in 1849, *The Tablet* observed that 'it is to his Episcopacy that posterity will trace the great development of ecclesiastical architecture which forms so distinctive a feature in the history of our period.'[2] A keen supporter of Pugin, Walsh oversaw the opening of a number of churches and institutions that were gems of the Gothic Revival: the future Cathedrals of Birmingham (St Chad's) and Nottingham, New Oscott, the Trappist monastery at Mount St Bernard's, the glorious churches at Cheadle and Derby, and the religious houses of Hanley, Ratcliffe and Aston. Many of these ambitious projects were made possible through the patronage of John Talbot, sixteenth Earl of Shrewsbury, and Ambrose Phillips de Lisle.

When the Rosminian Fr Gentili reported to Rome on the state of the English Church, he spoke highly of the bishop – not surprising given the support he had shown for his Institute:

> Walsh, though inferior in learning and talents to many of the others, preaches very sensible sermons that are full of unction, and so are the best sermons of all; just as there is no other bishop who has done or does now as much as he. He is a holy man and as such blessed by God. He has given a good example, and it is from his District that has come nearly all the good that now flows into the others, like retreats, building of churches and convents, the conversion of Protestant ministers, the wearing of more clerical garb, the reviving of the liturgy, and if the preaching of missions did not start in his District, both the Passionists and our missionaries belong to his District.[3]

However, the District was put under a huge financial strain, which led to Ullathorne's brief imprisonment for debt after Walsh's death. The bishop's actions also earned him many critics. After the consecration of Pugin's chapel at Oscott, for example, Bishop Baines delated him to Rome because of the 'gothic' vestments he had seen in use there. Elsewhere Walsh was

---

[2] *The Tablet*, 24 February 1849, 120.
[3] C. Leetham, *Luigi Gentili, A Sower for the Second Spring* (1965), 293.

criticised too for encouraging the singing of plainchant, approving of prayers for the conversion of England and promoting the work of the *Oeuvre pour la Propagation de la Foi*. This organisation, which originated in France, supported overseas missions but was seen by some as a drain on much-needed English Catholic resources.

Walsh took a special interest in the Oxford Movement, whose epicentre lay in his District, and was unique among the Vicars Apostolic of his time in seeing the potential of the Oxford converts. Walsh's vision for Oscott was to make it a centre of Catholic life and scholarship that would provide a home for many of the converts. Pugin was given the task of decorating and furnishing the chapel, using ornaments 'executed by ancient artists in the days of faith' but 'torn by heretical and revolutionary violence from their original positions in the noble churches of France and Belgium,' and restoring 'the ample and dignified vestments which were anciently used in this land.'[4] Walsh bought an impressive library that had been made available in Rome and appointed converts like George Spencer to high positions. When he finally succeeded in gaining Wiseman as his coadjutor (1840), the new bishop was appointed President of the College. If he lacked attention to details and was often absent due to illness or other responsibilities, Wiseman brought much energy and vision to the post. However, the college was dogged by financial problems and, towards the end of his episcopate, Walsh considered closing Oscott as a lay school and turning it into solely a seminary.

As Walsh grew older, he could justifiably expect to end his days in the Midlands. However his seniority amongst the bishops and his long experience made him the obvious choice, in Rome's eyes, to succeed Griffiths in London and eventually to become the first Archbishop of a newly-restored Hierarchy.

For his brief period in the London District, see pp. 82–3

Further Reading

Peter Dennison, 'Thomas Walsh's vision of Oscott: hopes and realities', in J. Champ (ed.), *Oscott College 1838–1988* (1988)

---

[4] Judith F. Champ (ed.), *Oscott College 1838–1988* (1988), 39.

NICHOLAS PATRICK STEPHEN WISEMAN

1802-65
TITULAR BISHOP OF MELIPOTAMUS (1840)
COADJUTOR TO BISHOP WALSH – CENTRAL DISTRICT (1840-47)
PRO-VICAR APOSTOLIC OF THE LONDON DISTRICT (1847-48)
COADJUTOR TO BISHOP WALSH – LONDON DISTRICT (1848-49)
VICAR APOSTOLIC OF THE LONDON DISTRICT (1849-50)
ARCHBISHOP OF WESTMINSTER (1850-65)
CARDINAL PRIEST OF SANTA PUDENTIANA (1850)

The name of Nicholas Wiseman is usually associated with a later era of Catholic history as the first Cardinal Archbishop of Westminster. But he belongs just as much to the period of the Vicars Apostolic, as their Roman Agent, coadjutor to Bishop Walsh and the last Vicar Apostolic of the London District.

He was the only Vicar Apostolic to be born in Catholic Europe – in Seville on 2 August 1802, where his father worked as a merchant. Both his parents, James and Xaviera, were Irish, though they had married at the Virginia Street chapel during a stay in London in 1800. James Wiseman died in 1804 and the family moved to Ireland, where Nicholas attended a boarding school in the Waterford area. Then in March 1810 he entered Ushaw, together with his elder brother James. Though he has been described as 'a somewhat gawky youth, with limbs all knit together, betokening the absence of all aptitude for athletics,'[1] he was gifted academically and noticed by the Vice-President, John Lingard.

In 1818 Wiseman was chosen as one of the first students for the newly-refounded English College in Rome. He felt at home immediately and within days of arriving found himself in audience with Pius VII, together

---

[1] W. Ward, *Life and Times of Cardinal Wiseman* (1897), i, 8.

with the other students. Ushaw's Vice-President wrote to the Rector, Robert Gradwell, that Wiseman's 'talents are unrivalled in Ushaw College, his piety fervent, and solid, and his character as a Christian scholar quite without a fault.' He thought that once the students grew accustomed to the ways of the Roman schools, 'Wiseman will not fear to enter the lists with any Italian that can stand forth against him.'[2] This prediction came to spectacular fruition in July 1824, when Wiseman was chosen to take the 'public act' or examination for his Doctorate of Divinity, in the presence of the future Gregory XVI, Cardinal Zurla, the Abbé Lamennais and many other dignitaries.

Wiseman was ordained to the priesthood on 10 March 1825. He stayed on in Rome, continuing his studies in the Oriental languages. By 1827 he was Vice-Rector of the College and had published his widely-acclaimed *Horae Syriacae*. The following year he became Rector and Roman Agent on Gradwell's appointment as coadjutor to Bishop Bramston. He was a popular Rector, who enjoyed good relations with his students, shunned strict discipline and played a full part in college life, even playing the organ and directing the choir. One of his students recalled that

> each Thursday (the weekly holiday) it was his habit to take us all to one of the Catacombs, or churches, or antiquities, or picture galleries, or the museums, or the studio of artists, and on such occasions we were often accompanied by some German scholar or other friend of his interested in Christian art … He was very fond of what he called an "outing." Sometimes he would take the whole of us in carriages to some place outside Rome, such as the spot known as the ruins of Veii, taking with us provisions for a picnic. One such occasions he was the most joyous of the party, and he liked to see others happy.[3]

Such was his reputation for scholarship that he was elected to the Royal Asiatic Society and the Royal Society of Literature. He was also named special preacher to the English-speakers in Rome and gave public lectures, some of which were later published as *The Real Presence of the Body and Blood of our Lord Jesus Christ in the Blessed Eucharist, Proved from Scripture* (1836) and *Twelve Lectures on the Connexion between Science and Revealed Religion* (1836). Beneath the success, Wiseman had to fight periods of depression and despair. In 1848 he told his nephew that 'many and many an hour have I passed alone, in bitter tears, on the loggia of the English College, ... fighting with subtle thoughts and venomous suggestions of a

---

[2] Schiefen, 7-8.
[3] Ward, *Wiseman*, i, 255-256.

fiendlike infidelity which I durst not confide to anyone.'[4]

Much as Wiseman felt at home in Rome, his thoughts were increasingly directed towards England. This was especially the case after his first visit to England since ordination in 1832 and the visits paid to him in Rome the following year by Newman and Froude. Wiseman thus became aware of the Oxford Movement and the great significance that this had not only for the Anglican Communion but the Catholic Church. He was concerned by the lack of interest and even hostility shown towards the Tractarians by the Vicars Apostolic.

Returning to England for a lengthy visit in 1835, Wiseman delivered lectures at Lincoln's Inn Fields and St Mary Moorfields, to which many non-Catholics flocked, and founded a Catholic quarterly, *The Dublin Review*, together with Daniel O'Connell and Michael Joseph Quinn. His intention in these lectures and writings was partly to provide a Catholic response to the Oxford Movement and attract Anglicans into the Church. It proved effective – Newman himself later admitted that a passage from St Augustine cited by Wiseman in his article 'The Anglican Claim of Apostolical Succession' had been the first serious blow to his understanding of the Anglican claim to represent the Church founded by Christ.

Wiseman's long stay in England was partly linked to Bishop Baines' desire to appoint him as President of Prior Park and eventually as his coadjutor. Baines differed from Wiseman on many points of ecclesiastical policy and a serious disagreement led to those plans being dropped. Bishop Walsh, however, began to apply pressure on Propaganda to get Wiseman nominated for his District. His wish was finally granted in 1840, when Wiseman was appointed coadjutor and Vicar General of the Midland District and President of Oscott. He was consecrated Titular Bishop of Melipotamus at the English College on 8 June 1840.

At Oscott, Wiseman was true to form: as in Rome, periods of intense work and energy were followed by periods of physical collapse and mental depression, and he was often absent from the college due to other projects. However, despite his inconsistent health and temperament, Wiseman achieved much at Oscott, making it the beating heart of the Midlands Catholic revival. Lord Acton, a student at the time, later noted that if the President failed in running the college he made it an exciting place to be, with many distinguished visitors: 'we used to see him with Lord

---

[4] Ibid., i, 17.

Shrewsbury, with O'Connell, with Father Mathew, with a Mesopotamian patriarch, with Newman, with Pugin, and we had a feeling that Oscott, next to Pekin, was a centre of the world.'[5] Newman himself wrote of how he was first brought to Oscott after his conversion and made 'the gaze of so many eyes ..., as if some wild incomprehensible beast, caught by the hunter, and a spectacle for Dr Wiseman to exhibit to strangers, as himself the hunter who captured it.'[6]

In 1847, following the latest breakdown of health, Wiseman visited Rome with Bishop Sharples to recuperate and also to negotiate over the restoration of a new Hierarchy in England and Wales. Blessed Pius IX had recently been elected and had amazed many by his 'liberal' reforms in the Papal States. He seemed open to the restoration of the Hierarchy but also asked Wiseman to seek an interview with Lord Palmerston, the Foreign Secretary. In particular, the Pope was keen for the British Government to hear of his reforms and appreciate his vulnerable situation in the face of calls for Italian Unification. Wiseman returned to England early on the news of the death of Bishop Griffiths. Despite his age and health, Bishop Walsh was appointed as successor and Wiseman moved with him to the London District.

For Wiseman's subsequent years in London, see pp. 84-6

Further Reading

B. Fothergill, *Nicholas Wiseman* (1963)

D. Gwynn, *Cardinal Wiseman* (1950)

E. E. Reynold, *Three Cardinals* (1958)

R. J. Schiefen, *Nicholas Wiseman and the Transformation of English Catholicism* (1984)

R. J. Schiefen, 'Wiseman's Oscott', in J. Champ (ed.), *Oscott College 1838-1988*

W. Ward, *Life and Times of Cardinal Wiseman*, 2 vols, (1897)

N. Wiseman, *Recollections of the Last Four Popes* (1856)

---

[5] Ibid., i, 348-49.
[6] J. H. Newman, *Autobiographical Writings*, ed. H. Tristram (1956), 255.

William Bernard Ullathorne, OSB

1806-89
Titular Bishop of Hetalona (1846)
Vicar Apostolic of the Western District (1846-48)
Vicar Apostolic of the Central District (1848-50)
Bishop of Birmingham (1850-89)
Titular Archbishop of Cabasa (1888)

For Ullathorne's early life and period as Vicar Apostolic of the Western District,
see pp. 239-243

Walsh was succeeded by Bishop Ullathorne, who was sorry to leave the Western District, especially since his plans for the Bristol and Clifton missions had to be left unfinished. He also found great relief in the Central District: 'for the first time in my agitated life I found myself placed in a peaceful jurisdiction, over a united clergy, conspicuous for their devotion to the episcopal authority.' Of course there were problems, in particular a large debt, and although 'Good Bishop Walsh explained to me the state of things as well as he could, ... he kept no regular accounts, and scarcely any documents.'[1] Ever the practical Yorkshireman, Ullathorne was forced to cut clergy incomes, issue a number of 'financial Pastorals' and establish a new fund for Church Education.

With the restoration of the Hierarchy in 1850, Ullathorne became the first Bishop of Birmingham. The details of his subsequent career have been told in detail elsewhere; suffice to say that he did much to replace the temporary expedients of penal times with the fullness of diocesan life, especially in the form of the Cathedral Chapter and a diocesan seminary – in 1873 the Church students moved from Oscott to the newly-created

---

[1] Ullathorne, *The Devil is a Jackass*, ed. L. Madigan (1995), 358.

St Bernard's Seminary, Olton. In recognition of his great contribution to ecclesiastical affairs in both hemispheres, the year before he died he was elevated to become titular Archbishop of Cabasa, while remaining Bishop of Birmingham. Earlier in 1865 he was Propaganda's choice to succeed Wiseman at Westminster, although he had to content himself with consecrating Manning at St Mary Moorfields.

Shortly before he died, the old Archbishop remarked to his doctor 'now that the old limbs are falling to pieces, I feel that I am beginning to live in the land of metaphysics.' He sternly told his Secretary that 'there must be no *Cardinal Wiseman's Last Illness* about this,' referring to Canon Morris' hagiographic account of the first Archbishop of Westminster's last days nearly twenty-five years before.[2] The last of the Vicars Apostolic died on the Feast of St Benedict, 21 March 1889, and was buried in the chapel of Stone convent near the three great women in his life – his own mother, Mother Margaret Hallahan, who had founded the Sisters of Penance of St Dominic with Ullathorne's help, and her successor, Mother Imelda Poole.

Further Reading

A. Bellenger, '"The Normal State of the Church": William Bernard Ullathorne, First Bishop of Birmingham', *Recusant History*, Vol. 25, no.2 (Oct. 2000), 325-334

D. A. Bellenger, *William Bernard Ullathorne* (2001)

C. Butler, *The Life and Times of Bishop Ullathorne*, 2 vols (1926)

J. Champ, *William Bernard Ullathorne: A Different Kind of Monk* (2006)

W. B. Ullathorne, *The Devil is a Jackass*, ed. L. Madigan (1995)

---

[2] C. Butler, *The Life and Times of Bishop Ullathorne*, (1926), ii, 293-294.

The Eastern District

(1840-50)

The Eastern District, created in 1840 out of part of the Midland District and part of the London District, consisted of Bedfordshire, Buckinghamshire, Cambridgeshire, Huntingdonshire, Lincolnshire, Norfolk, Northamptonshire, Rutland and Suffolk.

WILLIAM WAREING
1791-1865
TITULAR BISHOP OF ARIOPOLIS (1840)
VICAR APOSTOLIC OF THE EASTERN DISTRICT (1840-50)
BISHOP OF NORTHAMPTON (1850-58)
TITULAR BISHOP OF RHITYMNA (1858-65)

The future first Bishop of Northampton was born in London on 14 February 1791 and baptized two days later at the famous Sardinian Chapel in Lincoln's Inn Fields. He received his early education at Sedgley Park and then moved to Oscott in March 1806, when it was still run by John Bew and not yet 'refounded' by Bishop Milner. He was eventually ordained by Milner on 28 September 1815 and stayed on at Oscott as College Prefect. The following summer he moved to his other *alma mater*, Sedgley Park, as classics master and also acted as chaplain to the Whitgreave family at Moseley Court, where Mass was celebrated for Catholics of the surrounding area.

In 1819 Wareing moved to Creswell in Staffordshire, initially to assist a friend from Oscott, Thomas Baddesley, who had built a new chapel and mini-seminary. During this period, Wareing also acted as confessor to the English Benedictine nuns at Caverswall Castle, who had found a home there after being exiled from Ghent during the French Revolution.

After twelve years in Derbyshire, Wareing went to Grantham, where a chapel had been built by Mr Tempest, then a seminarian at Oscott. Wareing looked after the mission until its patron was ordained and in 1834 transferred to Stamford, where he erected a chapel and priest's house. Finally in 1838 he returned to Oscott as Vice-President and spiritual director.

When four new Districts were established in 1840, the senior staff at Oscott were seen as an obvious source of new bishops. It was hoped that the President, Dr Weedall, would take charge of the newly constituted Northern District. During an audience in Rome, Pope Gregory claimed that English Catholics desired his elevation. Weedall played this down by replying, 'Your Holiness does not speak *ex cathedra*' (from the chair). The Pope, who was standing, immediately sat down and playfully answered: 'Well, now I do speak *ex cathedra*'. Weedall managed to avoid the new dignity for reasons of health but his Vice-President was duly appointed to the Eastern District. Wareing was consecrated at Oscott by Bishop Walsh, assisted by Wiseman and George Brown, on 21 September 1840. He made Northampton his base and appointed Frederick Charles Husenbeth, the biographer of Milner, as his Vicar General.

In his first Pastoral Letter, Wareing referred to his District as an 'extensive and spiritually destitute tract of land, where the means of carrying on religion are slender, where our churches are few and our congregations small, where thousands are crying for bread and there is no one to break it to them.'[1] Indeed, in 1840 Huntingdonshire and Rutland had no places of worship, and three counties (Bedfordshire, Buckinghamshire and Cambridgeshire) had only one. Wareing's eighteen-year rule saw the opening of many chapels and missions, including St Peter's, Great Marlow (1846), which was designed by Pugin and paid for by James Scott-Murray of Danesfield.

Wareing also expressed in the 1840 Pastoral his wish to establish a seminary 'in which youths of approved piety and good abilities may be well grounded in their elementary studies and prepared to avail themselves of the pre-eminent advantage of St Mary's College, Oscott.' In time a modest seminary dedicated to St Felix was erected at Gifford's Hall in Suffolk and later transferred to Northampton, where the old chapel had been converted into apartments. It received a donation of £333 from the Association for the Propagation of the Faith at Lyons but, after a brief and shaky history, closed in 1853.

During his episcopate, Wareing received several notable converts into the Church who would make a significant contribution to the 'Second Spring'. On 17 November 1845 he received the future founder of the London Oratory, Frederick William Faber, and ten companions, and the following year, on 20 May, it was the turn of a Cambridge student, John Morris. Morris' biographer records that 'the only other person to be confirmed beside himself was a maid-servant, and while the two sat side by side on

---

[1] Pastoral of 1840.

two chairs in the middle of the otherwise empty chapel to receive the Bishop's homily, which was delivered to them with as much solemnity as if a large congregation had been present, the ludicrous aspect of the scene suddenly suggested itself to the young undergraduate so forcibly that he was seized with a fit of laughter and nearly choked himself in his efforts to suppress it.'[2] Wareing gained a place for Morris at the English College, Rome; after Ordination, Morris briefly acted as Wareing's Secretary and eventually became Secretary to Wiseman and thereafter a well-known Jesuit and an authority on the English Martyrs.

With the restoration of the Hierarchy in 1850, Wareing become the first Bishop of Northampton. Present in Rome for the definition of the Immaculate Conception in 1854, he was named an Assistant at the Pontifical Throne and finally resigned from the see on 11 February 1858. In retirement he was given the title of Bishop of Rhitymna and resided as chaplain at the Benedictine convent at East Bergholt, near Colchester. He died there on Boxing Day 1865 and a solemn Requiem was celebrated in the new year. The *Weekly Register* recorded that 'the solemn march was rather long, passing down the long gravel walks in the beautiful lawn and plantations of the Abbey, and winding among delightful shrubberies to the quiet, enclosed cemetery, where the honoured remains of the Bishop were finally deposited.' The old bishop, described as 'almost the last of Dr Milner's clergy', made a declaration on his deathbed that perhaps accurately summed up his varied life as a priest and prelate: 'I have no great talents; I have never done any great things; but I have always endeavoured to do my duty.'[3]

---

[2] J. H. Pollen, *The Life and Letters of Father John Morris* (1896), 44.
[3] *Weekly Register*, 13 January 1866, 25.

The Northern District

(1688-1840)

The Northern District, as created by Blessed Innocent XI in 1688, comprised a vast area – Cheshire, Cumberland, Durham, Lancashire, Northumberland, Westmorland and Yorkshire, together with the Isle of Man. The District included the historic towns of Carlisle, Chester, Durham and York, as well as the growing industrial centres of Hull, Leeds, Liverpool, Manchester, Newcastle and Sheffield, which boasted substantial Catholic populations towards the end of the period. Following the French Revolution, several important Catholic institutions moved from the continent to the Northern District: Douai continued at Crook Hall (1795) and then Ushaw (1808), which acted as the northern episcopal seminary; the Jesuit College at St Omer moved to Stonyhurst, near Preston, thanks to the patronage of the Weld family, and the English Benedictines of Dieulouard found a new home at Ampleforth (1802). The majority of the bishops lived in various locations east of the Pennines, though Dicconson was the first to live in the Catholic heartland of Lancashire.

JAMES SMITH
1645-1711
TITULAR BISHOP OF CALLIPOLIS (1688)
VICAR APOSTOLIC OF THE NORTHERN DISTRICT (1688-1711)

The first Vicar Apostolic of the Northern District, James Smith, was born at Winchester in 1645, the second son of Bartholomew and Frances Smith of Stoke Charity, near Winchester. In 1661 he was sent to the English College, Douai, and from there continued his ecclesiastical education at St Gregory's, Paris. In 1672 he returned to Douai as Professor of Poetry and was ordained a priest in 1677. Smith continued at Douai, teaching philosophy, and, having gained the Doctorate of Divinity (1680), became the College's tenth President on 28 August 1682. Shortly afterwards he inherited a substantial estate from his father, much of which he granted to his younger brother.

As early as 1684 James Smith's name had been included in a list of candidates for the episcopacy sent to Rome by the Chapter: it was proposed that Smith might be a possible suffragan or coadjutor to Cardinal Howard who, it was hoped, would become a Bishop-in-Ordinary in England. This scheme was not accepted by the Holy See but, with the erection of the four Vicariates in 1688, James Smith was appointed to the Northern District, which encompassed the vast area between the Humber and the Tweed. After a splendid episcopal consecration on 13 May at the royal residence of Somerset House in London, Bishop Smith journeyed to his District, finally arriving in York on 2 August. He was welcomed by a military guard of honour before proceeding to sing High Mass. According to John Kirk,

> he was received with great ceremony by the Clergy and Regulars of those parts, who sang *Te Deum* publicly upon the occasion. On the

Sunday following he appeared in the Chapel belonging to the Clergy in his Episcopal habit, and was present at a sermon preached by Mr. Parkinson, his Lordship's chaplain. In the afternoon he attended a service performed in the Friar's Chapel, where a sermon was also preached. The Commanding Officer of Lord Dumbarton's Regiment, which then lay in York, complimented him with the offer of a sentinel to stand at the door of his lodgings, but this honour Bishop Smith declined.[1]

The promise of the Catholic revival was soon extinguished by the Revolution of 1688. Unlike his brother bishops, Smith escaped arrest and took refuge at the home of his friend, Francis Tunstall, at Wycliffe Hall in Yorkshire. From that base he was to minister secretly among his scattered flock for the rest of his life, variously using the aliases of 'Harper', 'Tarlton', and 'Brown'. A letter written in 1709 to the Agent of the English Bishops in Rome, Laurence Mayes, describes his pastoral work, written in the customary 'secret code' of penal times:

I have been three months from home in the visits of such friends [his flock] as are dispersed up and down in Westmoreland, Lancashire and Cheshire: taking the opportunity of a present favourable calm, and doeing everything with as much caution and circumspection as was possible; goeing only with one companion and a servant; and performing everywhere by myselfe all parts of instruction and exhortation suitable to the occasion. These visits accompanied with such constant and almost daily performances [i.e. Confirmations], as they were very laborious, soe they have been of great comfort in the good dispositions and effects with which, through the mercy of God, I have reason to hope they have been everywhere blessed. Not to disappoint poor friends comeing in great numbers and to prevent the offence of unnecessary meetings, I seldom ended the burden and business of the day before 3 o'clock: a fault humbly submitted, and I hope easily pardoned by Fathers [Roman authorities] to us and our necessities.[2]

Smith showed great dedication to the Northern District, despite rumours of preferment to more prestigious positions. When Bishop Leyburn died in 1702 it was suggested that Smith should be translated to the London District. Likewise, following the death of Cardinal Howard in 1694 it was twice suggested that Smith should be raised to the cardinalate and become Protector of England. Even the exiled King supported the proposal but Smith was keen to avoid the limelight. In July 1701 the Pope told Dr Witham that of the two candidates that had been suggested to him for

---

[1] Hemphill, 18.
[2] Brady, 246-47.

the office of Cardinal Protector 'one had refused, and the other did not please.'[3] It was assumed that the one who had refused was Smith.

A letter from Smith (writing as 'Mr Harper') reveals his motivation:

> I am well pleased with what you write of Mr. Harper [i.e. Smith]. He is verie easy in his present service, as most comfortable to the will and ways of God: [he] would have great difficulties in leaving his poor wife and children [the Northern District and its flock] and is better contented to go on his little way, than be put in circumstances quite out of his talents and education. He has a deep sense of the honour and kindness designed to him. Contrary to his own judgement he submitted himself to the acceptance of the proposal; and he will alwaies be ready to comply with that or anything else more in the compasse of his parts. One great comfort of his life is to have been more under the direction of others than his own. He fears that he has been easy in that particular, in yielding to what he is; in resigning to what was proposed him to be. He begs you ... to joyn him in the prayer that nothing but the will and honour of God may be consulted and followed by him, and those that are to determine his post and service.[4]

Bishop Smith's labours came to an end on 13 May 1711, the twenty-third anniversary of his episcopal consecration. He had spent three months carrying out a visitation in the eastern part of Yorkshire during the summer of 1710. Having returned home to Wycliffe his health quickly faded as he suffered from dropsy and heart trouble and became an invalid for the last ten months of his life. He was buried at Wycliffe, but no memorial was erected to mark his grave.

A surprising 'relic' of Bishop Smith is the so-called 'Braganza Crozier' kept at York Minster and regularly used by the Anglican Archbishop. This was originally given to Bishop Smith by the widow of Charles II, Queen Catherine of Braganza, but passed into the hands of the Church of England. According to Brady, Smith was making a visitation when he was 'robbed of his beautiful silver crozier by the notorious Earl of Danby, the first Duke of Leeds, who triumphantly deposited it in York Minster.'[5] In the spirit of ecumenism, however, it has recently been loaned to the Catholic Bishops of Middlesbrough and Leeds for special occasions such as episcopal consecrations.

---

[3] Hemphill, 28.

[4] Ibid., 28.

[5] Brady, 247.

GEORGE WITHAM

1655-1725

TITULAR BISHOP OF MARCOPOLIS (1703)
VICAR APOSTOLIC OF THE MIDLAND DISTRICT (1703-16)
VICAR APOSTOLIC OF THE NORTHERN DISTRICT (1716-25)

For Witham's early life and his ministry as Vicar Apostolic
of the Midland District, see pp. 94-5

It took five years to appoint a successor to Bishop Smith. In 1713 Silvester Jenks, a noted controversialist and author of a popular book against Jansenism, was proposed by Bishops Giffard and Witham and subsequently named as the new Vicar Apostolic and Titular Bishop of Callipolis. Jenks was seriously ill and died at the end of 1714 before his consecration, which had been delayed at the request of the other bishops until the dissolution of the English Parliament to minimise any disturbance.

In the end, it was decided to transfer George Witham on 6 April 1716 from the Midland to the Northern District. The bishop was happy to return to the area of his youth, where he had previously worked as Vicar General, but by the time of the appointment his health was failing. In the years that followed, he considered resigning. In June 1718 he wrote to Mayes, the Roman Agent, hoping that 'a poor old weak man' might be allowed to lay down 'his too heavy burden that he may better prepare to dye,' and suggesting a number of suitable candidates, including his brother Robert.[1] He also wrote continually asking for a coadjutor, such as Mayes or Edward Dicconson.

Incipient dropsy, paralysis and other ailments blighted Witham's attempts to shepherd his flock effectively. He was based at Cliffe Hall,

---

[1] Hemphill, 119.

his birthplace, where he lived with his brother Robert. It was here he died suddenly on 16 April 1725. That day two priests had visited him to do business and

> he even walked over his floor to show them how active he was, yet when they were going home, he having desired his man to pull his chair to his study and lay him his book before him to say vespers, and come up again in a quarter of an hour; and accordingly his man coming up again to him found him leaning upon his book dead.[2]

Witham was buried at the church in Manfield. A memorial was later erected to him in the Victorian mausoleum at Lartington Hall.

---

[2] AAW B40, Ep. Var. VIII/247 (letter of Peter Brian Tunstall to the Roman Agent, 23 April 1725).

Thomas Dominic Williams, O.P.

c. 1661-1740
Titular Bishop of Tiberiopolis (1725)
Vicar Apostolic of the Northern District (1725-40)

Witham's successor, Thomas Dominic Williams, was the only Dominican Vicar Apostolic. Little is known with certainty about his early life except that he came from a Welsh Catholic family who owned the former Benedictine Priory of Monmouth. His uncle may have been William Dominic Williams, an English Dominican and second Prior of Bornhem.

It was perhaps natural, then, that Thomas should choose to enter Bornhem himself on 30 October 1685. He then proceeded to Ghent for his novitiate, finally being professed at Bornhem on 5 December 1686. Fra' Dominic, as he was now called, pursued further studies in Rome and Naples, where he was ordained in 1692. He became a professor at the newly established college of St Thomas Aquinas at Louvain on 15 September 1696 and five years later was appointed Regent of that college.

From 1708 Williams was Vicar Provincial in the Low Countries and in 1712 he became Provincial. He then returned to Louvain until he was elected Prior of Bornhem in 1724. Twice he was elected as Definitor for the Dominican General Chapters of 1721 and 1725, and on 25 July 1725 was once again elected Provincial. Around this time he was recommended for the episcopate by 'James III' and was appointed Vicar Apostolic of the Northern District on 11 December 1725 by Benedict XIII (himself a Dominican). He was consecrated as Titular Bishop of Tiberiopolis by the Pope on 30 December 1725 at the Quirinal Palace, the only Vicar Apostolic to have received his episcopal orders directly from the Successor of St Peter.

The secular clergy of the Northern District were highly sceptical of the appointment as their bishop of a friar who had spent most of his religious life on the continent. When news of the nomination was made public in December 1725, Ingleton wrote to Mayes:

> Just now I received yours of the 12th with the afflicting news of a Dominican Bishop. The Pope's resolution, if unalterable, will cause great confusion, as well as chagrin in a District which makes the most considerable part of the English Mission. There is but one poor Dominican in the whole District, and in all England only seven.[1]

As time went by the fear and resentment of the proposed Dominican grew and Ingleton wrote again six weeks later:

> Both the Clergy and the Gentry of the North received the news with the greatest surprise and trouble; and this the more because they are persuaded this choice was not made by His Holiness *ex proprio motu*, and without the advice and suggestion of others. ... Tis certain the choice of Bishop Williams will be attended with very ill consequences, and not less mortifying to him than to others. A friend of mine lately come from the North and well acquainted with the Catholic Families, assures me that not one Gentleman will give [the Bishop] a residence in that District. He is a stranger, a beggar. ... I have taken liberty to acquaint the King how much the Northern Clergy are offended at this choice, and that they will not believe it made by the Pope alone *ex motu proprio*.[2]

Bishop Williams arrived in his District during December 1727. The delay in arrival was in large part due to financial problems in supporting his new position. Letters from the Pope to the Kings of France and Spain requesting benefices for Williams failed to produce any fruit. The District's first Vicar Apostolic had left a large legacy for his successors, provided that they were members of the secular clergy, thus excluding Williams.

The bishop at first resided at Wycliffe, where Smith had lived and died, and then moved to Sir Edward Gascoigne's estates at Huddlestone Hall, near Pontefract, and Paylington Hall, where he consecrated the small chapel in 1733. Williams threw himself into a visitation of his vast District. In 1728 and 1729 he confirmed large numbers during his travels – including 580 at Fernyhalgh and 402 at Dunkenhalgh, a true demonstration of the strength of Lancashire Catholicism. Williams continued to face challenges and dangers, as a letter to Cardinal Petra reveals in 1733. The bishop was

---

[1] AAW B40, Ep. Var. VIII/339.
[2] Hemphill, 124.

actually obliged to fly to the most deserted and remote places, to escape prison and torture as the Pseudo-archbishop of York had issued a mandate for his capture, on account of his having made a conversion (which caused a great noise) of a Protestant Minister, who, instructed by bishop Williams, nobly resigned his rich prebend, and publicly declared himself a Catholic.[3]

Williams became much loved and respected in his District. He died at Huddlestone Hall on the morning of Holy Thursday, 3 April 1740, aged 73, and was buried the following day in the Catholic chapel of nearby Hazlewood, the home of the Vavasours. The Dominicans, meanwhile, would have to wait until 2000 for another Friar Preacher, Malcolm McMahon, to be appointed as an English bishop (of Nottingham).

---

[3] Brady, 254.

EDWARD DICCONSON
1670-1752
TITULAR BISHOP OF MALLUS (1741)
VICAR APOSTOLIC OF THE NORTHERN DISTRICT (1741-52)

Edward Dicconson was born at Wrightington Hall, north of Wigan, on 30 November 1670, the third son of Hugh Dicconson and Agnes Kirkby. His family had lived at Wrightington Hall since 1658, the original Tudor manor that the bishop would have known only being demolished in 1930 to make way for the Wrightington Hospital. In the late seventeenth and eighteenth centuries, the Hall boasted a resident chaplain and a small chapel dedicated to St Joseph, the ancestor of the present church in Wrightington of the same name. The Dicconson family was known for its strong Jacobite loyalties: Edward's eldest brother, William, became the tutor to Prince James Francis Edward at St Germain and treasurer to Queen Mary of Modena. Another brother, Roger, was involved in the 1715 uprising, though this did not lead to the forfeiture of his estates.

Dicconson entered the English College at Douai in 1683 and remained there until 1720. He was ordained priest in Douai in June 1701, having studied theology in Paris for two years, and stayed on at the college, successively holding the offices of Procurator (1701-08), Professor of Syntax (1708-9), Poetry (1709-10) and Philosophy (1711-12) and finally Vice-President and Professor of Theology. During the interregnum between the death of Edward Paston in July 1714 and the arrival of his successor, Robert Witham, in October 1715, Dicconson took charge of the college.

Dicconson helped 'Charles Dodd' (the alias of Hugh Tootell) compile his famous *Church History* and made copies of the college papers for this purpose. Dicconson also kept a personal diary, now preserved at Ushaw, which gives the reader a vivid picture of college life. For example, he recounts how a student, William Roe (alias Roberts), ran away from the college in August 1706 to join the Duke of Marlborough's army, stationed nearby during the War of the Spanish Succession. The boy was almost immediately captured by the French and only released through the college's connections with the exiled Stuart court. The future bishop also speaks of improvements made to his chamber in September 1706, for previously 'I could not have things in order (without which 'tis rarely a thing can be found when wanted) but was forced to fling things on heaps.' Moreover 'the rats and mice so molested my closets that no papers were secure. To this may be attributed the losse of so many writings of consequence which must once have belonged to this Colledge.'[1]

In the early eighteenth century accusations of Jansenism were thrown against the English College. These were originally directed against a Vice-President and talented theologian, Dr Edward Hawarden, but the attacks continued even after Hawarden's return to England in 1707. Dicconson attributed these rumours to the Jesuits and made great efforts to stress the college's orthodoxy. In October 1714 Dicconson and the Professor of Theology, Richard Kendal, added their names to the Faculty of Divinity's acceptance of *Unigenitus*, the Apostolic Constitution condemning Jansenism. The same day news reached Douai of Queen Anne's death and the accession of the Elector of Hanover as George I. Dicconson added in his diary that this happened 'without any opposition in favour of the true King, James the 3rd.'[2]

Dicconson was offered the opportunity to return to England around 1717 but showed reluctance, partly because he feared the temptations of missionary life (such as wearing lay dress) and partly because of worries about finance. He hoped to stay in Catholic Europe and petitioned Rome to gain a comfortable canonry in Cambrai. In 1720 he had spent time in Paris looking after the college funds. In search of a profitable investment, he gained little from the so-called 'Mississippi Bubble'. This was caused by a Scottish exile, John Law, who devised a scheme whereby portions of the national debt were exchanged for shares in his *Compagnie des Indes*, which had a monopoly on trading rights with the French American colonies. A 120% profit was promised to shareholders, leading to high demand for the available shares and inflation. However, the bubble burst and by the end of 1720 shares were valued at half of their nominal worth, ruining many.

Soon after, Dicconson left France and acted as chaplain to Mr Giffard of

---

[1] P. R. Harris (ed.), *Douai College Documents, 1639-1794* (Catholic Records Series vol. 63, 1972), 82.

[2] Ibid., 110.

Chillington in Staffordshire and as Vicar General to Bishop Stonor of the Midland District. His name was several times considered in connection with a mitre – as coadjutor in London in 1721 and the Northern District two years later. Reports then judged him 'a man of learning, application to business, and much dexterity in the management of affairs' although noting 'he had not ... been very successful in the economy of the Douay Seminary' and suffered from 'an impediment in his tongue, which made the practice of preaching difficult to him.'[3] Again he was considered for the now vacant Northern District in 1725 but the Dominican Thomas Williams was appointed in his place.

Dicconson spent four years in Rome in the continuing dispute with the regulars. He hoped that the Jesuit superior of the English College, Rome would be replaced by a secular priest but this was not to be. He was successful, however, in securing the ruling that members of the regular clergy should only be allowed to be established in England if they had the permission of the local bishop.

In 1740 Pope Benedict XIV appointed Dicconson as successor to Williams as Vicar Apostolic of the Northern District. However, he was not consecrated Titular Bishop of Mallus until 19 March 1741 (Passion Sunday) by Bishop Smits of Ghent. The new bishop returned to the college at Douai to confirm and ordain before returning to his new District.

Dicconson now took up residence at a property belonging to his family, Finch Mill, Appley Bridge, near Wrightington, and thus became the first Vicar Apostolic to be based on the western side of the Pennines, in the Catholic heartland of Lancashire. From the name of Finch Mill a pun was made that Dicconson was the Auditor of the Rota (*rota* being the Latin for mill and the name also given to the Roman Ecclesiastical Court). Dicconson was already a septuagenarian and petitioned for a coadjutor in 1750, suggesting Francis Petre, Charles Howard and William Maire as possible candidates. Petre was appointed and was consecrated by Dicconson in 1751.

The following year, on 5 May, Dicconson died at Finch Mill and was buried in the family vault at St Wilfrid's Church, Standish (near Wigan). He has a monument on the wall of this church, complete with crozier and mitre, and his library is now at Ushaw.

Further Reading

Dicconson's Diary in P. R. Harris (ed.), *Douai College Documents, 1639-1794* (Catholic Records Series 63, 1972)

---

[3] Brady, 257.

FRANCIS PETRE

1692-1775

TITULAR BISHOP OF AMORIA (1750)
COADJUTOR TO BISHOP DICCONSON (1750-52)
VICAR APOSTOLIC OF THE NORTHERN DISTRICT (1752-75)

Considerable obscurity surrounds the life of Francis Petre, not to be confused with his namesake who was Vice-President of Douai between 1730 and 1762. He was born at Fidlers, Essex on 2 October 1692, the third son of Joseph Petre, of the famous Catholic family, and his first wife, Catherine Andrews, who died when Francis was eight years old. Many members of the family had pursued ecclesiastical vocations. His uncle was Bishop Benjamin Petre and his grandfather, John, had ended life as a Jesuit lay brother (having been widowed). Francis' sister, Helen, later joined the English Poor Clares of Gravelines.

Details of Bishop Petre's early life and ministry remain exceedingly sketchy. He studied at the English College in Douai from April 1718 and was ordained priest in Tournai on 31 March 1720. He briefly returned to England on business in 1722 but spent several years in France, acting as tutor to John Wolf and pursuing further studies at the Paris seminary of Saint-Nicolas-du-Chardonnet and possibly also St Gregory's.

Petre returned permanently to the English Mission, though there few details concerning his labours. In 1729 he succeeded his brother Joseph to the estate of Fidlers, as the last male member of this branch of the family, and his new status gave him a secure income. He lived in many ways as a country gentleman and was said to have been very fond of hunting. In 1733 he was elected to the Old Chapter and on 12 July 1750 Benedict XIV confirmed his appointment as coadjutor to Bishop Dicconson. Other names considered were Charles Howard and William Maire, but it seems that Petre was favoured by 'James III', who still had considerable influence over the nomination of bishops. The following year, possibly on 27 July, Petre was consecrated Titular Bishop of Amoria, and soon succeeded as Vicar Apostolic in his own right.

The new Vicar Apostolic lived with the Walmesley family at Showley Hall, near Ribchester, and leased the property after the family left around 1756. As a bishop his personal wealth allowed him to live comfortably and be generous in his alms-giving and patronage. In 1767 he was granted the support of a young coadjutor, William Maire, but the latter died in 1769 and was replaced by William Walton, with whom he had a rocky relationship.

A report to Propaganda in September 1773 showed that the Vicariate's seven counties and 20,000 Catholics were served by 137 priests, of whom sixty-seven were secular and the rest Jesuit (forty-five), Benedictine (eighteen), Franciscan (four) and Dominican (three). Although there were many chapels (mostly in the upstairs rooms of the houses of the nobility and gentry), the Vicariate claimed only one consecrated church and one convent (the Bar Convent, York).

Petre died at Showley, aged 84, on Christmas Eve 1775. He was buried in the twelfth-century church founded by the Knights Hospitallers, St Saviour, Stydd, on the edge of the village of Ribchester in Lancashire, where his monument can be seen in the chancel. The parish burial register records: '1775, December 27, Francis Petre, Esq., Sholey [sic], a Romish Bis'p.' Although continuing to have occasional Anglican services, the church and lands at Stydd had been bought by a consortium of local Catholic gentry, with a view to obtaining burial rights. Stydd thus became the final resting place of a number of Catholics, including Sir William Vavasour, 'a reputed Romish priest', and, according to one tradition, the Elizabethan martyr, St Margaret Clitherow. After Petre's death, his chaplain, William Fisher, leased thirteen acres of land from the Walmesleys and built a church (Ss Peter and Paul) and presbytery (Stydd Lodge) in 1789, two years before the Catholic Relief Act.

WILLIAM MAIRE

1704-69
TITULAR BISHOP OF CINNA (1768)
COADJUTOR TO BISHOP PETRE (1768-69)

Briefly coadjutor to Bishop Petre, William Maire was the fifth son of Thomas Maire and Mary Fermor and was born at Lartington Hall on 3 January 1704 into a well-known Catholic family in the north-east. Between 1719 and 1730 he studied at the English College, Douai, together with his brother Marmaduke, and was finally ordained at Tournai on 23 December 1730 by an Irish Dominican bishop, Dominic O'Daly of Achonry. After a brief time in Paris, where his parents hoped he would learn French, Maire remained in Douai as Professor, first of Rhetoric and then Philosophy.

In 1735 he returned to England and acted as chaplain at the family home of Lartington Hall, with care of the Catholics in the Richmond area. He then served at Gilesgate in Durham and later moved to the mission of Old Elvet, where he succeeded his great-uncle as missioner. During the Jacobite Rebellion of 1745, Maire tried to avoid involvement with the Jacobites and assured the Deputy Lieutenant, George Bowes, in writing of his 'utter disinclination to any measures against the government.'[1] This did not remove him as the target of anti-Catholic mobs in 1746 and he was forced to write to the Bishop of Durham and the Duke of Newcastle for assistance.

Maire's abilities were recognized, together with his distinguished family background, and Bishop Dicconson suggested his name as a possible coadjutor in 1750. He became Vicar General for Durham and Northumberland and was elected to the Old Chapter in 1759. Maire also published a number of translations, including several works by St

---

[1] L. Gooch, *The Desperate Faction? The Jacobites of North-East England 1688-1745* (2001), 168.

Alphonsus and Charles Gobinet's *A Treatise of the Holy Youth of our Lord and Saviour Jesus Christ.*

In 1767 Maire was nominated as coadjutor to the ageing Bishop Petre and consecrated on 29 May 1768 (Trinity Sunday) by Bishop Challoner. Unfortunately, his health required him to spend much of his brief episcopate in retirement at Lartington Hall, where he passed away on 25 July 1769, aged 65. His body was interred in the Maire vault at the Anglican church of Romaldkirk. No inscription was placed over his tomb although a memorial was later erected in the mausoleum at Lartington.

WILLIAM WALTON

1716-1780
TITULAR BISHOP OF TRACHONITIS (1770)
COADJUTOR TO BISHOP PETRE (1770-75)
VICAR APOSTOLIC OF THE NORTHERN DISTRICT (1775-80)

Bishop Petre's second coadjutor and eventual successor was William Walton. Born in Manchester on 9 December 1716, he was the eldest son of Michael and Mary Walton. He entered the English College at Douai in October 1731 and was ordained a priest on 3 April 1741 by Bishop Dicconson. Until 1748 Walton acted as Professor of Theology at Douai, during which time Bishop Challoner presented him with his edition of the New Testament for examination and approval.

On 4 June 1748, Walton left Douai to serve on the English Mission and was posted as chaplain to Brian Barrett, at Milton Manor, near Abingdon, Berkshire. Barrett was a wealthy and well connected figure, lace-maker to the Royal Family and a close friend of Challoner, who was later buried in the chapel at Milton. This was beautifully decorated with a large painting of the Assumption as the altarpiece and a ceiling decorated in the Gothic style.

Barrett also had a London residence in Craven Street and often brought Walton with him on his trips to the city. The priest was well paid for his duties, though they were comparatively light. This enabled him to carry out pastoral work amongst the poor of the local area and, in 1756, publish a book, *The Miraculous Powers of the Church of Christ*. During this time he was Challoner's Secretary and Vicar General, Dean of the Old Brotherhood and treasurer of several charities. Not surprisingly Challoner requested that Walton be appointed his coadjutor and his name was also considered as Dr Green's successor as President of Douai. Walton was appointed however, on 25 June 1770, as coadjutor to Bishop Petre, and consecrated Titular Bishop of Trachonitis in December, possibly by his mentor, Challoner.

Walton kept a regular correspondence with Challoner and especially in his years as coadjutor often asked for the old man's advice. Petre was not an easy man to collaborate with and such were the difficulties between them that Walton considered resigning. Challoner persuaded him not to follow this resolution,

> as I am convinced that your call to the office was from God, and that your continuing in it is more agreeable to the will of God; waiving all other considerations, I earnestly recommend to you again and again to follow God, and to remain in the calling to which he has called you, and I make no doubt but that His divine majesty will ... give a plentiful blessing to your labours in that northern part of the vineyard which His divine providence has allotted to you.[1]

There were also questions of rubrics, which give a brief glimpse into the liturgical customs of eighteenth-century Catholics. Walton told Challoner, for example, that he did not insist on the kissing of the bishop's ring while distributing Holy Communion since it was 'liable to inconveniences, and instead of edifying, distracts the receivers.'[2] In another letter, Challoner advised his friend to discourage the giving of Benediction in English, which was not then allowed by the Church but which was seemingly the practice in parts of the Northern District.[3]

Walton succeeded Petre as Vicar Apostolic of the Northern District on Christmas Eve 1775. He had previously lived at Clayton-le-Dale, near Petre's place of residence but now moved to York (a recognition of the growing importance of urban Catholicism) and undertook a thorough visitation of his Vicariate. He was confronted by problems caused by the lay committees that managed some of the town missions, most notably at Liverpool. Here the chief priest, Joseph Gittins, felt that he should have control over finance, while his assistant complained that his income was hardly adequate and that the lay trustees would be better at managing temporalities. The bishop tended to agree with this, so that the clergy could concentrate on what they were ordained to do, although he also preferred individual communities to solve their own problems.

---

[1] Burton, ii, 157.
[2] Ibid., 155.
[3] Ibid., 173.

Walton asked for the assistance of a coadjutor but died before this request could be granted. He passed away on 26 February 1780 at York, aged 64, and was buried at the ancient church of St Michael's-le-Belfry, near the gate of York Minster.

MATTHEW GIBSON

(1734-90)

TITULAR BISHOP OF COMANA (1780)

VICAR APOSTOLIC OF THE NORTHERN DISTRICT (1780-90)

Walton's successor as Vicar Apostolic was Matthew Gibson, one of the priests he had recommended as coadjutor. Born at Stonecroft, Northumberland, on 23 March 1734, Gibson was the fourth son of Jasper Gibson and his wife, Margaret Leadbitter. The couple produced twenty-one children, including four priests, two of whom, Matthew and William, became bishops. His uncle, Thomas, was a well-known member of the Old Chapter.

Matthew Gibson entered the English College at Douai on 29 September 1747 and was ordained a priest ten or eleven years later. Then, like so many of the Vicars Apostolic, he became Professor of Philosophy and, subsequently, Theology at Douai.

For reasons of health Gibson returned to the Northern District in 1768. He received his faculties from Bishop Maire and acted as chaplain to that bishop's family at Lartington Hall in the North Riding. Two years later Gibson was elected to the Old Chapter with the titular position of Archdeacon of Kent and Surrey. After the death in 1771 of John Maire, his widow, Mary, moved to Headlam Hall near Darlington and Gibson moved with them. Bishop Walton appointed him as Vicar General in 1776 and Special Vicar in 1777, thus paving the way for Gibson's nomination to succeed him upon his death in 1780. He was named as Vicar Apostolic and consecrated Titular Bishop of Comana on 3 September by Bishop James Talbot, assisted by Bishop Challoner, then in his ninetieth year.

The new bishop continued to reside at Headlam Hall but after the death of Mary Maire in April 1784, he moved to the Jacobean Stella Hall in Blaydon-on-Tyne, then belonging to the Eyre family. In the same year he published *The London, or Little Catechism*, which hoped to draw Catholics away from some of the inaccurate catechisms then in circulation.

Gibson entered into controversy with the former Jesuits, the Society having been suppressed by Clement XIV in 1773. When they sold a mission, together with its property and land, to the Benedictines, the bishop stepped in since he considered the ex-Jesuits to be secular priests under his authority and thus unable to transfer property at their whim. In 1786 he applied to Cardinal Antonelli, the Prefect of Propaganda, for a rescript, duly granted on 15 July, prohibiting the alienation of former Jesuit property. Indeed, all ex-Jesuits were compelled to leave their property to the Vicar Apostolic at death. The former Jesuits counter-attacked by claiming that Gibson's appeal to Rome was in violation of the oath he had taken under the 1778 Relief Act, by which, in the words of Fr William Strickland (President of the Liège Academy), 'we have declared in the clearest terms that we do not admit in this kingdom any foreign jurisdiction in temporal concerns.'[1] The ex-Jesuits involved the Catholic Committee in the issue, who went on to argue in a printed address to the English Catholics of 1787 that government by Vicars Apostolic (as opposed to Bishops-in-Ordinary) was an infringement of the statutes of 'Praemunire' which limited papal jurisdiction in England.

Gibson is perhaps best remembered for his early opposition to the Catholic Committee and its negotiations with the Government over Catholic relief, initially without reference to the Vicars Apostolic. While the Talbot brothers showed little desire actively to check the activities of the Committee, partly because of their aristocratic backgrounds, Gibson teamed up with Walmesley in defending episcopal prerogatives. In 1789 he condemned the oath with the controversial words 'Protesting Catholic Dissenters' and prohibited anyone in his District from taking it. In January 1790 the bishop attacked the Committee in a Pastoral, referring to their 'Infernal Stratagems'. When the Committee invited the bishops to attend a meeting a few months later, Gibson flatly refused. Some of the Lancashire clergy suggested appointing future bishops by election but Gibson rebutted the idea. Defending the

---

[1] *Dawn*, i, 105.

Hierarchy of the Church, he also was wary of lay committees running missions and suspended Mr Harris, the assistant priest in Liverpool who had sided with the trustees against the senior missioner.

In his final years, the bishop suffered much from the old complaint of gout. He died at Stella Hall on 17 May 1790 and was buried at Newbrough church, near Stonecroft, Northumberland.

WILLIAM GIBSON

1738-1821
TITULAR BISHOP OF ACANTHOS (1790)
VICAR APOSTOLIC OF THE NORTHERN DISTRICT (1790-1821)

Uniquely in the history of the Vicars Apostolic, Matthew Gibson was succeeded by his younger brother William, characterised by Bernard Ward as having 'more than his share of roughness of manner and bluntness of speech, and this, added to a tendency to autocratic action, created for him enemies throughout his life.'[1] The appointment of the second Bishop Gibson was clearly the wish of his brother, who died without a coadjutor, although some of the Northern clergy, influenced by the Catholic Committee, tried to engineer an 'election' for his successor.

Born on 2 February 1738, William Gibson, like his brother, was sent to Douai. In 1757, having spent seven years at the college, he was directed to teach the junior class, a task that he carried out for the following three years until, in 1760, he commenced studying divinity. In 1764 he was ordained priest a year earlier than his contemporaries so that he could return to England to help his frail uncle, George Gibson, on the Tyneside Mission. By the end of the year William was back at Douai but was unable to complete his studies due to a long illness that followed a skating accident. Returning to England once more in June 1776, he was appointed chaplain to the Silvertop family at Minsteracres in Durham (a house that is now a Passionist retreat centre). From 1775 William Gibson lived in London but it is not known in what manner of work he was engaged.

On 31 May 1781 Gibson succeeded Henry Tichborne Blount as the sixteenth President of the English College, Douai. During the following nine years he embarked on a major refurbishment of the college buildings

---

[1] *Dawn*, i, 55.

and updated the syllabus of studies. Gibson's governance, though praised by many collegians, was accused of extravagance and resulted in a heavy debt. Indeed the College Procurator, Gregory Stapleton (the future bishop), saw the financial dangers of Gibson's reform and resigned in 1785; Bishop James Talbot refused for a while to send his students to Douai and others even attempted to have the President removed from office.

When his brother Matthew died in May 1790 at the age of 57, Gibson was chosen to succeed him, partly because of his known opposition to the Catholic Committee, which he compared to the French Parlements. He was consecrated Titular Bishop of Achantos at Lulworth Castle on 5 December 1790 by Bishop Walmesley, another keen critic of the Committee. Only two weeks later Gibson presided over the consecration of John Douglass, the new Vicar Apostolic of the London District. Meanwhile, he kept an eye on Douai and suggested two names as his successor: Edward Kitchin, chaplain at Lartington, and John Daniel, Vice-President of the College. The former was chosen but resigned after three months, to be replaced by the latter, who would be Douai's eighteenth and last President.

Gibson, along with Douglass, was immediately enjoined in the battle against the Committee and the controversial oath that was to be enshrined in a second Catholic Relief Bill. Gibson hosted a number of important meetings for the English bishops to discuss these issues at Durham in 1809, 1812, 1813 and 1814. Gibson was aware of his status, for much of his administration, as the senior Vicar Apostolic in the country. During the vacancies in the Midland District following the deaths of Bishops Berington and Stapleton, Gibson claimed jurisdiction, which was confirmed by Rome. In 1799 he not only issued a Lenten Pastoral with certain dispensations from fasting, but deprived Fr John Wilkes of his faculties and wrote to each of the Staffordshire clergy asking them to retract their liberal principles.

A further challenge for Bishop Gibson came as a result of the French Revolution. Not only did a number of French clergy seek refuge from the terrors of their homeland but also the communities of the English colleges, including that of Douai. Gibson had acquired many enemies among the secular clergy during his Presidency of the college and this did not help him in finding a quick solution to its relocation. Finally, on 2 October 1799, he secured the purchase of an estate at Ushaw in County Durham. While the college's community continued their exile at Crook Hall in north-west Durham, building work began at Ushaw in 1804. It was only in 1808, with three sides of a massive quadrangle built, that the staff and students moved into their new home.

Another notable relocation involved the former Jesuits of Liège, who settled in 1794 at Stonyhurst, near Blackburn, which was owned by the Welds. The original colony consisted of three priests, four ecclesiastical students, two servants and twelve students (later referred to in Stonyhurst lore as 'The Twelve Apostles'). The following year Gibson protested to Rome about the invasion of ex-Jesuits but a rescript of Pius VI dated 14 February 1796 confirmed that Stonyhurst was the same institution as Liège, with all the rights and privileges of a missionary seminary. The bishop came to see the advantages of having such an institution in his District and tried to transform it into the seminary of the north, claiming any newly-ordained priests of Stonyhurst for his District alone. A rescript of 1802 eventually cleared the matter up by denying that Stonyhurst men were bound to work in any particular District. Stonyhurst was not an episcopal seminary, as Ushaw would be.

Whilst, undoubtedly, Gibson's reputation has been clouded by those who had crossed him in the past and by the long years of his illness, there is no doubt that he was a most single-minded character and considered unnecessarily autocratic. He often tried to control affairs at Ushaw, successfully resisting the appointment of the scholarly but independent-minded John Lingard as President. The bishop was even accused of acting as the College's 'President, Procurator, and everything else.'[2] Yet he achieved much during his priestly life and episcopate. Beyond all that Douai had profited from, both in its old and new location, Gibson oversaw the expansion of Catholicism in his District and the building of thirty churches and many schools.

The physical and psychological pressures of these activities contributed to the slow and irreversible breakdown of his health. He suffered from gout and in 1798 was further afflicted by a stroke. He hoped that he would be allowed his younger brother, Richard, to act as his coadjutor but this was unacceptable to the clergy. In 1807 Gibson's former Procurator at Douai and Secretary, Thomas Smith, was appointed coadjutor, although he was not consecrated for almost three years due to problems getting the correct documents from Rome.

Gibson had already ruled the District for seventeen years and was reluctant to share his authority. According to Smith's Brief of appointment, the coadjutor was not permitted to 'interfere' in the affairs of the District without his superior's permission. This may have suited the new bishop's

---

[2] Milburn, 126.

character, preferring to stay in the background as second-in-command, but it put him in an increasingly awkward position as Gibson's health declined. By 1819 the old bishop needed two men to lift him out of his chair and the other bishops appealed to Propaganda for a Brief withdrawing the restrictions in Smith's Brief of appointment and giving the coadjutor authority to act in those matters with which Gibson was unable to cope.

There were many issues to be dealt with. In Gibson's final years a grave situation developed in Wigan. The existing chapel had become too small and the Jesuits, together with the chapel trustees, decided to build a larger structure. These plans were opposed by Gibson, who was hostile to congregational pretensions and unsure about the status of the Society of Jesus, recently restored by Pius VII in 1814. The bishop started collecting funds for a new church in Wigan that would be served by the secular clergy and thus be fully under his control. The trustees of the original chapel, however, called a meeting of the congregation that resolved to ignore Gibson's injunctions and go ahead with their own project, since they were surely entitled to rebuild the chapel without the bishop's permission. The result was that in 1818 Wigan found itself with two new Catholic chapels: the gothic St Mary's (under the seculars) and the classical St John's (under the regulars). Gibson considered placing the latter under Interdict but a compromise was reached, with the help of Bishop Milner, in which the bishop authorised both places of worship and confirmed he had rights of appointment in both. John Bossy has called this a 'victory of congregationalism'.[3]

Gibson's last years were marked by increasing infirmity and senility. By 1819 he was virtually paralysed and needed the assistance of two men to lift him from his chair. His mind was also starting to be affected. Encouraged by the three Grand Vicars of the Northern District, Bishop Poynter petitioned Propaganda to grant Smith extraordinary faculties. Cardinal Fontana signed a Brief to this effect on 8 May 1819, though Gibson continued to be Vicar Apostolic in name. The old man finally died at 33 Old Elvet, Durham, on 2 June 1821, aged 84. He was buried at Ushaw, with which he had been so closely connected throughout his life.

Further Reading

David Milburn, 'William Gibson, President of Douai', *The Ushaw Magazine*, vol. 66 (1956) and vol. 67 (1957)

---

[3] John Bossy, *The English Catholic Community 1570–1850* (1975), 346.

THOMAS SMITH

1763-1831

TITULAR BISHOP OF BOLINA (1810)
COADJUTOR TO BISHOP GIBSON (1810-21)
VICAR APOSTOLIC OF THE NORTHERN DISTRICT (1821-31)

William Gibson was succeeded by his self-effacing coadjutor, Thomas Smith, who had formerly been a colleague of his at Douai. Smith was born at Brooms in County Durham on 21 March 1763, the second son of John Smith and his wife Mary Fewster. The chapel that was opened at Brooms at the beginning of the nineteenth century was built on land donated by the future bishop's father. Thomas was educated at Sedgley Park, near Wolverhampton, between 1774 and 1777 and then went on to the English College, Douai, where he was noted for his piety and obedience to the rules. He was ordained priest by the Bishop of Arras in June 1787 and continued to live at Douai acting as Professor of Philosophy and Procurator at a time when the college faced an increasing debt. By this time William Gibson had taken over the Presidency of the college and Smith would enjoy a close relationship with him for nearly thirty years.

Smith's time at Douai was cruelly terminated when, in 1793, he was incarcerated along with others from the college by the French Republicans, finally being permitted to return to England on an American ship in 1795 and being given the responsibility of returning the students back to their parents. By the time the collegians reached London, they were an extraordinary sight, wearing clothing given to them by soldiers and Smith himself looking rather awkward in a sailor's jacket. Such was their appearance that the landlady of the Blue Boar, Holborn, hesitated in offering them hospitality.

Smith was actively involved in finding a new home for Douai and first assisted in the establishment of a seminary at Old Hall Green in the London District. From November 1795 he was given charge of the Catholic community in Durham but his reputation was such that he was swiftly marked out for other important work. He remained close to Gibson, who was now Vicar Apostolic of the Northern District, and acted as his private secretary. In 1798 he was considered as a future Vicar Apostolic for the Midland District and four years later as coadjutor in London and also declined the Presidency of the Royal English College, Valladolid. Smith was appointed treasurer of the fund that had been initiated for the building of a 'new' Douai. After having looked into the potential of sites in Lancashire, Yorkshire and Durham, it was Smith who finally signed the document, on 26 March 1799, by which the site at Ushaw was procured.

On 17 April 1807 Smith was nominated Titular Bishop of Bolina and coadjutor to Bishop Gibson. The mandate for his consecration, however, was lost in transit and a new one did not arrive until 1809. Thus it was not until 11 March 1810 that Smith was consecrated at St Edmund's College, Ware, by Bishop Poynter, an old companion from Douai, with Bishops Gibson and Collingridge as the co-consecrators. Gibson was an authoritarian who did not tend to delegate his authority and he forbade his coadjutor from involvement in Vicariate affairs without his explicit permission. As the bishop grew older and became affected by paralysis and senility, this stubbornness caused serious problems and the three other Vicars Apostolic wrote to Propaganda, without Smith's knowledge, to request that full faculties be given to the coadjutor. These were granted in 1819 and two years later the old man died.

Although he was only 58 years old by the time of his succession, Smith was said to have been as old then as his predecessor had been at eighty. He predicted that 'if the change from a life of confinement to one of action and almost continual motion does not make a material improvement in my health, I feel I must not expect to last long.'[1] His health had improved by October such that he was able to confirm close to one-and-a-half thousand over several days in Manchester. He wrote to Poynter that 'the consolation I have derived from visiting this part of my flock is enough to revive anyone. In this place in particular which may in many respects be compared with your Metropolis, I have shed tears of joy at the great good

---

[1] AAW A59 (Smith to Poynter, 31 July 1821).

which is doing in spite of the general corruption of the times.'[2] In 1823 Smith reported to Propaganda on the state of his District, particularly noting the lack of priests, chapels and money.

Smith's delicate health underlined the importance of gaining a coadjutor. In January 1824 Thomas Penswick was appointed and he generally looked after affairs west of the Pennines. Unlike Gibson, Smith was happy to work as part of a team. Despite the perennial lack of money, many new chapels were opened under Smith's benign rule, mostly in urban locations, including Pleasington Priory (1819), St Augustine's, Manchester (1820), Ashton-under-Lyne (1825), St Patrick's, Liverpool (1826), Blackburn (1826), Durham (1828), Berwick-upon-Tweed (1828), Oldham (1829), Rochdale (1830) and St Patrick's, Leeds (1831).

On 5 July 1831 Smith petitioned Rome that he might be able to resign due to his weakened state but on 30 July 1831, before his resignation could be effected, he died at Ushaw, where he was buried three days later. Smith was thought highly of by many of his contemporaries. Bishop Poynter was a close friend and Bishop Sharrock had said of him, 'to know him was to love him.'[3] However, in summing him up, Mgr John Dunne has noted that 'his long standing ill health, his years of subservience to a dominant superior combined perhaps with a temperament ill suited to involvement in public affairs resulted in an episcopate that appears pedestrian rather than inspiring.'[4]

Further Reading

J. T. Dunne (ed.), *The Northern Catholic Community in 1823: A Report to Rome* (Leeds Diocesan Archives 2007)
J. M. Hagerty, 'Notes on the Northern District under Bishop Thomas Smith 1821-1831', *Northern Catholic History*, Spring 1988

---

[2] AAW A59 (Smith to Poynter, 20 Oct 1821).
[3] Brady, 274.
[4] J. T. Dunne, *The Northern Catholic Community in 1823* (2007), 12.

THOMAS PENSWICK

1772-1836
TITULAR BISHOP OF EUROPUM (1824)
COADJUTOR VICAR APOSTOLIC OF THE NORTHERN DISTRICT (1824-31)
VICAR APOSTOLIC OF THE NORTHERN DISTRICT (1831-36)

Thomas Penswick was born on 7 March 1772 at the manor house of Ashton-in-Makerfield, Lancashire, where his father Thomas was steward to the Gerard family. The future Vicar Apostolic was first educated at Peter Newby's School at Fernyhalgh and then (from 1786) at the English College at Douai. He was a second philosopher when the French occupied the college and, together with three classmates, was given the daring task of burying some of the plate outside the town walls and another lot on the site itself. When Thomas's younger brother, John, peeped through a keyhole to witness the secret burials, he was severely reprimanded. At the same time, the most important relics were secretly hidden, including the body of St John Southworth that now rests in Westminster Cathedral. Many years later, in 1863, the treasure buried by Penswick within the college was recovered, at the request of Cardinal Wiseman and with the permission of Napoleon III. The rescued valuables included two Giffard goblets (given to Oscott) and a mounted salver given by the Duke of Norfolk in 1701 (deposited at St Edmund's).

Penswick managed to escape imprisonment, together with Thomas Gillow, and continued his studies at Old Hall Green and then transferred to Crook Hall – if tradition be believed, he and several companions walked all the way with their belongings in a wheelbarrow. Bishop William Gibson eventually ordained him to the priesthood on 1 April 1797 and he was appointed to Chester where, very swiftly, he built a fine new chapel on Queen Street. His dedication to his flock was proved by his resisting an offer to be transferred to the mission at York in 1810. Penswick insisted that he would not leave Chester until a replacement had arrived and, since no replacement was forthcoming, he stayed put.

Four years later, however, Penswick was moved to the mission based around the new chapel of St Nicholas, Copperas Hill, Liverpool, which was to become the Pro-Cathedral at the restoration of the Hierarchy in 1850. The work of the mission was intense and described by Penswick's successor as one of the worst in the Northern District. This did not stop him from founding (in conjunction with a lay committee) the mission of St Patrick's, Park Place, to serve the growing Irish masses and even laid the foundation stone himself, in the absence of the bishop. He raised funds for the building, although the process was damaged by unfounded rumours that an English priest was going to be given charge of the church. Penswick sung the High Mass at the church's opening on 22 August 1817 and, such was the congregation's poverty, pew rents were not charged.

On 1 December 1823 Penswick was appointed Titular Bishop of Europum and coadjutor to Bishop Smith, who was too infirm to preside at the consecration. Penswick was thus consecrated at Ushaw on 29 June 1824 by Poynter, assisted by Smith and, with special permission since a third bishop could not be found, John Gillow, the College President. Smith asked his new assistant to take responsibility for the area of the District that lay west of the Pennines.

On the death of Bishop Smith on 30 July 1831, Penswick became Vicar Apostolic. He proved to be a greater disciplinarian than his predecessor and suspended the famous Biblical scholar, George Haydock, the result of a long-term conflict over financial irregularities at the mission of Whitby. The bishop managed to block Haydock's appeals to Rome and faculties were not restored until after Penswick's death.

The bishop followed his old master's advice by quickly appealing for a coadjutor. John Briggs was appointed in 1833 and for a time acted as both coadjutor and President of Ushaw. During Penswick's relatively short tenure as Vicar Apostolic several new missions were established in the District, especially in the growing cities, including St Anthony's, Scotland Road, Liverpool (1833).

Bishop Penswick died at his brother's house at Ashton-in-Makerfield on 28 January 1836. He was buried in the Catholic burial ground at Windleshaw Abbey, near St Helen's, and was commemorated with a monument at Copperas Hill Chapel where he had been working at the time of his appointment to the episcopacy.

JOHN BRIGGS

1788-1861
TITULAR BISHOP OF TRACHIS (1833)
COADJUTOR TO BISHOP PENSWICK (1833-36)
VICAR APOSTOLIC OF THE NORTHERN DISTRICT (1836-40)
VICAR APOSTOLIC OF THE YORKSHIRE DISTRICT (1840-50)
BISHOP OF BEVERLEY (1850-60)

Bishop Penswick was succeeded by his coadjutor, John Briggs. Born in Barton Moss, Manchester, on 20 May 1788, he had been educated at Sedgley Park, near Wolverhampton, and then Crook Hall and Ushaw. On 19 July 1814 he was ordained a priest at Ushaw and stayed on as Professor of Rhetoric, numbering among his students Nicholas Wiseman, the future first Cardinal Archbishop of Westminster.

In 1816 Briggs was sent to the mission at St Werburgh's, Chester. His flock included Sergeant Grant of the 71st Highlanders, whose son, Thomas, served Briggs' Mass and soon revealed his intention to become a priest. The young boy lived with Briggs for a time, to be grounded in Latin and theology, before going on to Ushaw and Rome, with Briggs' financial assistance. Grant later became the first Bishop of Southwark.

Briggs was renowned as a zealous pastor and, with the help of the other three priests in Cheshire, helped set up new missions, such as Congleton, Dukinfield and Wrexham (beyond the Welsh border). Briggs frequently wrote to the local papers to defend the Catholic position regarding the various issues of the day and supporting the Irish community. In 1833 Briggs was called back to Ushaw to take up the appointment of President. That same year, on 22 January, he was appointed coadjutor to the Northern District and consecrated Titular Bishop of Trachis on the

Feast of Ss Peter and Paul, 29 June 1833, by Bishop Penswick, assisted by Bishops Baines and Walsh.

For three years the new bishop helped administer the vast District and continued as President of Ushaw. At the college he managed to build a new lodge and decorate the interior. Then, on 28 January 1836, he succeeded Penswick as Vicar Apostolic of the Northern District, resigning the college presidency and moving from Ushaw to Fulford House, York. In the second half of 1838, Briggs began a comprehensive visitation of his District which continued into the following year. In June 1839, for example, the bishop managed to visit thirteen separate missions in Northumberland and still keep up-to-date with his heavy correspondence. The visitation was both a fact-finding exercise and an opportunity for the bishop to meet his flock and, most importantly, administer the sacrament of Confirmation.

While English Catholic hagiography continues to celebrate the martyrs of the sixteenth and seventeenth centuries, the heroism of the priests of the early Victorian era is often forgotten. Not only did they sacrifice much in establishing and expanding missions, but they suffered physical danger – not the rack and rope of the earlier period but the diseases that spread so quickly in the growing towns and cities. Many priests fell victim during epidemics of cholera, typhoid or typhus as they went about their sacramental ministry. In 1838, for example, Briggs noted that no less than 26 of his priests had died from disease in only eighteen months.

In April 1838 Briggs hosted a meeting of the Vicars Apostolic at Fulford House to discuss the proposed creation of four new Districts. This took effect in 1840 and the Northern District was the most drastically re-ordered, being divided into three new vicariates. For the next decade Briggs took charge of the new Yorkshire District.

For his subsequent years as Vicar Apostolic of the Yorkshire District, see pp. 195–6

Further Reading

G. T. Bradley, 'Bishop Briggs' Visitation of Durham and Northumberland in 1839', *Northern Catholic History*, Spring 1976

The Northern District

(1840-50)

In *1840* the old Northern District was split into three: the Northern, Lancashire and Yorkshire Districts. The new Northern District comprised Cumberland, Durham, Northumberland and Westmorland. Despite its decade of existence, the new Northern District was governed by no less than three Vicars Apostolic.

Francis George Mostyn

1800-47

Titular Bishop of Abydus (1840)
Vicar Apostolic of the Northern District (1840-47)

With the creation in 1840 of four new Districts, new Vicars Apostolic were required to serve alongside the original four. Usually a Vicar Apostolic requested the Holy See for the assistance of a particular priest who, if approved, was ordained bishop and was given right of succession. In the case of the new Northern District, however, there was no right of succession and so the senior Vicar Apostolic made the nomination. In 1840 this particular duty fell to Bishop Thomas Walsh. His first choice had been Henry Weedall, the President of Oscott, but Weedall declined for reasons of health, although not before he had been assigned the titular see of Abydus. Francis Mostyn was Walsh's second choice, a man described as being 'of illustrious family, wealthy, of exceeding piety, competent, zealous, whose ministry had been crowned with continual conversions.'[1]

Francis Mostyn was born in 1800 at Kidlington, Oxfordshire, the third son of Charles Mostyn and his wife Mary Tucker. The future bishop belonged to a prominent Catholic family based at Talacre, Flintshire, and his grandfather was Sir Edward Mostyn, fifth Baronet. Francis entered Oscott on 18 August 1813 and, despite leaving the college in 1816, resumed his studies in December 1822 and was finally ordained priest on 1 March 1828. His first and only experience of life on the mission was the twelve years he spent at Ss Peter and Paul, Wolverhampton.

On 21 December 1840 he was consecrated at Ushaw by Bishop Briggs, assisted by Bishops Walsh and George Hilary Brown. He was assigned the very titular see of Abydus that had at first been intended for Weedall.

---

[1] Brady, 344.

The ceremony lasted four hours and it was reported that 'at an early hour the roads leading to the College were crowded with carriages, chaises, gigs and every description of vehicle.'[2]

Not being known to the priests of his new District, Mostyn was destined to receive a cool welcome. John Lingard wrote, 'I heartily disapprove . . . But while I admit the abuse, I know not where to discover a remedy which may not prove a worse evil.' Lingard went on to describe the new bishop as being 'with no outstanding ability, a man more likely to be led than to lead.'[3]

Mostyn did not enjoy good health and frequently had to recuperate at Ventnor and Bristol Hotwells. Ever aware of his physical frailty, he gained the appointment of William Riddell, a well-respected Northumbrian priest, as his coadjutor. Mostyn supported Ushaw through various difficulties and enjoyed a warm relationship with the President. He left money for the establishment of a preparatory school at the college. Mostyn also encouraged the project for building St Mary's in Newcastle, the church that was to become the Cathedral of the Diocese of Hexham and Newcastle. After years of poor health, the bishop finally died of consumption on 11 August 1847 and was buried at Ushaw, leaving the District briefly in the hands of Bishop Riddell.

Less than fifty years later another member of the Mostyn family briefly served as Vicar Apostolic. In 1895 Francis Edward Joseph Mostyn was appointed to the newly created Apostolic Vicariate of Wales, which had been carved out of the diocese of Cardiff. Three years later the Vicariate became the new diocese of Menevia – true mission territory with a small Catholic population facing much opposition.

---

[2] *Orthodox Journal*, vol. XII, 31.
[3] Milburn, 182.

WILLIAM RIDDELL

1807-47

TITULAR BISHOP OF LONGO (1844)
COADJUTOR VICAR APOSTOLIC OF THE NORTHERN DISTRICT (1844-47)
VICAR APOSTOLIC OF THE NORTHERN DISTRICT (1847)

Although conditions for Catholics had vastly improved in the early nineteenth century, the life of a missionary priest was still hard. In 1994 Cardinal Basil Hume preached at the 150th anniversary of the foundation of the Cathedral of St Mary's, Newcastle, and spoke of the parish's first two priests as 'martyrs of charity'. These included William Riddell, briefly Vicar Apostolic of the Northern District in the fateful year of 1847.

Riddell was born at Felton Park Hall, near Morpeth, Northumberland, on 5 February 1807, the third son of Ralph Riddell and his wife Elizabeth Blount and a member of a distinguished Catholic family. Felton Park had only recently passed to the Riddells, who undertook major remodelling work, and the house remained in their hands until the twentieth century. After receiving his early education at Stonyhurst (1817-23), the future bishop proceeded to the English College, Rome, to train for the priesthood (1823-30). He was ordained priest in the Eternal City in March 1830.

After a brief spell as Cardinal Weld's secretary, Riddell returned to England in 1832 to work as assistant to Fr James Worswick at St Andrew's in Newcastle. In July 1838 Riddell chaired a public meeting of the Catholics of Newcastle that decided to erect a new church dedicated to 'St Mary'. A resolution was passed 'that ... it behoves the Catholic Body to endeavour to erect a large and handsome Church, that may be at the same time an honour to their religion, an ornament to the Town, and capable to afford sittings for about twelve hundred persons.'

Although the Catholics of Newcastle were mostly poor, by 1842 they had raised sufficient funds to engage an architect (Augustus Welby Pugin) and purchase some land. While the church was being built, on 22 December 1843, Riddell was appointed coadjutor to Bishop Mostyn. On 17 March the following year he was ordained Titular Bishop of Longo by Bishop Briggs of the Yorkshire District. On 21 August 1844 the church was opened and Riddell combined his duties as coadjutor with caring for the new mission.

Riddell succeeded as Vicar Apostolic of the Northern District on 11 August 1847, but he was not to live for long. In 1847 typhus ravaged the dwellings of the poor of Newcastle and those who ministered to the victims knew that they could easily fall foul of the pestilence. Riddell was among those who visited the houses of the sick, where many others dared not go. By this stage all the other priests in Newcastle were either too ill or had died from the fever. In late October 1847, having visited the sick and just completed the funeral rites of one of his priests, he began to feel unwell and returned to his house at 7 Charlotte Square. Ten days later, on 2 November, All Souls' Day, he died, aged only 41. It was reported that 'his death, occurring as it did in the discharge of his pastoral office to the sick and dying, has occasioned a painful sensation in this district, for his courtesy and urbanity as a gentleman, his zeal and unwearied devotion as a priest, his grace and dignity as a prelate, and his successful efforts towards raising the splendid church of St Mary's-in-Clayton-Street, had deserved and secured the admiration, esteem and love of all.'[1]

Further tragedy ensued when, as his mortal remains were being carried to St Mary's for the Requiem Mass, the crowds lining the streets were so great that a wall on Charlotte Square collapsed under the pressure of the throng, killing a seven-year-old boy. After the Requiem Mass, Bishop Riddell's coffin was interred in a newly constructed crypt at the church. Within a few months the crypt was reopened for the interment of Bishop Riddell's assistant priest, Fr William Fletcher, another victim of the disease. After this, despite the fact that there was room for twenty coffins on the ledges of the crypt, the chamber was sealed and covered over with soil. Over the years its exact location was forgotten and only discovered during redevelopment work in 2003. The crypt was subsequently made available once again for use and so

---

[1] *Dolman's Magazine*, vol. VI, 411.

Bishop Riddell was joined by the bodies of his modern successors, Bishops Kevin Dunn (†2008) and Hugh Lindsay (†2009).

Bishop Riddell's nephew, Arthur, later became Bishop of Northampton (1880-1907) – the fulfilment, it is said, of a prophecy uttered by St John Vianney as he held the baby boy in his arms during a pilgrimage to Ars.

WILLIAM HOGARTH

1786-1866
TITULAR BISHOP OF SAMOSATA (1848)
VICAR APOSTOLIC OF THE NORTHERN DISTRICT (1848-50)
BISHOP OF HEXHAM (1850-61)
BISHOP OF HEXHAM AND NEWCASTLE (1861-66)

The name of William Hogarth is inextricably linked to Darlington, where he lived as priest and bishop for over 40 years. However, his birthplace lay on the other side of the Pennines – at Dodding Green, two and a half miles north of Kendal and on the edge of the Lakes, which was an important Catholic centre for the area. He was born on the Feast of the Annunciation, 25 March, 1786.

William Hogarth joined his elder brother, Robert, in discerning a call to the priesthood. The family, which had managed to keep both their faith and their lands throughout the years of persecution, sent the two boys to Crook Hall in County Durham in 1796. This was the northern base for the students of Douai College that had left France after the Revolution. In 1808 the community moved to Ushaw, and it was there that Hogarth was ordained on 20 December 1809 by Bishop William Gibson.

His brother had been ordained earlier that year and was immediately immersed in pastoral work, while William was called upon to remain at Ushaw as a professor, Prefect General and, from 1811, Procurator. Charles Newsham and Nicholas Wiseman were among his pupils at this time. Hogarth worked extremely hard, often retiring at midnight and sleeping for only five hours. Unsurprisingly, his health collapsed in 1816 and he moved as chaplain to Cliffe Hall, near Darlington, with responsibility for the 600 or so Catholics who lived in the area.

In November 1824 Hogarth moved to Darlington, which had just been merged with the Cliffe mission, a reflection of the growing importance of urban Catholicism. Here he oversaw the building of a new church dedicated to St Augustine, designed by Bonomi and opened on 29 May 1827. He was able to welcome the arrival of the Poor Clare and Carmelite nuns. A second mission was also founded during his tenure there.

From 1838 Hogarth served as Vicar General to Bishops Briggs, Mostyn and Riddell. After the latter's sudden death in August 1847, Hogarth succeeded as Vicar Apostolic, aged 62. He was consecrated Titular Bishop of Samosata at Ushaw on 24 August 1848 by Bishop Briggs, assisted by Bishops George Brown and Wareing. The new bishop continued to live in Darlington and look after the mission. This provided him with the means to live, the bishop's revenue otherwise only amounting to about £100 a year. Just over two years later, with the restoration of the Hierarchy by Blessed Pius IX, Hogarth was named the first Bishop of Hexham (renamed Hexham and Newcastle in 1861). The appointment was new in dignity but not in territory, since the boundaries of the new diocese were identical with those of the old Vicariate.

Hogarth was a man of great pastoral zeal, energetically overseeing and promoting the growth of the new diocese. New churches were built, old ones enlarged and the ambitious plans for expanding Ushaw of his former student, Charles Newsham (the College President), encouraged. At Hogarth's Jubilee in 1860, an address of congratulations claimed that every church in his diocese had either been erected or rebuilt by him. The bishop was known as a kind and generous man who lived simply because, as he used to point out, he had a large family to provide for and many mouths to fill. He did not seek a prominent role on the playing field of national ecclesiastical affairs, although he acted as a *confidant* of Cardinal Wiseman.

Hogarth died suddenly at Paradise Row, Darlington, from an attack of apoplexy on 29 January 1866, having celebrated the parochial Sunday Mass the day before. His body was laid in state for two days at St Augustine's and a solemn Requiem was celebrated on 1 February. Afterwards his body was taken through densely packed streets of mourners to Ushaw for burial. In the Pugin chapel, that he had himself consecrated on 27 September 1848, a Mass was offered and a sermon delivered by Bishop Ullathorne.

The people of Darlington, both Catholic and non-Catholic, later contributed towards the erection of an obelisk, made of polished granite and standing thirty feet high, which was designed by E. W. Pugin. It recorded that Bishop Hogarth had been 'the Father of his clergy and the poor, who by a saintly life, great labours and charity unbounded, won love and veneration from all.'

The Lancashire District

(1840-50)

The Lancashire District was created in 1840 out of the old Northern District. It comprised Cheshire, Lancashire and the Isle of Man. From 1850 this area was covered by the new Dioceses of Liverpool and Salford, as well as part of the new Diocese of Shrewsbury.

GEORGE HILARY BROWN

1786-1856
TITULAR BISHOP OF BUGIA (1840)
TITULAR BISHOP OF TLOA (1842)
VICAR APOSTOLIC OF THE LANCASHIRE DISTRICT (1840-50)
BISHOP OF LIVERPOOL (1850-56)

George Hilary Brown was born in January 1786 in Clifton, Lancashire, the son of William Brown and Helen Gradwell. His elder brother, Richard, later became the principal Catholic publisher in London, succeeding John Peter Coughlan in this role around 1800, and his first cousin, Robert Gradwell, became coadjutor of the London District.

He was first educated at Banister's school at Mowbreck and then moved on to Crook Hall (1799-1808) and Ushaw (1808-10). It is said that Dr Lingard, the great historian, considered Brown his favourite student. After priestly ordination on 13 June 1810, he stayed at Ushaw as Professor of Theology, Prefect of Studies and Vice-President. In 1818 five Ushaw students were sent to Rome as the vanguard of the re-founded English College under Robert Gradwell, including James Sharples, Brown's future coadjutor, and Nicholas Wiseman, whom Brown 'pronounced above all praise … I think Mr Wiseman will not fear to enter the lists with any Italian that can stand forth against him.'[1]

In 1819 Brown become a missioner at St Peter's, Lancaster, where he remained for 21 years. Writing to his old classmate, Wiseman, in April 1826, Brown reported that

> our congregation continues increasing in numbers notwithstanding the ravages that have been made in it since I came. For the last two years the chapel has been fuller than I ever saw it before and since my return from

---

[1] Milburn, 144.

Rome I have reconciled six converts, one of whom was a Quaker whom I baptized on H[oly] Saturday ... I have continual applications on behalf of others and when the days are longer I mean to give lectures.[2]

He established a Catholic lending library, encouraged his flock to play a lively part in civic affairs and published a *Supplement to the Diurnal* (1833). Despite working with great enthusiasm, it is fair to say that his gifts did not mark him out for higher office, especially since his health was extremely delicate, requiring him to be absent for long periods. Even Lingard, who was fond of his former student, described Brown in 1839 as a 'walking shadow' who trembled like a man of ninety and was often unable to celebrate Mass.

However, with the creation of four new Districts in 1840 Brown was appointed the first and only Vicar Apostolic of the Lancashire District and was duly consecrated at St Anthony's, Liverpool, on 24 August 1840 by Bishop Briggs. The new bishop initially retained charge of the Lancaster mission until October 1841, though his nephew and eventual successor, Richard Melchiades Brown, took care of practical affairs. Brown's titular see was originally Bugia but was changed to Tloa in 1842. In 1843 he was also appointed Assistant at the Pontifical Throne, thus making him a member of the papal *famiglia* with the rank of Count of the Apostolic Palace.

The day after his consecration, Brown presided at the opening of St Bartholomew's, Rainhill. His episcopate was marked by the huge exponential growth of his flock, particularly due to the massive immigration of Irish Catholics, the building of 16 new churches between 1841 and 1851, and the invitations extended to various religious Orders to assist him in the care of his District, including the Oblates of Mary Immaculate, Passionists and Redemptorists. In 1844 the bishop announced in his Pastoral that the lay committees which controlled the finances in many of the missions would be abolished and replaced by a District Board made up of clergy. He also established the Lancashire Mission Fund (later the Liverpool Diocesan Mission Fund) which organised an annual collection and distributed money for church extension and the maintenance of poor missions. Further collections were initiated for Ecclesiastical Education and the Poor Schools. Like all the Vicars Apostolic, Brown had to cope with insufficient resources for an ever-expanding Catholic community. The availability of priests was severely affected by the dangers inherent in

---

[2] Schiefen, 18.

the mission. Between April and September 1847, for example, as many as ten priests died from typhus in Liverpool.

Brown's other problem was that he lacked self-confidence and relied increasingly on his trusted Vicar General, Richard Thompson of Blackbrook. He also continued to be absent for long periods on grounds of health, creating resentment amongst the clergy. In 1843 he received a coadjutor, James Sharples, who had once been his student at Ushaw. The appointment of this energetic young priest seems to have been against Brown's wishes and the two often clashed, although they managed to live together in Sharples' property at Bishop Eton on the outskirts of Liverpool.

The restoration of the English and Welsh Hierarchy by Blessed Pius IX in 1850 brought about Brown's appointment as the first Bishop of Liverpool. Brown was strongly opposed to the division of Lancashire into the Dioceses of Liverpool and Salford, especially since the original plans would have meant him travelling through part of Salford (the Hundred of Leyland) to reach the northern areas of his diocese, such as Preston and Lancaster. He initially administered the new Diocese of Salford until the appointment of his Vicar General, William Turner, as bishop in 1851, and used this period successfully to petition Propaganda for the transferral of the Leyland Hundred to Liverpool.

Brown left his residence at Bishop Eton and moved into a more centrally located house on Catharine Street. During his brief time as Bishop of Liverpool, he saw the opening of nine churches, five convents and two secondary schools. In 1853 he called the first Diocesan Synod, which strengthened episcopal authority, and supported the opening of Fr Nugent's Catholic Institute for the education of middle-class boys on Hope Street. Brown named St Nicholas, Copperas Hill, as his Pro-Cathedral and became the first of the new diocesan bishops to erect a Chapter, although it frequently clashed with the bishop over matters of policy and finance.

Meanwhile, Brown's health was fast declining and his doctor despaired of his life in 1851, though he lived another five years. Sharples having died in 1850, Brown reluctantly asked for a coadjutor and recommended the Provost of the Chapter, Canon Cookson, but Propaganda instead appointed Canon Alexander Goss, who was consecrated by Cardinal Wiseman at Copperas Hill on 25 September 1853. Brown resented Goss' appointment and even failed to acknowledge his presence or offer him full faculties. Since Brown failed to provide his new assistant with a suitable income, a fund was created for him by the Liverpool Chapter. Brown, who felt insecure in his position as his health further declined, feared that Goss, like Sharples before him, would become a focus of division and threaten his own authority.

Despite his poor health, Brown died quite suddenly at Catharine Street on 25 January 1856. His Requiem was held at the Pro-Cathedral, during which Mozart's Requiem was performed, and his body was then taken in a hearse drawn by four black horses to the cemetery at St Oswald's, Old Swan. Despite his indecision, paranoia and the 'tangled skein of confusion' that marked his administration, Brown achieved some notable successes and prepared the foundations for the future Archdiocese of Liverpool.

Further Reading

Peter Doyle, 'A Tangled Skein of Confusion: The Administration of George Hilary Brown of Liverpool, 1850-56', *Recusant History*, Vol. 25, no.2 (Oct. 2000), 294-303

JAMES SHARPLES

1797-1850

TITULAR BISHOP OF SAMARIA (1843)
COADJUTOR TO BISHOP BROWN (1843-50)

James Sharples was born in Liverpool on 19 October 1799, the son of Thomas and Elizabeth Sharples, and was baptised shortly afterwards at St Peter's, Seel Street. He was educated first at Ushaw (1809-18) and on 18 December 1818 entered the newly re-established Venerable English College, Rome, his fellow students including Nicholas Wiseman. Like Wiseman, he quickly adapted to studies at the Gregorian and won prizes in theology and Hebrew. He was ordained priest in Rome on 30 November 1823 and returned home the following July, taking temporary positions at Lea and Kirkham.

In 1825 Sharples took charge of the mission of St Alban's in Blackburn. The foundations of a new church had been built on a large five acre site and it was up to the young priest to finish the job and raise the money. He also provided the parish with schools and a fine organ. Controversy was caused when Sharples placed a brass plaque saying 'Rectory' at the entrance of the clergy house, offending Anglican sensibilities and even leading to questions being asked in Parliament. However the sign remained in place for over a century. His fourteen years at Blackburn were marked by a rapidly growing congregation, thanks largely to Irish immigration and the process of urbanisation, and Sharples founded a mission at nearby Darwen to accommodate the numbers.

In 1839 Sharples was appointed to St Marie's, Sheffield, which would eventually become Hallam Cathedral. An enthusiast of the Gothic Revival, Sharples was instrumental in building the church of St Bede at Masbrough (Rotherham) in the Decorated style in 1842.

Sharples had also gained a reputation as a skilled preacher and an able controversialist, having written articles in support of Catholic Emancipation and the abolition of tithes. Given his proven success also as a pastor, it was little surprising that he was called to Rome at the end of 1842 and appointed coadjutor to Bishop Brown of the Lancashire District. He was consecrated Titular Bishop of Samaria on 15 August 1843 in the church of Sant' Agata dei Goti, which then was part of the Irish College, by Cardinal Fransoni, the Prefect of Propaganda.

Soon after returning from Rome, the new bishop blessed the foundation stone of St John's, Salford (now Salford Cathedral), on 30 May 1844. As coadjutor, Sharples' youthful energy was a contrast to the ageing Brown and it often seemed as if the coadjutor was in reality his master. This was facilitated by Brown's long absences due to sickness. Sharples purchased a property, Eton House, jointly with his brother Henry, a local timber merchant. The house became known as Bishop Eton and later became a Redemptorist monastery. In Sharples' lifetime it was the official residence of the two bishops and a base for the clergy – it was used for retreats, including one preached by the Rosminian, Fr Luigi Gentili in 1847. One of the Italian's pet hates was public dances and he criticised Sharples and Brown for attending a Charity Ball in Liverpool.

Sharples had ambivalent feelings towards his alma mater of Ushaw and was perceived to be an ally of the Jesuits. He enthusiastically supported the foundation of a school at Domingo House, Everton, dedicated to St Edward, which led to a row with Ushaw, who feared the school would be turned into a diocesan seminary and thus remove Lancastrian funding from St Cuthbert's. Tensions were heightened when Sharples laid claim to Ushaw monies. St Edward's went on to become a seminary and later moved to Upholland.

Negotiations were taking place for a restored Hierarchy and Sharples was chosen, with Wiseman, to form a deputation from the Vicars Apostolic to Rome. They arrived in the Eternal City on 9 July 1847 and were received by Blessed Pius IX. Cardinal Acton, who was cautious of a Hierarchy, had just died and the Pope celebrated Mass on three occasions for guidance on the issue, finally deciding that the time was indeed opportune. However, the unexpected death of Bishop Griffiths meant that Wiseman had to return to London and Sharples remained in Rome until October. He brought back with him a commission to the English Vicars Apostolic to propose the division of the eight Districts into twelve dioceses, and a

James Smith

William Gibson

Thomas Smith

PMVS IN CHRISTO PATER AC DNVS DNVS IOANNES BRIGGS
PRIMVS POST HIERARCHIAM ANNO MDCCCL A PIO P.P. IX RESTAVRATAM EPVS BEVERLACENSIS
PRAELATVS DOMESTICVS SVAE SANCTITATIS ET SOLIO PONTIFICIO ASSISTENS
PIE OBIIT IN DNO EBORACI DIE IV IANVARII A.D. MDCCCLXI ANNOS NATVS LXXI
EPVS TRACHINENSIS A.D MDCCCXXXIII RENVNCIATVS
COADIVTOR PRIMO VICARIVS APLICVS POSTEA A.D MDCCCXXXVI DISTRICTVS SEPTENT
POST EIVSDEM IN TRES DISTRICTVS DIVISIONEM DISTRICTVI EBORACENSI PRAEFECTVS.

John Briggs

William Hogarth

George Hilary Brown

THE YORKSHIRE DISTRICT

John Briggs

Philip Michael Ellis, OSB

William Laurence York, OSB

Charles Walmesley, OSB

Peter Bernardine Collingridge, OSF

Peter Augustine Baines, OSB

Charles Michael Baggs

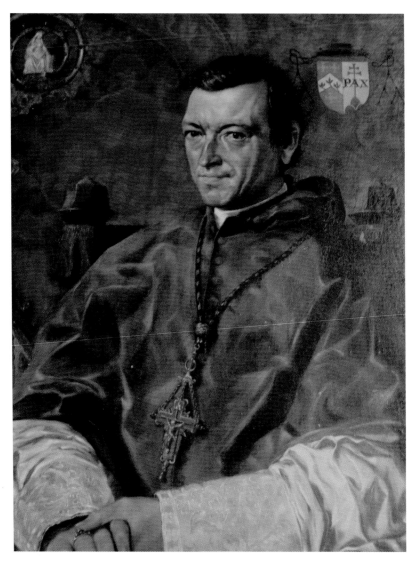

William Bernard Ullathorne, OSB

THE KIDNAPPER.—A CASE FOR THE POLICE.

Kidnapper. "THERE 'S A BE-AUTIFUL VEIL !!! GIVE ME YOUR PARCEL, MY DEAR, WHILE YOU PUT IT ON."

Punch cartoon of Joseph William Hendren, OSF

Thomas Joseph Brown

meeting of the bishops was arranged at Wiseman's residence in Golden Square on 11 November.

Sharples returned from Rome not only with this promising news but with poor health, from which he never recovered. In 1850 he retired to Singleton for recuperation. The doctors pronounced his condition as hopeless in June and he died on 11 August 1850, aged only 48, on the seventh anniversary of his appointment as coadjutor. He was buried in the churchyard of St Mary's, Great Eccleston. Tragically for him, given his great efforts, he died only a few weeks before the restoration of the Hierarchy.

The Yorkshire District

(1840-50)

Created out of the old Northern District in 1840, the Yorkshire District, as its name suggested, consisted of the county of Yorkshire.

JOHN BRIGGS

1788-1861

TITULAR BISHOP OF TRACHIS (1833)
COADJUTOR VICAR APOSTOLIC OF THE NORTHERN DISTRICT (1833-36)
VICAR APOSTOLIC OF THE NORTHERN DISTRICT (1836-40)
VICAR APOSTOLIC OF THE YORKSHIRE DISTRICT (1840-50)
BISHOP OF BEVERLEY (1850-60)

For Briggs' early life and his ministry as Vicar Apostolic of the old Northern District, see pp. 175-6

In 1840 Briggs, the outgoing Vicar Apostolic of the Northern District, took charge of the new Yorkshire District and remained at Fulford House, York. He continued to be an energetic shepherd of his ever-expanding flock, overseeing the building of churches in such places as Bradford, Leeds, Sheffield and York. Further challenges to his work came about through the untimely deaths of some of his clergy during the typhus epidemic of 1847; five priests were lost in Leeds alone.

With the restoration of the Hierarchy by Blessed Pius IX, Briggs was appointed on 29 September 1850 as Bishop of Beverley, the see that was subsequently renamed the Diocese of Leeds (20 December 1878). Since there was no suitable church in Beverley, St George's, York became the Pro-Cathedral. Briggs was one of the oldest of the newly appointed bishops and suffered from frequent bouts of ill health. His episcopal motto revealed his determination to continue: *Non recuso laborem*, 'I do not refuse the work'. He saw to it that his new diocese was furnished with new churches, served by the religious Orders that he invited into his see and equipped with a sound structure of lay associations. For the guidance of his priests he wrote *Admonitions and Exhortations*, a work that had a wide influence.

Briggs did not always see eye-to-eye with Wiseman, who tended to play the part of Primate rather than Metropolitan, and the Cardinal even suspected Briggs of being a Gallican. The bishop could certainly be stubbornly independent, as seen in his refusal to appoint a coadjutor, despite this being the Pope's express desire. However, Briggs was also a much respected figure in the English Church. He was particularly praised for his appeal throughout the country for funds to alleviate the effects of the Irish famine and it was Briggs who was the celebrant of the Mass of the Holy Ghost at the Provincial Synod held at Oscott, on 13 July 1852, on which occasion John Henry Newman preached his celebrated *Second Spring* sermon. He was affectionately known as 'the late Dr Briggs' due to his tendency to unpunctuality, caused partly by his reluctance to end the conversation of the previous meeting.

Poor health finally caused Briggs to resign his see on 7 November 1860 and two months later, on the evening of 4 January 1861, he died at his home in York. The Requiem Mass was celebrated at the Pro-Cathedral by Thomas Grant, the Bishop of Southwark and his former protégé. The funeral pall had 'a large red cross, surmounted with beautiful mitres, beneath which were the letters "J.B." and below these again was a splendid scroll with the word "Beverley" worked thereon.'[1] Briggs' body was then buried at the ancient church of St Leonard's, next to the Vavasour's manor at Hazlewood, near Tadcaster. He was succeeded at Beverley by the outgoing Rector of the Venerable English College, Rome – Robert Cornthwaite.

---

[1] *Weekly Register*, 19 January 1861, 2.

The Western District

(1688–1850)

Created in 1688, the Western District consisted of the Principality of Wales and the counties of Cornwall, Devon, Dorset, Gloucestershire, Herefordshire, Somerset and Wiltshire. It was the District with the smallest Catholic population and the Vicars Apostolic had constantly to struggle for sufficient funds. In 1840 the District was divided into two to create the new Western and Welsh Districts. With the exception of Baggs (a secular), all the Vicars Apostolic of the Western District belonged to either the Benedictine or Franciscan Orders, thus assuring the presence of a regular amongst the English and Welsh episcopate. Important centres included Bath and (in the nineteenth century) Bristol. In the aftermath of the French Revolution, the monks of St Gregory's, Douai eventually settled at Downside.

Philip Michael Ellis, OSB

1652-1726

Titular Bishop of Aureliopolis (1688)
Vicar Apostolic of the Western District (1688-1705)
Bishop of Segni (1708-20)

Philip Ellis' extraordinary family was a microcosm of the divisions in the body politic and ecclesiastic of the time. Born on 8 September 1652, the future bishop was the third son of John Ellis and his wife, Susannah Welbore. His father was the Anglican Rector of Waddesdon, Buckinghamshire, who had made his name as a religious controversialist. Philip's eldest brother, John, became Under Secretary of State to William III and to Queen Anne between 1695 and 1705, and died a man of substantial wealth. Alexander Pope even hinted that he had had a liaison with the Duchess of Cleveland. Another of the Ellis brothers, Sir William, stood on the opposite side of the political spectrum, becoming Secretary of State to the exiled James II at St Germain-en-Laye and then controlling court finances under the 'Old Pretender'. He died in Rome in 1732 although remaining loyal to the Anglican faith of his baptism. Other brothers included Welbore Ellis, later Church of Ireland Bishop of Kildare and then of Meath; Samuel, Marshall of the King's Bench under James II; and Charles, a clergyman in the Church of England.

Along with his other brothers, Philip was sent to Westminster School in 1667, but converted to Catholicism the following year and went overseas. A nineteenth-century edition of *The List of the Queen's Scholars of St Peter's College, Westminster* claimed that Ellis had been 'kidnapped by the Jesuits from Westminster School, and brought up by them in the principles of the Romish faith, at St Omer. He was not heard of by his family for many years; and might never have been discovered, but for his having at St

Omer the nickname of "Jolly Phil", by which he had also been known at Westminster.[1] He was professed at the Benedictine priory of St Gregory at Douai on 30 November 1670, taking the name Michael. After final profession Ellis proceeded to study at the University of Douai.

In 1681 Ellis was appointed the first official annalist of the English Benedictines and in this role he wrote the *Chronology* – biographies of the Congregation's great and good and a record of the privileges accorded the Order. Poor health meant that he had to employ a secretary to complete this task.

With the accession of James II, Ellis found himself back in England as a member of the newly-established Benedictine community at St James' Palace. The young monk became one of the King's chaplains-in-ordinary and preachers, being known as 'the great pulpit man' of the Catholics, 'his method, stille, and delivery being far above the common, and very much admired even by Protestants.'[2] Some of Ellis' sermons were printed, including the celebrated one given on 13 November 1686 in which he announced he had been authorized by the Order to renounce all claims to the monastic lands held before the Reformation, thus reassuring many a lay landowner. All that the Benedictines wanted restored to them, Ellis proclaimed, was their good reputation.

In 1688 Blessed Innocent XI divided England into four ecclesiastical Districts and Ellis was among the new bishops, appointed first Vicar Apostolic of the Western District and Titular Bishop of Aureliopolis in Lydia by Letters Apostolic dated 30 January 1688. He was consecrated at the Chapel Royal in St James' on 6 May by the Papal Nuncio, Archbishop Ferdinand d'Adda. The four Vicars Apostolic were to be paid an annual salary of £1,000 out of the royal exchequer and a further £500 each as they commenced office.

At first, all went well: the new bishop confirmed at the new Jesuit school in the Savoy and, it is said, reconciled the Earls of Sunderland and Melfort to the Church on 30 August. However, it does not seem that Ellis ever actually resided in his District. Revolution broke out in November 1688 and with it died Catholic hopes. Bishop Ellis was arrested, having been betrayed by a serving girl, and incarcerated in Newgate Prison. There he was visited by a representative of William III, Gilbert Burnet, who ordered that the bishop be well treated. In early January 1689 Ellis was

---

[1] *The List of the Queen's Scholars of St Peter's College, Westminster* (1852), 164.
[2] *Dodd's Church History of England*, ed. M. A. Tierney, III, 295.

released and travelled to the exiled court of St Germain, never to return to England again. In France he became chaplain to the Queen, Mary of Modena and, due to a misunderstanding concerning his surname, became known as the 'Bishop of Ely'.

In early 1693 Ellis travelled to Rome and became Secretary to the English Dominican Cardinal, Philip Howard. It was rumoured that Ellis was to be appointed the King's Roman Agent but this never came about, although he acted on behalf of the exiled monarch semi-officially during his residence in the Eternal City. The bishop was closely connected to the English College, beside which he lived, and witnessed the great rebuilding work that Howard sponsored. He was with the cardinal during his last illness and wrote to the King in June 1694 of the cardinal's temporary recovery thanks to the 'efficacy of St Philippi Nerius's cap [biretta], for soon after it was applied to my Lord, he voided several stones, when he had not the least suspicion of that temper.'[3] The 'Cardinal of Norfolk' died shortly afterwards and left his Secretary a generous grant of money and the cardinalatial coach and horses.

Ellis moved to the English Dominican house at Ss Giovanni e Paolo on the Celian Hill. In 1696 he was appointed by Innocent XII as an Assistant Prelate to the Pontifical Throne, a small step up the ecclesiastical ladder. He was forced to leave Ss Giovanni e Paolo in 1698, since the house by that time had been given to the Lazarists. Fr Ralph Postgate, the Jesuit Rector of the English College, petitioned the Pope that Ellis should not be given lodgings at the *Venerabile* since the presence of an English bishop would destroy student discipline and lead to the growth of an anti-Jesuit faction. The two men had, in fact, had a disagreement over the will of Sir William Godolphin, Ambassador to Spain and a convert to Catholicism, who died in 1696 unmarried and childless. Ellis believed that money had been left for the establishment of a seminary in Rome for the Western District and claimed that Postgate, who had translated the will into Italian, had altered it. In Rome, Ellis also acted as Procurator for the English Benedictines and in October 1699 gained for their chapels certain privileges granted by the 1633 Bull, *Plantata*.

Not surprisingly, Ellis was accused of abdicating his responsibilities towards his District and preferring a privileged life in Catholic Italy to a life of hardship in Protestant England. Ellis was aware of these accusations and in January 1702 wrote to Bishop Giffard:

---

[3] A. Bellenger (ed.), *Fathers In Faith: The Western District 1688-1988* (1991), 24.

I heard of nothing but coldnesse in some places and untimed expressions in others; misrepresentations and ill offices from abroad and at home, were supposed not to be wanting to make my exile look like an abdication. But at length my repeated instances to obtain permission to return ... are become so public that they can no longer be called in question, but on the contrary are charged upon me as a fault and where before I was taxed for want of zeal. Now some would render me suspected of want of duty and leaning too much on the government. But the divine goodness has more than recompensed these little mortifications, by giving me frequent opportunities to serve my religion and my country, in the place where I am, by rectifying many persons' understandings, taking off prejudices, and sweetening the sharpe humours of those who had power and disposition to do us harm.[4]

He further protested that 'some years past, persons well acquainted with the aspect of your court were of opinion a license to return [to England] would not be denied me: but then my old master that is gone [James II], would not allow that I should ask it: but when I understood he was not so much against it, the face of things was much changed, and the permission, tho' not denied, yet not granted but rather deferred.'[5]

That Ellis' future lay overseas was made signally clear when he transferred to the Italian Benedictines at Subiaco on 13 November 1703. He became life Abbot of the College of St Gregory the Great *de Urbe* in Rome and was supported by a number of other benefices. On 19 September 1705 Ellis finally resigned from the Western Vicariate and was appointed the following year to the legation of Bologna.

Finally, on 3 October 1708, Clement XI translated him to the Diocese of Segni, a hill town in the Volscians, south-east of Rome but still within the Papal States. He solemnly took possession of the cathedral on 28 October. The bishopric dated from the end of the fifth century and Ellis must have been interested to learn that Pope Alexander III had canonised St Thomas of Canterbury at Segni in 1173. Writing nearly two hundred years after the arrival of Ellis, Augustus Hare noted that 'nothing can be more kind than the reception which the inhabitants of Segni give to strangers' and that 'excellent cherries and peaches abound; and the woods supply chestnuts for a coarse bread which is considered very nourishing, and abundant acorns for the maintenance of the black pigs which feed here in vast numbers.' When the people returned from the fields with their animals at sunset,

---

4 Brady, 286.
5 Ibid., 286.

the steep streets were 'blocked up for a time, and the cries, the shouts, the braying, the barking, and, above all, the squeaking and grunting, baffle description.'[6]

Ellis had been a bishop for twenty years and yet for most of that time had virtually been without a flock. Now at Segni, he exercised his office with great energy. During his first two years as bishop, he only left the diocese three times – an impressive record for an early modern prelate. Within three months he had succeeded where his predecessor failed and founded a seminary and secondary school in a disused Poor Clare convent at the top of the town, although the use of this property led to a lengthy legal dispute.

'Mylord Ellis of Wales,' as he became known, carried out regular parish visitations, widened roads and organised missions, with the help of the famous Jesuit preacher, Blessed Anthony Baldinucci. He repaired the episcopal palace and cathedral, which was in a poor state; indeed, the bishop's chief means of entering his cathedral was at first through a wine cellar. He added a new roof and choir-stalls, promoted devotion to 'Our Lady of the Mountains' and erected statues to two local saints: Pope St Vitalian and St Bruno, a twelfth-century Bishop of Segni. In November 1710 Ellis oversaw the first diocesan synod, which was held in the choir of the *duomo*. About seventy of the clergy attended and Ellis had to provide them with hospitality in his palace, seminary and elsewhere. It became something of a model for other dioceses in the Papal States and Clement XI ordered the decrees to be published.

Ellis was still interested in English affairs and remained close to the Jacobite court, which was now settled in Rome. He was present at the birth of 'Bonnie Prince Charlie' in 1720 and gained chapter rights with the English Benedictines in 1725. In Rome he was also involved in the process that led to the canonisations of Pius V, Andrew Avellino, Felix of Cantalice and Catherine of Bologna in 1712.

Ellis had, at first, been shocked by the condition of his flock. 'The people of Segni,' he wrote, 'are only a little more civilized than the ancient Volscii, their ancestors. They appear to take no interest in education and culture and, what is far worse, seem to be quite averse from religion. For the most part they do not even know the basic truths of the faith.'[7] The people, on their part, had been suspicious of Ellis' reforming zeal. However, by the

---

[6] A. Hare, *Days Near Rome* (1907), 136-37.
[7] Bellenger (ed.), *Fathers in Faith*, 27.

time of his death from dropsy of the chest on 16 November 1726, aged 74, Ellis was much-loved by the *Segnini* and he is still regarded as one of their most important bishops. He was buried in the chapel of his seminary, to which he left most of his belongings.

Ellis' episcopal ring, along with his library, was eventually given to Bishop Baines by Leo XII for the use of his successors in the Western District and then the Diocese of Clifton. In 1981 Segni was united to Velletri to make a new suburbican diocese, a see administered by a bishop but also given as a title to one of the senior curial cardinals at the Vatican. Between 1993 and 2002 Joseph Ratzinger was Bishop of Velletri-Segni, before becoming Dean of the Sacred College and Bishop of Ostia. Thus, in a sense, Benedict XVI can claim to have been a successor of Philip Michael Ellis.

Matthew Prichard, OSF
1669-1750
Titular Bishop of Myra (1715)
Vicar Apostolic of the Western District (1713-1750)

The exile of Ellis led to a lengthy period without a bishop for the Western District. The Pope had asked for names of possible candidates to replace Ellis in 1704 and among those suggested was Robert Witham, superior of the Paris seminary, his brother Thomas Witham, President of Douai, and John Gother, the noted author and mentor of the young Challoner. Mary of Modena, on the other hand, was keen that a regular should be appointed. Bishop Giffard, who occasionally ventured into the Vicariate to administer the sacrament of Confirmation, was instrumental in obtaining the appointment of his brother, Andrew, as Vicar Apostolic following Ellis' resignation in 1705. Despite being granted the titular see of Centuriae, he refused to accept the nomination due to poor health and advancing years. In the summer of 1706, after the names of eight other secular priests had been submitted and refused by Rome, Bishop Smith of the Northern District wrote in coded language:

> . . . Old Andrew is stiff and not going to be moved from his resolution. He is hardened against all that was offered, and gives no other answere but that he cannot, will not agree to what is desired; and as it appears to me, required by God and his friends. This peremptory refusal puts us hard to it to find out an excuse for the good man, for he will not write himself [to Rome], and, to offer another that may be acceptable to Mr Clement [the Pope], has talents, and will accept of the farm [the Western District]. Such, is hoped may, in some measure, be Mr Saltmarsh, who, though in some particulars less qualified, yet *omnibus consideratis* is as, or more, fit than any we could pitch on. But in all appearance the management of that farm will by Mrs Grace's [Queen Mary of Modena] interest, and other

insinuations, be put into other hands, and provided he be an able, good man and a good neighbour, tis no great matter who he be, or of what cote, or parish [i.e. secular or regular].[1]

The Vicars Apostolic proposed Gerard Saltmarsh as an alternative but his appointment was blocked since the Internuncio at Cologne accused him of being a friend of the Jansenists. Appointments to the Vicariate always saw the flaring up of old animosities between the secular and regular clergy, often to the consternation of Rome. Not until September 1713 was the Western District to have a new Vicar Apostolic, the Franciscan Matthew Prichard (or Pritchard), and even then he was not consecrated until 1715, some ten years after Ellis' resignation.

Born at Graig, near Newport, in 1669, Matthew Prichard was the only Vicar Apostolic of the Western District to be a native of that area. As a youth he settled on joining the Franciscans and entered the novitiate of the friary of St Bonaventure, Douai. After priestly ordination in 1693 he returned to England to minister at Perthyre in Monmouthshire under the patronage of the wealthy Powell family. He then returned to the continent to teach philosophy and theology at Louvain for twelve years.

This life of conventual and academic duties was interrupted in 1713 by Prichard's nomination to the Western District, largely due to the influence of the exiled 'James III', who expressed his wishes through the Paris Nuncio. Those who supported the appointment of a secular complained that not since the days of King John had the reigning monarch been permitted to make such nominations. Prichard was finally consecrated at Whitsun, 9 June 1715, in Cologne.

The Western District had been without a resident bishop since its creation nearly thirty years previously. Prichard kept a low profile and threw himself into his work with an ardour measured by prudence. He resided with his old patrons, the Powells, at Perthyre, although he travelled extensively throughout his territory. He was severely limited by the penal laws and the state of the District's finances, which necessitated papal subsidies in 1721 and 1723.

In 1736 Prichard became the only Vicar Apostolic appointed in the eighteenth century to travel to Rome. He sought financial aid and the appointment of a coadjutor, but also hoped to defend the rights and privileges of the religious Orders. Rumours quickly circulated that Prichard was in the pay of the Jesuits and was fighting for their cause.

---

[1] Hemphill, 38-39.

In the autumn of 1736 Prichard set out on his journey, stopping at Douai and Paris on the way and protesting in both places that he was not going to Rome as the Jesuits' agent. Whilst at table at St Gregory's College in Paris he made it clear that the only aim of his visit was to procure funds from Rome. On his return journey in March 1737 Prichard was described by Dicconson as being 'mightily satisfied with the success he met with at Rome' and proceeded to give support to the removal of the Jesuits from the English College.[2]

Prichard refused to accept the papal decree of 1745 that gave the bishops the right to grant faculties to the regular clergy and received a reprimand from Rome. His concern for the regulars led to suspicion – Christopher Stonor wrote in 1749 that 'Mr Prichard is to have a gentle reprimande, for his having had a greater regard to his former brethren than his present dignity.'[3] However, the President of Douai, Dr Robert Witham, himself an opponent of the regulars, spoke well of Bishop Prichard:

> . . . I have a late letter from Bp. Prichard, a very worthy Prelate, and who has shown himself not only just and impartial to the Clergy [seculars], but I have reason to say, he has shown himself a particular friend to me and to this House [Douay] even more than every Bishop has done of our Body [i.e. than any secular bishop]; having a true zeal for the King's service, as I can truly say in this we have been always of the same sentiments. . . . But now Bishop Prichard has so ill-health and is so poor that he desired me in his last letter to let his Master [the King] know that he hoped he would not take it amiss that he desired of the Pope to be freed from his present charge of his District, not being able to acquit himself of those obligations.[4]

In 1741 Prichard was granted the assistance of William Laurence York as his coadjutor. Bishop Prichard died at the age of 81, having been a bishop for 37 years, on 22 May 1750 at Perthyre. He was buried in the local parish church, St Kenelm's in Rockfield, Abergavenny, where above his tomb was placed the communion table. A later minister at that church sought to remove the memorial stone and the ensuing episode was recorded by the then Catholic parish priest:

> The late incumbent was a bigoted parson. In doing some repairs to the church he had this [tombstone] and two other Catholic tombstones removed, and offered for sale as waste materials! This I herd from some

---

[2] Ibid., 139.
[3] Dockery, *Collingridge: A Franciscan Contribution to Catholic Emancipation* (1954), 212 (fn).
[4] AAW B41, Ep. Var., IX/217.

of the Protestant parishioners; so I walked over, and saw the stones reared against the boundary wall. The Vicar happened to call upon me, with his wife, a few days after on some business; so I asked him why he had removed the Bishop's tombstone. He said he did not think it right to have a 'Romish' bishop's tombstone there. I said, "Are you not going to replace it?" He replied, "No, certainly not." Then I said, "I will write to my friend the Rev. Dr Oliver of Exeter, who has published the history of Bp Prichard with a full description of his Lordship's burial there and the inscription on the stone, and I will get him to put a footnote in the next edition to the effect that, through the bigotry of the Rev.- this monument was removed in such a year." He then said he would have it replaced immediately. I said, "If you don't, I will hand down your name to posterity like Pontius Pilate's in the Creed." It has been replaced, and his successor, I am told, still repeats the anecdote to visitors.[5]

---

[5] *Miscellanea* (Catholic Records Society 9), 1911, 165 (letter from Fr Abbott to Alfred Williams).

WILLIAM LAURENCE YORK, OSB
1687-1770
TITULAR BISHOP OF NISIBIS (1741)
COADJUTOR OF THE WESTERN DISTRICT (1741-50)
VICAR APOSTOLIC OF THE WESTERN DISTRICT (1750-70)

The Franciscan Bishop Prichard was succeeded by his Benedictine coadjutor, William Laurence York. Born in London during the reign of James II, York was sent to St Gregory's, Douai, for his early schooling and was subsequently professed as a monk there in either 1704 or 1705, taking the name Laurence. In December 1711 he was ordained a priest at Douai where he taught and carried out various duties until, having been a vocal critic of the English Benedictine President-General, Dom Laurence Fenwick, he was sent on the English mission. In 1721 York was appointed Prior of St Edmund's, Paris. After serving his four year term he returned to his own monastery in the same capacity. A brief appointment as secretary to the President-General, Dom Thomas Southcote, ensued before York finally returned to England in 1730 to take charge of the important mission at Bath, which was usually staffed by Benedictines and frequently found a prominent place on the agenda of Provincial Chapter meetings.

The Bath mission was based at Bell Tree House, at the corner of Binbury Lane and Beau Street, with a chapel on the second floor and lodgings for Catholic visitors to the popular spa town. The chapel was well-appointed and according to a 1725 inventory boasted '3 vestments and antependiums, viz: one of Moehair crimson with silver lace; an other of Purple adorned with open silver lace, the 3rd of black; a good Albe, Altar-stone, 2 large Reliquaries of Silver, a Crucifix, two Silver bread boxes, Cartes, tynn Thurible, etc.'[1] York seems to have been successful as missioner here and,

---

[1] J. A. Williams, *Bath and Rome: The Living Link* (1963), 27.

in 1740, was deemed to be 'exceedingly agreeable to all the chief of both Protestant and Catholick nobility that frequent that place … He preaches in a publick chapel … and is a man fit to appear in the best company.'[2]

York's subsequent appointment as coadjutor to Bishop Prichard in 1741 promised continuity with the traditions of the Western District. He was firstly a member of the regular clergy – Ellis had been a Benedictine and Prichard was a Franciscan. Secondly, he had strong Jacobite tendencies – Ellis had been close to the exiled Stuart court and Prichard was also known for his Jacobite sympathies. Indeed, the influence of the 'Old Pretender' was an important factor in York's appointment by Propaganda.

On 20 August 1741 he was consecrated Titular Bishop of Nisibis at Douai and, back in England, continued to reside at Bell Tree House, which was also to become the residence of his two successors, Walmesley and Sharrock. Prichard, meanwhile, remained in Wales. Due to the destruction of much of the early archives of the District during the Gordon Riots, there are many gaps in our knowledge of York's episcopate. Perhaps the most dramatic incident occurred at the time of the 1745 Jacobite rebellion, when an anti-Catholic troublemaker forged a letter from Prince Charles to York thanking him for his support and promising him the bishopric of Carlisle after the Stuarts had reclaimed the Throne. The letter was taken to the Mayor of Bath who thought it a forgery but, for the sake of the bishop's safety, advised him to leave the city for a while. This Bishop York did and he remained away for eighteen months. In a letter to Propaganda of 1747 York recounted the situation in which he and the elderly Prichard found themselves:

> We are compelled to fly from house to house, from city to city. Bishop Prichard is ill, I his unworthy coadjutor have been a fugitive from my ordinary residence and as yet I have no fixed abode.[3]

Around the same time, York joined Prichard in opposing the papal brief *Emanivit nuper* (1745) which gave the power of granting faculties for the regular clergy to the local Ordinary. In England the full implementation of this bull was delayed owing to the rebellion of 1745 but the issue was clarified once and for all by the Bull *Apostolicum ministerium* (1753). It further demanded that English regulars were to spend three months in every six years living under the roof and rule of a continental religious house of their Order, this time to include a fifteen-day retreat. Such a

---

[2] G. Scott, *Gothic Rage Undone* (1992), 88.
[3] Brady, 293.

scheme would have caused disarray in the Western District, where the majority of priests belonged to religious Orders.

With the death of Prichard on 22 May 1750, York took full control of the Vicariate and before long began looking for a coadjutor, which was so necessary given the size of the Vicariate. York, of course, wanted his assistant to be a Benedictine, although his brother Vicars Apostolic were not of the same opinion. The Holy See had asked the bishops to put forward the names of two secular priests and two regulars but Stonor, with the support of Petre and his coadjutor Challoner, suggested that they should refuse to offer the names of any member of the regular clergy. Once again, however, a Benedictine with Jacobite sympathies was eventually appointed, with the help of the exiled Stuart Court – the renowned scholar Charles Walmesley. He was consecrated a coadjutor with right of succession in 1756.

York's health was declining by this time, and he was allowed to retire to Douai in 1764. Walmesley took charge of the District's administration, although he only formally succeeded *per coadjutorium* at York's death. The old bishop lived a further six years and died in April 1770 having suffered a stroke while celebrating Mass at St Gregory's.[4] Like a surprising number of the early Vicars Apostolic he lived to a remarkable age for his time, being about 83 at his death.

---

[4] A Bell Tree House document cited in J. A. Williams, *Post-Reformation Catholicism in Bath*, *1*, 176, dates his death as 14 April 1770. According to the DNB other sources suggest the date as 20 April.

CHARLES WALMESLEY, OSB
1722-97
TITULAR BISHOP OF RAMA (1756)
COADJUTOR TO BISHOP YORK (1756-70)
VICAR APOSTOLIC OF THE WESTERN DISTRICT (1770-97)

When Bishop York petitioned Rome for a coadjutor in 1755, Cardinal Spinelli of Propaganda wrote to the Vicars Apostolic asking for suitable names. Bishop Stonor saw this as a valuable opportunity to put a secular priest in charge of the Western District and Christopher Stonor, Charles Howard and James Talbot were all suggested. In the end, however, Rome continued the practice of appointing a regular to the District and followed York's own recommendation of Charles Walmesley, Prior of the English Benedictines of Paris.

Born at Wigan Lane House, Standish, Lancashire, on 13 January 1722, Charles was the eleventh of the twelve children of John and Mary Walmesley of Westwood House, near Wigan – and their seventh son. In later life he was never happier than when he returned to Westwood House to visit family and to fish for perch and tench. The family was staunchly Catholic and Benedictine. One of his brothers, Richard, was professed at St Gregory's, Douai, as Dom Peter and a cousin, Teresa, was a nun of Cambrai who died in prison during the French Revolution. Charles himself, after being educated at St Gregory's and then St Edmund's, Paris, entered the latter house and was clothed in the Benedictine habit on 28 September 1738. He progressed quickly both in the community and academia, acting as Prior of St Edmund's between 1749 and 1753 and gaining the coveted Doctorate in Divinity from the Sorbonne – a qualification that brought with it the benefice of Saint-Marcel, near Châlons-sur-Marne.

Alongside his Benedictine life was a passion for mathematics and science, making him a somewhat unusual figure amongst the Vicars Apostolic. As Prior of St Edmund's he founded a literary and scientific society. He published learned papers, became a fellow of the Royal Society of Berlin and the Royal Society of London in 1750 and was involved in the discussions around Great Britain's adoption of the Gregorian Calendar in 1752. In December 1748 he attempted to persuade Alexis-Claude Clairaut, by means of Newtonian mathematics, about the source of the discrepancy in calculating the motion of the moon's apse. He followed this up with a book, *Théorie du Mouvement des Apsides en Général, et en Particulier des Apsides de l'Orbite de la Lune* (1749; English trans., 1754), based on Newton's propositions and a theorem of John Machin.

In 1754 Walmesley was sent to Rome to act as the English Benedictine *procurator in curia,* a position that chiefly entailed fighting by artful persuasion for the cause of the privileges granted to priests of religious Orders in England against the attempts of the seculars to have those privileges considerably weakened. He took the opportunity also to make a field trip to Mount Etna, make the acquaintance of his fellow Newtonians Paolo Frisi (a Barnabite) and François Jacquier (a Minim), and write his celebrated *De inaequalitatibus motuum lunarium* (1758).

It was also during his Roman sojourn that Walmesley learnt of his appointment as coadjutor to Bishop York. He was consecrated as Titular Bishop of Rama in the Sodality Chapel at the English College, Rome, on 21 December 1756 by the Protector of England, Federico Marcello Cardinal Lante Montefeltro Della Rovere.[1] With the virtual retirement of Bishop York in 1763 Walmesley took over the administration of the Vicariate, being based at Bath, finally becoming Vicar Apostolic of the Western District upon the death of York in 1770.

The onerous responsibilities of being Vicar Apostolic did not stifle Walmesley's scientific researches. In 1770 he published a commentary on the Book of Revelation under the pseudonym 'Signor Pastorini'. The title, *The General History of the Christian Church from Her Birth to Her Final Triumphant State in Heaven*, revealed the chief theme of the book: that the Apocalypse, with its prophecies, exhibited 'a summary of the whole history of the Christian Church,' divided into seven ages corresponding to the seven trumpets (trials), vials (punishments) and seals (building of the Kingdom).

---

[1] This being the second of only three episcopal ordinations at which the cardinal presided – the third being the episcopal ordination of the future Pope Clement XIV, suppressor of the Jesuits. In this last consecration he was assisted by the Cardinal Duke of York.

This commentary on the Book of Revelation was followed, in 1778, by *Ezekiel's Vision Explained*: both volumes prophesying troubled times ahead. Walmesley believed that his prophecies had come true with the Gordon Riots in 1780. In the latter part of his life Walmesley turned his back on science. Charles Butler attributed this to his experience while saying Mass one morning, when the bishop realised he was drawing geometric diagrams on the corporal with the paten! However, he continued to welcome the opportunity to discuss scientific topics in conversation.

Walmesley had for many years tried to obtain a coadjutor from the Benedictine Order, although this was opposed by the seculars and the other Vicars Apostolic. When Propaganda asked Bishop Challoner about the three monks suggested by Walmesley, he stated 'that he did not think Mr Walmesley really wanted an assistant.'[2] In 1780 Propaganda finally appointed Dom Gregory Sharrock as coadjutor and he was consecrated in 1780 at Wardour.

Indeed, 1780 would prove to be a dramatic year for the Western District – not only did it gain a coadjutor but also an elegant church on St James's Parade in Bath. At least that was the intention, for two days before its official opening it was severely damaged in the anti-Catholic Gordon Riots. The mob had tried to vent their fury on the priest, Fr Brewer, but he had managed to escape through the back door of a local inn, 'The White Lion', which for many years subsequently enjoyed the custom of Catholic clients. A man was glimpsed in one of the houses on St James's Parade wearing a nightgown with gold flowers, and the cry went out that this was the Pope himself. The rioters stormed through Walmesley's rooms and destroyed his clothes, books and papers – meaning that little documentation has survived regarding the early Vicars Apostolic of the Western District. The new church on St James's Parade was damaged beyond redemption but in 1786 the Benedictines opened a chapel in Corn Street, by which time Walmesley had moved to a house in Chapel Row.

Bernard Ward said that Walmesley's 'speech, like his writings, was blunt to the verge of roughness, a defect which was emphasised by a partial deafness with which he became afflicted, and which helped to isolate him from those with whom he lived.'[3] This bluntness can be clearly seen in his strong reaction against the Catholic Committee, making him the most outspoken of the bishops at the time. Like many 'old' Catholics, he was

[2] Williams, *Bath and Rome*, 50-51.
[3] *Dawn*, i, 5.

cautious about bringing the repeal of the penal laws into the public forum and his fears seemed justified after the Gordon Riots. If the condition of Catholics was improved, he feared negative consequences for religion – 'when so very few Catholics become mixed with such a multitude of Protestants,' he asked, 'what religious duties can we suppose they will observe?'[4] Although he initially signed the Committee's Protestation, he later withdrew his name and issued a Pastoral at the end of 1789 attacking the Committee. Shortly before his death Walmesley told his priests that if any of the signatories of the second and third Blue Books or the 'Staffordshire Creed' came into the District, they could not exercise any ecclesiastical functions or participate in the sacraments 'until they have explicitly and publicly disavowed or withdrawn their signatures from those scandalous and erroneous acts.'[5] When Douglass criticised this censure, the bishop advised him that the same should be done in the London District. Walmesley became known in some circles as 'Old Apocalypse' – an apt nickname given his Scriptural scholarship. A particular *cause célèbre* was Walmesley's suspension in 1791 of Joseph Wilkes, a Benedictine who lived right under the bishop's nose in Bath and was seen as one of the Committee's theological masterminds. The subsequent controversy dragged on for several years.

When the Sepulchrine nuns of Liège briefly found a home in his District at Dean House, near Salisbury, the bishop insisted that they wear their habits. This brought him into conflict with Mgr Erskine, later a cardinal, who announced he had special faculties from Rome to look after the English convents and gave the nuns dispensation not to wear their habits out of prudence. The bishop strongly disagreed and failed to recognise Erskine's faculties, forcing the *monsignore* to back down. Walmesley was indeed a force to be reckoned with.

Perhaps Walmesley's most far-reaching action was his consecration of John Carroll as first Bishop of Baltimore and 'Father of the American Hierarchy'. This historic event took place on 15 August 1790 at the chapel of Lulworth Castle, the home of the Welds. As was common practice in eighteenth-century England, the consecrating bishop had two priest-assistants, Charles Plowden and James Porter, and one of the servers was Thomas Weld, the future Cardinal.

Walmesley died at Bath on 25 November 1797 and was buried at St

---

[4] Ibid., i, 6.
[5] Ibid., ii, 148.

Joseph's Chapel, Trenchard Street, Bristol. His health had long been declining and some attributed the severity of his reaction to the Catholic Committee to his infirmities. The immediate cause of death was due to an accident, as Douglass recorded in his diary: 'the Bishop, whilst taking the air in his go-cart or chair (common at Bath), was overturned by some passenger and received a bruise. This fall happened in the beginning of the week. A mortification took place all down one thigh, and of this he died.'[6] In 1906 his remains were transferred to a new tomb at Downside Abbey upon which was inscribed in Latin these lines by Bishop George Ambrose Burton: 'Proud Lancashire bore me, Rome consecrated me, and Bath, which I cared for, carried me off'.

6 Ibid., ii, 150.

WILLIAM GREGORY SHARROCK, OSB

1742-1809
TITULAR BISHOP OF TELMESSA (1780)
COADJUTOR TO BISHOP WALMESLEY (1780-97)
VICAR APOSTOLIC OF THE WESTERN DISTRICT (1797-1809)

Bishop Walmesley was succeeded by his coadjutor and fellow Benedictine, William Gregory Sharrock. Born on 30 March 1742 at Friar Gate, Preston, Lancashire, he seems to have been one of twenty-two children. The young man went to St Gregory's, Douai in 1755, being professed on 29 September 1758 and taking the name of Gregory. Indeed, the Sharrock family had a close relationship with the Order for two other brothers also became Benedictines at St Gregory's: James (Dom Jerome) and John, while Walter became a lay brother at Dieulouard and then Ampleforth.

Ordained in 1766, Dom Gregory Sharrock became Procurator of his community the following year and held this office until succeeding Augustine Moore as Prior on 15 June 1775. He also took the Doctor of Divinity at Douai University.

In 1779 Prior Sharrock was appointed as Walmesley's coadjutor. However, the President of the English Benedictines applied for the consecration to be postponed on account of the quadriennium. Sharrock was eventually consecrated Titular Bishop of Telmessa by Walmesley on 12 August 1781 at Wardour Castle, the chapel of which had been formally opened five years previously. According to the nineteenth-century historian of the Western District, George Oliver, the consecration ceremony was marked with 'a solemnity unprecedented until then in England since the reign of Queen Mary [Tudor]. Thirteen priests attended, and Henry, eighth Lord Arundell, spared no expense to do honour to the ceremony.'[1] Sharrock was

---

[1] G. Oliver, *Collections Illustrating the History of the Catholic Religion in the Counties of Cornwall,*

succeeded by his brother James as Prior of St Gregory's.

As coadjutor, Sharrock based himself in Wales and concentrated on that part of the District while Walmesley remained in Bath. Conditions were not easy with the lack of missions and Welsh-speaking priests, and Sharrock had to make do with a meagre income of £110 per year.

After Walmesley's death in 1797 Sharrock succeeded as Vicar Apostolic and, like his two predeccessors, lived in Bath. He took a more conciliatory line than Walmesley with regard to the Catholic Committee and removed the censure on the Staffordshire clergy. In 1803 he sent a report of his District to Rome, listing nearly fifty chapels serving about 5,500 Catholics, including twelve noble families. Perhaps the most significant development was the arrival of religious communities and émigré priests who had fled to England during the French Revolution. These included the English Dominican nuns of Brussels who took up residence at Hartpury Court, Gloucester (1794-1839) and eventually settled on the Isle of Wight at Carisbrooke. The English Carmelites of Antwerp settled at Lanherne in Cornwall and the Teresians of Hoogstraet went to Canford House, Dorset. By the time of Sharrock's death, three additional missions had also opened at Newport, Swansea and Holywell.

Sharrock's health was not good and he soon began looking for a coadjutor. In 1806 Propaganda appointed his own brother, Dom Jerome, as coadjutor and Titular Bishop of Themiscyra in Cappadocia. However, he refused the mitre, which was perhaps just as well since he died two years later, aged 58. In his place a Franciscan, Peter Bernardine Collingridge, was appointed and consecrated at St Edmund's College, Ware by Bishop Poynter of the London District on 11 October 1807, Sharrock himself being too ill to preside personally. He was able to send letters of direction to his new assistant, stressing the importance of a bishop writing regular Pastoral Letters and getting to know his scattered flock: 'I would have the Bishop the life and soul of his District, animating all, felt everywhere and not appearing as it were only administering Confirmation.'[2] Unable to walk, speak clearly and celebrate Mass, Sharrock effectively retired and passed over the administration of the District to his assistant – 'I make you Vicar General, I make you Pro-Vicar and I give you all the powers that I can give you, and all the powers you can inherit at my demise.'[3]

Devon, Dorset, Somerset, Wilts, and Gloucester (1857), 409.

[2] Dockery, op. cit., 77.

[3] Ibid., 78.

Bishop Sharrock died in Bath at four in the afternoon on 17 October 1809, aged 67 – a relatively young age compared to his predeccessors. He was buried near Walmesley at the Trenchard Street chapel in Bristol.

Peter Bernardine Collingridge, OSF
1757-1829
Titular Bishop of Thespiae (1807)
Coadjutor of the Western District (1807-1809)
Vicar Apostolic of the Western District (1809-1829)

Peter Collingridge was born at Fritwell, Oxfordshire on 10 March 1757, the son of Peter and Mary Collingridge. Little is known of his early days, although he admitted in later life to feeling an attraction to both the Franciscan and Jesuit vocations. He finally threw his lot in with the former and on 26 June 1773 received the Franciscan habit at the friary of St Bonaventure, Douai, taking the name Bernardine. All records of his priestly ordination have been lost, perhaps destroyed during the French Revolution. His gifts were swiftly recognized for he was lecturing in philosophy and theology before his ordination and was elected Guardian of his friary in 1788.

Having lived for nearly twenty years at Douai, Collingridge returned to England in 1791 as Director of the Franciscan Academy at Baddesley Clinton in Warwickshire. He also worked briefly at St George's Fields (now St George's Cathedral, Southwark), Coventry and the Sardinian Chapel at Lincoln's Inn Fields. On 28 July 1794 he was granted the honorary title of Guardian of Oxford, where a Franciscan house had stood before the Reformation and on 15 October 1806 was elected Minister Provincial. It was at about this time that he began to experience bouts of ill health, an affliction that he was to endure for the rest of his life. He suffered a mild paralytic stroke on the Feast of the Epiphany 1807.

Yet it was at this juncture that Collingridge's name was being considered as a possible coadjutor to Bishop Sharrock. On 2 January 1807 Collingridge was appointed as Titular Bishop of Thespiae, but he took several months to make up his mind as he recovered from the stroke and struggled with his conscience. He was finally consecrated on 11 October, by Bishop Poynter at St Edmund's College, Ware. There was plenty for him to do, for Sharrock was unable to walk or say Mass, and he effectively handed over administration of the District to the new bishop. One of his first duties was preaching at the profession of Francis Hendren, a future Vicar Apostolic of the Western District, at the Franciscan house in Abergavenny.

Collingridge succeeded Sharrock on 17 October 1809. Throughout his episcopate he variously lived at Chepstow, Taunton, Clifton, Bristol (Trenchard Street) and the Benedictine Convent at Cannington, near Taunton. Unlike Sharrock, he never resided in Bath.

Much ink was spilt at the time over Catholic Emancipation and the 'securities' or checks placed by the Government upon Catholics to guarantee their allegiance. Especially controversial was the wording of the oath that would be taken by Catholics in public office and the possibility of a government veto over episcopal appointment. Collingridge favoured compromise and signed the Catholic Board's 'Fifth Resolution' at the St Alban's Tavern in London in 1810, cautiously approving of a veto in principle. He was joined in this by Poynter, his great ally in ecclesiastical politics, but on this occasion and many others found himself the subject of Milner's ire. His biographer, Dockery, states that 'Collingridge's point throughout was that he would be failing in his duty to the Catholic body if he refused to second their efforts to recover their civil rights. He felt too, that, by not accepting even an imperfect emancipation, numbers of non-Catholics were being prevented from entering the Church.'[1]

Collingridge facilitated the entrance of a number of religious Orders into the District. Most notably, the Benedictines (formerly of Douai) moved from Acton Burnell in Shropshire to Downside in 1814 and Collingridge frequently visited the community. Dockery recalls a memorable occasion, illustrating a practical consequence of having so few bishops:

> In 1818 Collingridge consecrated the Holy Oils for the whole country, as the other three Vicars Apostolic were out of England at the time. It took place in the little parlour chapel at Downside which was used by the Monks and boys until 1823. The oils had been placed in wine decanters and the bottom of one of them gave way and the oil was oozing out on to the table when a Brother Abram … put in the stopper, inverted the bottle and thus saved most of the oil … The exacting Bishop Collingridge cried, "The table must be burnt, the table must be burnt!" but it is recorded that the

---

[1] Dockery, op. cit., 88-89.

more practical Procurator of the Abbey saved it from immolation.[2]

Perhaps even more provocatively to some minds, Collingridge was the first of the Vicars Apostolic to welcome the Jesuits to his District after their rehabilitation in 1814.

Like his predecessors, Collingridge soon petitioned Rome for a coadjutor, especially after serious illness in 1812. Propaganda approved of the bishop's preferred choice, Charles Francis McDonnell, the Franciscan Provincial, but he refused, giving the usual reasons of poor health and unworthiness. However, his brother, Daniel McDonnell, later gained a mitre when he became Vicar Apostolic of Trinidad. Collingridge's on-going poor health necessitated Poynter to step in sometimes and officiate at Ordination and Confirmation ceremonies.

In 1823 Collingridge was finally given the assistance of a Benedictine, Peter Augustine Baines, as his coadjutor. Collingridge was too ill to consecrate him and the ceremony was performed in Dublin by Archbishop Daniel Murray. Baines flung himself into his new work with great energy, although his high-handed, overly-assertive manner often brought him into conflict with his superior. He displayed little of the subservience that Collingridge had shown as coadjutor and often followed his own agendas, most notably his fledging plans for a seminary for the District. In 1826 Baines travelled to Rome to convalesce after a bout of poor health, probably much to Collingridge's relief, but ended up staying three years. Although Baines was successful in negotiating with Propaganda over the retention of a Franciscan Provincial in England, Collingridge was concerned by his assistant's prolonged absence. He commented that having Baines in Rome was worse than having no coadjutor at all and appointed Dom John Augustine Birdsall, the President of the English Benedictines, as Vicar General and Administrator of the District. Baines was only to return after Collingridge's death.

Franciscan simplicity remained a characteristic of Collingridge throughout his life – while living at Chepstow as coadjutor he enjoyed tending his vegetable garden and he is recorded as begging for hay for his horse. Despite suffering from years of poor health, Collingridge's death came suddenly at Cannington on 3 March 1829. The convent chaplain, Fr Dullard, wrote that he was called in the middle of the night and 'hastened to [the bishop's] room and found him speechless. Immediately I gave him the Absolution and sent for the Holy Oils. The Sacrament of Extreme

---

[2] Ibid., 169.

Unction was no sooner administered to him than he placidly resigned his soul into the hands of God.'[3] One of the bishop's last acts was to write to his flock about the recent death of Pope Leo XII. Collingridge was buried at Cannington on 10 March, which happened to be his 72nd birthday. In 1914 his mortal remains were translated to a new, simple tomb at Downside, close to his coadjutor Baines. Examination of his skull testified to the accuracy of a drawing made of the bishop from life by Sister M. Magdalen Scott, which shows an unusual formation of his head.

Further Reading

J. B. Dockery, *Collingridge: A Franciscan Contribution to Catholic Emancipation* (1954)

---

[3] Ibid., 322.

PETER AUGUSTINE BAINES, OSB

1786-1843
TITULAR BISHOP OF SIGA (1823)
COADJUTOR TO BISHOP COLLINGRIDGE (1823-29)
VICAR APOSTOLIC OF THE WESTERN DISTRICT (1829-43)

Bishop Baines, the most controversial of the Vicars Apostolic of the Western District, was a figure of paradox. Attracting strong reactions from all who encountered him, including stern rebukes from the Pope, he nevertheless accomplished much as a bishop and provided foundations for future generations. Sheridan Gilley has noted 'a contradiction in his public image between the fledgling prince-prelate fired by memories of the Teutonic abbatial splendours of Lambspring Abbey in the last days of the Holy Roman Empire, and the moderate compiler of the statistics which so offended papal optimism by proving England's conversion as "morally impossible as the return of the negro's skin to its antediluvian whiteness."'[1] Neither Gallican nor Ultramontane, he loved Rome and its liturgy and was even rumoured to be in line for a red hat, and yet he was suspicious of devotion to the Sacred Heart and seemed to Gregory XVI to represent all that was bad about the 'old' English Catholics. Moreover, despite being a Benedictine monk, he nearly succeeded in destroying both Ampleforth and Downside in his quest for an episcopal seminary.

Peter Baines was born on 25 June 1786 at Pear Tree Farm, Kirkby, near Liverpool, the eldest son of James Baines and his second wife, Catherine. James Baines was a 'farmer and yeoman' and part of a family line that had remained faithful to Catholicism throughout the years of persecution. At the age of ten, Peter Baines was sent to the Benedictine school of Scholes in Prescot and then went as a border to the school

---

[1] S. Gilley, 'Battling Bishop: Baines of Bath', *South Western Catholic History*, no.3 (1985), 13-14.

attached to the English Benedictine Abbey of Lambspring in Hanover, one of the most impressive parts of the English Catholic diaspora, boasting extensive estates and the largest baroque church in northern Germany. There was also a lake used for skating in winter. Even as a bishop, Baines professed to be a keen skater and was reputedly able to cut the shape of an eagle on the ice. He remained at Lambspring until the school was suppressed in 1802 by the invading Prussians. Together with eleven other students, he returned to England and, with two of them, joined the Benedictine community of St Laurence, only recently settled from Dieulouard at Ampleforth in Yorkshire. Here he was clothed on 27 May 1803 and took the name Augustine. As a novice, Baines wrote twice to the Benedictine Bishop Sharrock of the Western District, complaining about the austere lifestyle being promoted by the Prior, Thomas Appleton. In 1810 he was ordained priest by Bishop Thomas Smith in the monastery chapel.

For seven years Baines worked as a priest, teacher and (from 1814) Prefect of Studies at Ampleforth. For the times, the syllabus of studies and pedagogical methods were highly imaginative – the students covered subjects such as history, geography, science and modern languages, mnemonic systems were used and there was no corporal punishment. Baines was also already noted for his gracious manners and his eloquence as a preacher.

In 1817 Baines was appointed to Bath, the fashionable spa town then being celebrated in the novels of Jane Austen, the most important mission of the Western District and the most prestigious in the hands of the Benedictines. Arriving in the late summer, Baines set to work repairing and renovating, letting and renting, buying and buying still more to raise the standard of the dilapidated buildings, replacing any lodgers whom he deemed unsuitable and furnishing his presbytery. Money seemed to be of little importance until he was made aware by his superiors that he was living beyond his means. The frenetic activity of overseeing the buildings and premises did nothing to dampen his pastoral zeal. He was assiduous in visiting the sick and the dying, in hearing confessions and in all that pertained to the worthy celebration of the Mass. Preaching continued to receive his most careful attention and the highest praise. Cardinal Wiseman was to recall in later years, having witnessed Baines' preaching during a sojourn in Rome in the late 1820s:

The church, which was nearly empty when preachers of inferior mark

occupied it, was crowded when Bishop Baines was announced as the orator
... He was happiest with unwritten discourses. The flow of his words was
easy and copious, his imagery was often very elegant, and his discourses
were replete with thought and solid matter. But his great power, was in
his delivery, in voice, in tone, in look, and gesture. His whole manner was
full of pathos, sometimes more even than the matter justified; there was a
particular tremulousness of voice, which gave his words more than double
effect, notwithstanding a broadness of provincial accent, and an occasional
dramatic pronunciation of certain words. In spite of such defects, he was
considered, by all that heard him, one of the most eloquent and earnest
preachers they had ever attended.[2]

In 1821, the same year as Baines' appointment as Bishop Collingridge's
Vicar General, a rather unusual element entered this monk's life in the
form of Anna de Mendoza y Rios, the daughter of a Spanish admiral who
had settled in Bath. Both of Anna's parents died before she had come of
age and she had been left as a ward to the Vicar Apostolic of the Western
District and a lady known as Madame Chaussegros. Bishop Collingridge
was living in a convent and Madame Chaussegros could only look after
Anna for short periods of time. Thus it came about that Anna, along with
her companion and maid, took up residence in Baines' presbytery.

Baines became a prolific writer of letters, articles and books, including
A Defence of the Christian Religion published in 1822. He showed great
promise and in 1823, at the age of only 36, he was appointed coadjutor to
Bishop Collingridge and consecrated Titular Bishop of Siga in Bath by
Archbishop Murray of Dublin.

One of his chief aims from the start was the establishment of a
seminary, for the Western District was the only one without such an
institution. Money being short, Baines settled upon the idea that it should
be established at the monastery of Downside, meaning that the monks
would come directly under the bishop's authority and that only church
students would be accepted in its school. The monks resisted, seeing clearly
how this would alter the nature of the monastery, and the result was war.
In his history of Downside Abbey, Herbert von Zeller contrasted the two
main belligerants:

> In the clash of principles there was also the clash of personalities. You have
> Dr Baines, the enthusiast, the man with a mission, the dazzling talker,
> the hot-headed protagonist with unusual good looks. You have Dom
> Bernard [Barber, the Prior], "not a man of brilliant parts, distinguished

---

[2] Wiseman, *Recollections*, 326.

acquirements or popular manners, but provided with an eminent degree of common sense, with great firmness and remarkable prudence."[3]

Baines, himself a monk, was not anti-Benedictine but had a particular vision of what a monastery should be. At a time when English monks never wore habits and often worked on the mission, he dreamt of a Benedictine Vicariate, with a monastery (Downside) at its centre and monks, under the bishop's direct authority, training the clergy and working the missions. It perhaps did not seem a large leap for the Western District, for it had had five Benedictine bishops and greatly depended on the Order for personnel.

Given the opposition at Downside, it was suggested that Ampleforth and Downside should exchange buildings so as to allow for Baines' grand plan, though this came to nothing. With few other possibilities, particularly given the reluctance of Bishop Collingridge to push the District's limited finances to establish a seminary, Baines realised that he would have to wait until he himself held the purse strings.

In the summer of 1826 Baines' health broke down and he was advised to spend the winter in a warmer climate. Thus at the end of August of that year he travelled to Rome where he was to remain until December 1829. During this time Baines made many friends, attended the most fashionable salons and enjoyed the special favour of Pope Leo XII, who paid him an annual pension, appointed him as an Assistant at the Pontifical Throne and apparently considered raising him still further to the Sacred College. The Holy Father had himself been created a cardinal by a Benedictine Pope (Pius VII) and he wanted to elevate a Benedictine out of reverence for his predecessor. Baines certainly believed this to be the case. He asked Collingridge for money, so that he could live according to his new dignity, and moved out of his private apartments in the Palazzo Costa to the monastery of San Callisto. His hopes were dashed by the Pope's unexpected death in February 1829.

Baines had taken to Rome his charge, Anna de Mendoza y Rios. She became the object of the desire of a young Italian *galante*, who taught his native language to visitors and conducted them around the Forum, the catacombs and the other tourist sites in and around the Eternal City. Baines made sure that his advances were not returned and this great disappointment led to the young man's profound religious conversion.

---

[3] H. Van Zeller, *Downside By and Large: A Double Figure in Praise of Things Lasting and Georgian* (1954), 38-39.

The rejected lover's name was Luigi Gentili. In the words of the Rosminian historian Claude Leetham, 'the hand that struck the blow to Gentili's pride was destined to be the instrument of providing Gentili a few years later with the opportunity of fulfilling his apostolic mission in England.'[4] He became a priest of the Institute of Charity and devoted his life to preaching in England and Ireland. The famous Rosminian priest, William Lockhart, later recalled that 'when the English newspapers sometimes mentioned his name as "a remarkable preacher among the Roman Catholics," I remember a relative of mine, a Protestant, much used to Roman society, saying, "Can this be that Luigi Gentili with whom we used to sing duets in Rome?"'[5]

The bishop made full use of his time in Rome to further his various plans. He won over the Camaldolese Prefect of Propaganda, Cardinal Cappellari (the future Gregory XVI), who even urged the Prior of Downside to collaborate with Baines. He also worked behind the scenes in defence of the Jesuits. Although the Society had been restored by Pius VII in 1814, all the Vicars Apostolic (except Milner) had opposed the bull's enactment in their territory. It was largely thanks to Baines' efforts in Rome that a rescript was issued on New Year's Day 1829 restoring the Jesuits to full canonical status in England.

Back in England, the year 1829 also saw Catholic Emancipation and the death of Bishop Collingridge, requiring Baines finally to return to his District. It seems that the new Pope, Pius VIII, offered him a position in Rome that would have led to a red hat, but Baines declined:

> My predecessor had just died; I felt in better health and spirits; I was home-sick and anxious to return to my friends and native air; I preferred just then the position of an English Vicar Apostolic, immeasurably though it was beneath the Cardinalatial dignity, and I was eager to found the Seminary for the Western District, and to promote by my presence the interests of religion in that part of England.[6]

Now in charge, Baines pushed forward his plans for a seminary with renewed vigour. He had already asked Propaganda to investigate the canonical establishment of the English Benenedictine houses. Downside sent two monks to intervene, including the future Vicar Apostolic of Wales, Dom Joseph Brown. In an attempt to gain control of Downside, Baines claimed that the vows made by the English Benedictines were

---

[4] C. Leetham, *Luigi Gentili, A Sower for the Second Spring* (1965), 12.
[5] W. Lockhart, *Life of Antonio Serbati Rosmini* (1886), ii, 87.
[6] Ward, *Life and Times of Cardinal Wiseman*, i, 101.

'null and void' and withdrew all their missionary faculties. Ullathorne later recalled how a priest would travel to Downside for the sake of the congregation and 'heard their Confessions in the brewery, seated on a tub, as being outside the precincts of the monastery.'[7] The bishop was soon required to back down, as Cardinal Cappellari became disillusioned with the imprudent Baines.

Baines was thus forced to follow his other option. For some time he had had his eyes on the mansion of Prior Park, built by Ralph Allen and situated on the former land of Bath Priory, and at the end of 1829 he had purchased it at the considerable cost of £22,000. He persuaded the community of Ampleforth to commit itself to supporting the venture, in terms of personnel and finance, and amazingly only one monk declined. Baines used the familiar argument that the monastery had not been properly erected and that the monks were therefore not bound to monastic obedience and were free to assist at Prior Park. Baines moved in with Dr Brindle and three senior monks of Ampleforth, soon to be joined by the first pupils, a housekeeper and a herd of cattle. Things started promisingly as Baines set about transforming the mansion into a school, seminary and episcopal residence. Perhaps one day it would become a university too. However, Rome made it clear in a decree of 13 March 1830 that Ampleforth, along with Downside, should be considered duly established. If monks were to live at Prior Park, they would first need to be secularised.

In desperate need of staff, Baines introduced three Fathers of Charity to Prior Park in 1835, including Luigi Gentili, who started work as Professor of Philosophy. The Italian priest's principal importance, however, was in introducing the practices of continental Catholicism to the Western District. Gentili had been shocked by the situation he had found at Prior Park – priests did not say daily Mass unless there was a specific need and there was no lamp burning before the Tabernacle in the often locked chapel. Under the Italian's guidance, the boys were vested in cassock and surplice, the ceremonial and chanting were firmly modelled on Roman usage, and in Passiontide 1836 he preached one of the first public Retreats after the Jesuit manner in the country. The Fathers also assisted in Catholicizing the mansion. According to Ullathorne, Fr Gentili often wandered about the house

> in distress of mind, saying that he verily believed that "the devil was in the place." I have heard an amusing story from eyewitnesses of his having set

---

[7] Ullathorne, op. cit., 48.

the boys to pull down the statues of pagan gods from the central mansion to the wings, then erected into two Colleges ... [Fr Gentili] had got a rope round Hercules and the boys were put to the other end of it, and he directed them: "When I say the third time come down, you great monster, all of you pull together!" He had given the signal once, and twice, when Dr Baines put his head out of a window and stopped the destruction. It is a literal fact that after the great flight of steps were constructed up to the portico, a feature which spoiled the architect's design, and pulled down the elevation of the whole facade to the eye, these pagan gods were taken down from their elevated position, manipulated with canvas and plaster, and made to represent two rows of saints, standing on the two sides of this broad flight of steps; and that Hercules with a tiara, a plaster cope and a triple cross in his hand in place of his concealed club, did duty for St Gregory the Great.[8]

The College of St Peter continued the progressive educational lines that Baines had favoured at Ampleforth, as was shown in his *A Course of Studies* (1838). Children were 'to form their own ideas' and teachers were admonished to abstain from 'teasings and scoldings', 'a cross and surly tone' and 'irksome drudgery in lessons'. The school received high praise and in later years was recommended by Newman and others. However, in 1836 a fire resulted in damage worth a small fortune (£15,000), only about a third of which was covered by insurance, and the re-building work was a further burden on the bishop's finances.

Further trouble was caused by Baines' relations with the Rosminians. Gentili had become President of St Paul's College but the relations disintegrated when two of the bishop's most trusted members of staff, Moses Furlong and Peter Hutton, decided to join the Institute. Gentili also complained that his authority in the college was being undermined by the bishop, who had grown wary of the Italianate usages and had banned some of the devotions. Shortly afterwards the Fathers left Prior Park and were offered Old Oscott (now Maryvale) by Bishop Walsh, the forward-thinking Vicar Apostolic of the Midland District.

Baines had strong opinions about almost everything and showed resistance to 'new' ideas. He was especially distrustful of converts. The last great controversy of his life concerned the Pastoral of Lent 1840, in which he attacked the 'new' devotions of the Sacred Heart and the Immaculate Conception and Fr Ignatius Spencer's prayer campaign for the conversion of England, which had been blessed by the Pope. Fr Spencer had hoped

---

[8] Ibid., 285-286.

that it would be warmly welcomed by the Vicars Apostolic. Walsh showed great enthusiasm, while Briggs and Griffiths were at best lukewarm. Baines, on the other hand, reacted characteristically by openly venting his anger. Having cited in his Pastoral examples of real and possibly increased hostility to Catholics, Baines went on severely to criticize recent converts to Catholicism, condemning their lack of humility. He launched his attack on the prayer crusade:

> So far, therefore, from approving this novel and extraordinary project, we disapprove it, and strictly forbid any of our clergy to offer up publicly in their churches and chapels the weekly prayers above mentioned. At the same time we earnestly exhort them to pray, as has been customary, for all spiritual and temporal blessings in favour of our country, and for the conversion of such erring souls as God, in His mercy, may be pleased so to favour, and of whom we doubt not there will be a great and continually increasing number.[9]

Baines favoured a gradualist approach to the conversion of England and, according to J. C. H. Aveling, was in many ways 'a child of late-eighteenth-century practical liberalism' who 'got on famously with Protestants' and 'never wanted to convert the mass of Protestants: he sought only to put the old Catholic house in such good Christian order that Protestant prejudices against it would die a natural death.'[10] Nevertheless, Baines was summoned to Rome in the summer of 1840 to explain his position. He was received by Gregory XVI, who as Cardinal Prefect of Propaganda had been so disappointed by the bishop's treatment of Downside. The Lenten Pastoral seemed to go against the Pope's Encyclical *Mirari vos* (1831), which condemned liberalism and indifferentism. Baines' audience lasted an hour and he wrote to Briggs that the Pope 'put on an air of coldness that I had never seen before . . . he then gave me to understand that I was sent for as one of the Vicars Apostolic of whom he had the most serious occasion to complain.'[11] The Pastoral was reproved by the Pope by Letters Apostolic on 16 January 1841 and Baines had no choice but to submit and put his name to certain declarations.

A wiser man would have let the matter be closed but Baines was not that kind of man. He proceeded to compose a history of the writing, denunciations and Papal involvement in the affair, which he circulated amongst his brother bishops, together with his version of

---

[9] *Sequel*, i, 215.
[10] Aveling, op. cit., 345.
[11] P. Gilbert, *The Restless Prelate: Bishop Baines 1786-1843* (2006), 231.

the declarations that he had been required by the Holy See to make. On various points Baines' version of the declarations differed from the actual ones that he had agreed to. For example, in the Roman version Baines promised:

> I solemnly engage that as soon as favourable opportunity shall present itself, I will carefully endeavour to repair any scandal that may have arisen out of the Pastoral by declaring that I most fully approve whatever the Holy See approves relative to the devotion of the Sacred Heart and the Immaculate Conception.

In Baines' version this became,

> I declare that in no part of the Pastoral did I mean to disapprove of the Devotion to the Sacred Heart as far as it has had the approbation of the Holy See.[12]

In July 1841 he published at Prior Park *A Letter to Sir Charles Wolseley, Bart., on the Lenten Pastoral of 1840*, in which he denied – with a certain economy of truth – that he had been required to apologize for or retract any part of his Pastoral. This reached the Pope's attention and resulted in a stern rebuke:

> Since, however, the Bishop of Siga, instead of responding to our clemency as he should have done, has published new pamphlets in which he perverts almost every fact, and, quoting one letter of ours, that dated 19th March, after he had made his Declarations, omitted other things which had happened before, and finally, as if celebrating a triumph, endeavoured to persuade his own people that the Pastoral Letter in question, written by him, had been held to be free from the taint and suspicion of error and not worthy of censure, we feel it due to our office that we should by no means permit such boasting and untruthfulness from which great dishonesty to the Apostolic See and the Christian Religion might arise to prevail against the truth. Here we have thought well to send the aforesaid documents to your fraternity, as well as to your colleagues, the Vicars Apostolic of England, that you may learn the whole matter and, at the same time, take measure according to your wisdom to guard against all scandal, and reasonably and prudently to inform those whose ignorance of these things might be harmful . . .[13]

Baines vigorously campaigned against the new gothic vestments encouraged by the likes of Pugin and wrote to Propaganda with his complaints. In September 1839 he advised Griffiths that if he was going to

---

[12] Ibid., 240.
[13] Ibid., 243.

attend the opening of the new Derby church, 'in all probability the new fashioned vestments will be used, which I consider unlawful and which I do not think we can conscientiously countenance by our presence. I went to Utoxeter from Alton to the opening of that new church, but left the place at an early part of the service, feeling that it might be criminal to remain.' He included in his letter a drawing of the offending chasuble, noting that 'the whole costume bears no apparent resemblance to that of a Latin priest but is not unlike that of an oriental one.'[14]

As we have seen, Baines was for several years a supporter of the Fathers of Charity and tolerated (at least temporarily) the introduction of Italianate customs at Prior Park. He was also a 'friend' of the Jesuits, although he tried to remove them from Trenchard Street in Bristol in order to gain more control of this important mission. The chapel had been opened in 1790, while the Jesuits had still been suppressed, and so, the bishop argued, the Society had no claim to the mission. The Jesuits were unhappy to lose the largest congregation in the Western District and the 'Bristol Cause' was brought before Propaganda. The issue had still not been settled by Baines' death, but his last act had been to establish a new chapel in Bristol, most clearly in the hands of the secular clergy. St Mary's on the Quay was formed out of a chapel used by the Irvingites and, much to Baines' delight, included a seventeenth-century altarpiece and Corinthian columns. It was opened by the bishop on 5 July 1843.

Baines died in his sleep at Prior Park that night. Although his health had been failing and he had suffered a mild stroke the previous year, his death came without warning and a coroner's inquest was held. At first his body was buried according to his wishes in the chapel at Prior Park but with the closure of the school ten years later his mortal remains were transferred to Downside, the monastery that he had tried so hard to 'take over' and whose faculties he had briefly suspended. The irony was heightened by the fact that in his funeral effigy, the bishop wears the gothic style of vestment that he so energetically campaigned against.

Bishop Clifford, himself once a pupil at Prior Park, eventually bought back the premises and reopened the school on becoming Bishop of Clifton in 1866. Its more recent alumni include Cormac Cardinal Murphy-O'Connor.

Cardinal Wiseman, one whom Baines considered unsuitable for the office of Vicar Apostolic, evaluated the bishop's character in his *Recollections*

---

[14] AAW A80/189-191 (Baines to Griffiths, 25 September 1839).

of the Last Four Popes:

> He had a power of fascinating all who approached him, in spite of a positive tone and manner which scarcely admitted of difference from him in opinion. He had sometimes original views upon a certain class of subject; but on every topic he had a command of language, and a clear manner of expressing his sentiments, which commanded attention, and generally won assent. Hence his acquaintances were always willing listeners, and soon became sincere admirers, then warm partisans. Unfortunately, this proved to him a fatal gift. When he undertook great and even magnificent works, he would stand alone: assent to his plans was the condition of being near him; any one that did not agree, was soon at a distance; he isolated himself with his own genius, he had no counsellor but himself; and he who had, at one time, surrounded himself with men of learning, of prudence and of devotedness to him, found himself at last alone, and fretted a noble heart to a solitary death.[15]

Further Reading

Pamela Gilbert, *The Restless Prelate: Bishop Baines 1786-1843* (2006)
Sheridan Gilley, 'Battling Bishop: Baines of Bath', *South Western Catholic History*, no. 3 (1985), 13-18
Bernard Green, 'Augustine Baines, OSB 1786-1843', *The Ampleforth Journal*, vol. 42/1 (Spring 1987), 18-31; and vol. 42/2 (Autumn 1987), 18-24
J. S. Roche, *A History of Prior Park and its Founder, Bishop Baines* (1931)

---

[15] Gilbert, op. cit., 254.

Charles Michael Baggs

1806-1845

Titular Bishop of Pella (1844)
Vicar Apostolic of the Western District (1844-45)

The larger-than-life Baines died without a coadjutor. A number of names were considered, including Bishop Brown of the Welsh District and Dom William Bernard Ullathorne, who was also considered to be Brown's potential replacement in Wales. The choice of Propaganda eventually fell on the gifted but retiring Rector of the English College, Rome, Charles Michael Baggs – a striking contrast to his fiery predecessor. Ullathorne suggested that the appointment came down to the personal choice of Gregory XVI, who had cried out in the midst of discussions with Propaganda: 'No, no, questo Monsignor Baggs.'[1]

The future bishop was born on 21 May 1806 at Belville in County Meath, the eldest son of Charles Baggs and his wife, Eleanor Kyan – the only one among the Vicars Apostolic to have been born in Ireland. His father was a member of the Church of Ireland, a barrister who became judge of the vice-admiralty in Demerara. For his education Charles was sent to a Protestant academy at Englefield Green in Surrey. However with the death of his father in 1820, Baggs was transferred by his Catholic mother to Sedgley Park in Staffordshire. A year later Baggs gained a place at St Edmund's, Ware, as an ecclesiastical student, at the instigation of Bishop Poynter.

Baggs was an outstanding student and on 9 June 1824 entered the Venerable English College in Rome, a city that was to become his home for nearly twenty years. He achieved impressive results in his studies and was awarded first prizes in scripture, Hebrew, mathematics and physics.

---

[1] Ullathorne, op. cit., 273.

He was also highly gifted linguistically, being proficient in French, Italian, Spanish and German. On 5 December 1830 he was ordained to the priesthood by Cardinal Zurla, the College's Protector, before whom he had recently triumphantly defended his theological theses.

After ordination Baggs stayed at the college as Professor of Hebrew and, from 1834, Vice Rector. A further responsibility of Baggs was as *cameriere d'onore*, which involved the presentation of English visitors, both Catholic and Protestant, to the Pope. He became a noted controversialist, as seen in two publications of 1836: the *Letter Addressed to the Rev. R. Burgess, Protestant Chaplain at Rome* and *On the Supremacy of the Roman Pontiffs*, the latter being based on a polemical lecture delivered at the Gesù e Maria church on the Corso. He also studied the Roman Liturgy (like Wiseman) and produced *The Papal Chapel Described and Illustrated from History and Antiquities* (1839), *The Ceremonies of Holy Week at the Vatican and S. John Lateran's: Described and Illustrated from History and Antiquities* (1839) and *The Pontifical Mass sung at St Peter's Church on Easter Sunday, on the Festival of SS. Peter and Paul, and Christmas Day, with a Dissertation on Ecclesiastical Vestments* (1840).

At the beginning of 1840, when names were being discussed for the four new Vicars Apostolic, Baggs was considered but deemed unsuitable since he lacked experience of the English mission and was virtually unknown in that country. However, after the consecration of Wiseman as bishop on 8 June 1840, Baggs was appointed Rector and Roman Agent and became pre-eminently *episcopabile*. After all, his two immediate predecessors had become bishops.

As Rector, Baggs inherited a mixed legacy from Wiseman – the college had superb academic results and a proud tradition but faced financial difficulties, partly due to a reduced papal grant. By the early 1840s the college could only afford to take twenty students and these were selected from the names put forward to the Cardinal Protector. Despite such troubles, the college was honoured by the visit of Gregory XVI on 25 February 1843, on which occasion Cardinal Acton and Bishops Griffiths and Brown (of the Lancashire District) were present. According to the report in *The Tablet*:

> His Holiness immediately proceeded to the chapel of the College to adore the Blessed Sacrament; and, after he prayed there for a short time, entered the Geographical Hall, where the throne had been erected. The Cardinal Protector and two Vicars Apostolic were seated by the Pope's direction, close to the throne, while the inmates of the College approached

in succession to kiss His Holiness's foot. They were followed by some of the English Ecclesiastics, and other distinguished English Catholics resident in Rome. After this customary token of veneration had been paid to His Holiness, some Latin verses were recited in his honour by Mr English, one of the students. The Pope then proceeded to the Library, where refreshments had been prepared, and there also delighted all who had the happiness to be near him, by his condescension, his affability, his cheerfulness, and unaffected kindness of heart. The Cardinal Protector and the two Vicars Apostolic were seated next to him, and the President and Vice-President [of the College] were standing by his side. Before his departure His Holiness inspected the site of the old English church, dedicated to the Holy Trinity in honour of St Thomas, which was destroyed during the French invasion. He was accompanied to the College door by those who had had the honour to receive him; and, according to custom, Cardinal Acton shut the door of His Holiness's carriage, as his Eminence had opened it at the Pope's arrival.[2]

The following day Baggs accompanied the two bishops to the papal palace to offer thanks to Pope Gregory for his visit to the college, the second of his Pontificate.

Baggs remained a popular figure on the Roman scene. On 23 December 1840 he was chosen to preach the funeral discourse for his cousin, Lady Gwendoline Talbot, the Princess Borghese, at San Carlo al Corso. With her beauty, kindness to the poor and untimely death, the Princess Gwendoline enjoyed a posthumous cult similar to that of Diana, Princess of Wales 160 years later.

Even the responsibilities of being Rector did not suppress Baggs' learned pursuits, his most notable academic contribution being a dissertation explaining the contemporary situation of the Church of England and the 'Puseyite' faction. The paper was read to the highly-respected Accademia di Religione Cattolica on 30 June 1842 and published, together with another academic paper 'On the Present State of the Church of England', in the *Annali delle Scienze Religiose*.

After the death of Bishop Baines, Baggs was chosen as Vicar Apostolic of the Western District. On 28 January 1844 the Prefect of Propaganda, Cardinal Fransoni, assisted by Bishop Brown (Vicar Apostolic of Lancashire) and Bishop Bernard Collier (Bishop of Port Maurice in Mauritius) consecrated Baggs Titular Bishop of Pella. The consecration took place in Rome at San Gregorio on the Caelian Hill, where Baggs

---

[2] *The Tablet*, 18 March 1843, 167.

was well aware of the historical connections. He wrote to his new flock that 'on the same spot once stood the house of Saint Gregory the Great, whence he sent our English Apostles; and over the religious house which still exists, there formerly presided his worthy successor, Gregory XVI.'[3] Despite being held at the early hour of eight in the morning, the ceremony was witnessed by a large congregation and afterwards 'almost all who had been present in the church thronged into the noble hall of the monastery to offer their congratulations to the new bishop; and nothing could be better timed or placed, as it tended to relieve his lordship from the intense emotion under which he laboured.'[4]

The new bishop remained in Rome for several months to settle affairs at the English College, where he was to be succeeded by Thomas Grant, later first Bishop of Southwark. Mindful of his new District, Baggs issued a Pastoral Letter 'given outside the Flaminian Gate' for the first Sunday of Lent 1844 and asked his priests to prepare their congregations for an imminent visitation and Confirmation. Meanwhile he was created an Assistant at the Pontifical Throne and was further honoured by celebrating High Mass on Passion Sunday before the Pope in the Sistine Chapel.

Baggs formally took possession of the Western District on 30 May 1844, being welcomed at Prior Park by clergy and laity alike. Two days later he celebrated his first ordination and, within his first year, reorganized his District into four deaneries and introduced conferences and spiritual exercises for the clergy. He undertook a series of lectures at St John the Evangelist, Bath, on the supremacy of the Pope and divided the Bristol mission into three: Clifton, Trenchard Street and St Mary's. In doing so, he managed to reach an agreement with the Jesuits. Baggs, it seems, threw himself into the work entrusted to him with great fervour.

However, the English climate and the daily tribulations faced by a bishop proved too much for the scholarly Baggs, despite his good intentions. In the summer of 1845 he suffered a nervous breakdown and withdrew to Lord Clifford's residence at Teignmouth for recuperation. From this seaside retreat, he wrote to Bishop Griffiths: 'my physicians assure me that my attack is not organic, but one of dyspepsia and the nerves. They do not require me to go abroad: indeed they tell me that in a couple of months I shall with God's blessing be fit for work again.' The bishop looked forward to returning to his duties and even offered to

[3] Pastoral for Lent 1844, 5.
[4] *The Tablet,* 17 February 1844, 102.

go to Rome to negotiate 'our common cause of the hierarchy.' He noted that 'the amicable arrangement of the Bristol question with the Jesuits will give me some personal influence' and stated his opinion that 'if the hierarchy is granted, the archiepiscopal See ought to belong to the present London District, in which Canterbury as well as London are situated.'[5] However, Baggs never returned to the Eternal City, nor did he see the Hierarchy restored, for having gone back to Prior Park his health further declined and he died there aged only 39 on 16 October 1845, a week after Newman's reception into the Church. Originally buried in the chapel at Prior Park, Baggs' remains were subsequently transferred to the nearby Midford Chapel, only to be moved again to the Holy Souls cemetery at Arnos Vale, Bristol.

Further Reading

A. Burton, 'College Rectors II: Charles Michael Baggs', *The Venerabile*, IV, 112-116

---

[5] AAW A80/780-82 (Baggs to Griffiths, 8 August 1845).

William Bernard Ullathorne, OSB

1806-89

Titular Bishop of Hetalona (1846)
Vicar Apostolic of the Western District (1846-48)
Vicar Apostolic of the Central District (1848-50)
Bishop of Birmingham (1850-89)
Titular Archbishop of Cabasa (1888)

Baggs died young and was replaced by a forty year-old Benedictine who had already travelled to the ends of the earth: William Bernard Ullathorne. His youth more or less ensured that he would become, in his old age, the last surviving of the Vicars Apostolic. When he finally died in 1889, the *Weekly Register* called Ullathorne 'a link between the days of declining persecution and the age of School Boards'[1] and Cardinal Manning considered him 'the last of the old and great race.'[2]

Ullathorne wrote an autobiography that gives many details of his childhood and youth that otherwise would have been lost. Born in Pocklington in the East Riding of Yorkshire on 7 May 1806, he was the eldest of the ten children of William Ullathorne, a general trader, and his wife Hannah Longstaff, who had converted to Catholicism before getting married. Through his mother, the future bishop could claim to be the direct descendent of St Thomas More. Ullathorne's descriptions of his childhood experiences of the Church paint a vivid picture of Yorkshire Catholicism in the Regency period:

> We had a little chapel at Pocklington with its two windows, but recently enlarged, a small priest's house and a long slip of garden. The priest was the Abbé Fidèle, a venerable French emigrant, long remembered there

---

[1] C. Butler, *The Life and Times of Bishop Ullathorne* (1926), ii, 256.
[2] Ibid., ii, 295.

and at York for his piety, simplicity, and charity. He used to kneel before the little altar in a Welsh or worsted wig, saying his prayers, until Miss Constable, the patroness of the mission, arrived in the vestry, which was also his dining-room and parlour; he then rose up and entered the vestry, where in sight of the little flock he pulled off his wig, powdered his head, and came in vested with his two servers for the Mass. I was told at a later period that he had four written sermons, and that when he had read the first words of one of them the congregation knew the rest by heart. Other French emigrant priests occasionally came, and visited our house, and I remember one was Dr Gilbert, a man of great dignity of bearing, who told dreadful narrations of his escape from the guillotine.[3]

When the Ullathorne family moved to Scarborough, a priest only visited once every six weeks and on the other Sundays the congregation had to make do with a lay-led service:

On the five Sundays intervening between the sacerdotal visits, it was arranged that the flock should attend chapel morning and afternoon as usual. My father and a Mr Paxton, an Ushaw Church student, who had given up the idea of the Ministry, officiated as lectors on alternate days. First the usual English prayers were said aloud, then all in silence read the prayers for Mass in the *Garden of the Soul*, making a sort of spiritual Communion, and then the lector for the week read one of Archer's sermons, which my father preferred doing from his usual seat, but Mr Paxton standing in front of the sanctuary rails, facing the people. In the afternoon the psalm prayers were chanted aloud: "All ye works of the Lord," etc., and the Catechism was heard … No one of us youths had made our first Communion, though we had been from time to time to Confession. And as to Confirmation, no one of us children had ever seen a Bishop, either at Pocklington or at Scarborough.[4]

Ullathorne's education took place at the village school in Burnby and then at Mr Hornsey's school in Scarborough. Although he was withdrawn from formal education at the age of ten to start working in the family business, he loved books and the reading of works such as *Robinson Crusoe* developed a passion for the sea. He decided that he wanted to become a seafarer and in 1819 his parents reluctantly allowed him to become a cabin boy.

It would be a period both of high adventure, as colourfully recounted in his autobiography, and of lukewarmness regarding the Faith, for despite taking with him a copy of the *Garden of the Soul* he had few opportunities

---

[3] Ullathorne, op. cit., 6.
[4] Ibid., 13.

or perhaps much desire to practise his Catholicism. However, everything changed during his second voyage when he attended Mass with a shipmate in the Baltic town of Memel (now Klaipėda, Lithuania): 'the moment I entered, so awestruck was I with the simplicity and fervour of what I beheld that it threw me into a cold shiver, and turned my heart completely round upon myself. I saw the claim of God upon me, and felt a deep reproach within my soul.'[5] He followed up this experience by reading the few Catholic books he could find on board, namely Marsollier's *Life of St Jane Frances de Chantal* and Gobinet's *Instruction of Youth,* and began to consider a religious vocation.

Ullathorne may well have decided to train for the secular priesthood, for he took French lessons with Mr Paxton and enjoyed hearing his tales of Ushaw. However, the young man's fate was sealed by one of the serendipities of life:

> There happened to visit our house a Knaresborough linen-manufacturer who had a son studying for the Church at Downside. He took a great fancy to my brother James, who had a good boy's voice, and was a chief singer in the chapel. He pressed him to go to Downside for the Church, and spoke much to my parents about it, but my brother did not feel the attraction; whereupon I made known how much I should like it. My father wrote at once to Dr Barber, the then Prior of the Monastery, and the matter was settled to my great delight.[6]

And so Ullathorne entered Downside in February 1823, even though the deficiencies in his religious education meant that he had not yet made his First Communion. He took his first vows on 5 April 1825 and was known as 'Old Plato' on account of his reading into the early hours of the morning, although by this time he had replaced adventure stories with the lives of the Desert Fathers. He spent some time at Ampleforth as Prefect of the school and during this period was ordained priest at Ushaw on 24 September 1831. Having had a disagreement with the Prior of Ampleforth, he returned to Downside and volunteered to assist one of his fellow monks, William Placid Morris, who had just been appointed Vicar Apostolic of the Cape of Good Hope, Madagascar, Mauritius and its dependencies – a loose phrase effectively covering much of Oceania, Australia and New Zealand.

In September 1832 Ullathorne set sail for New South Wales on the *Sir Thomas Munro.* Despite not being able to say Mass, he enjoyed the five-

---

[5] Ibid., 34.
[6] Ibid., 35.

month journey and, surrounded by his library of 500 books, treated his cabin as a 'floating hermit's cell'. The voyage was broken at Cape Town, where he was hosted by an Ampleforth monk, Dom Clement Rishton – showing the English Benedictines' growing presence around the British Empire. Ullathorne finally arrived at Sydney on 18 February 1833 and began his work as Vicar General, supported by an annual state salary of £200. His youthful appearance and inexperience caused initial problems in asserting his authority over the likes of Fr John Joseph Thierry, who had served the Catholics of the colony for thirteen years. He enjoyed good relations with the civic officials and oversaw the building of the first church in Sydney on land that had been purchased by Thierry. In 1835 his former novice master from Downside, Bede Polding, arrived as the new Vicar Apostolic of New Holland and Van Diemen's Land and Ullathorne acted as his right hand.

Ullathorne returned to the old world in 1836 to recruit priests and raise money for the Antipodes and was called to Rome to give an account of the mission. When Gregory XVI met him, he exclaimed *Quel giovane!* (What a young man!) but was impressed by his ability and awarded him a Doctorate of Divinity. Ullathorne, who empathized with the lot of the convict, gave public lectures in England on the subject, publishing *The Horrors of Transportation* in 1837 and appeared as a witness before the Molesworth Committee in London the following year. Transportation to New South Wales finally ended in 1840.

Though Polding saw Australia as an English Benedictine mission, Ullathorne had the foresight to see it as a predominantly Irish church and during a visit to Ireland recruited eleven priests. He also helped prepare the way for the erection of a proper diocesan hierarchy, which came about in 1842 with Polding as Archbishop of Sydney. In 1840 Ullathorne was offered the Dioceses of Hobart and Adelaide, but declined. In truth, Ullathorne's final period in Australia was deeply unhappy. He was frustrated in his working relationship with Polding and unpopular with some members of the clergy, who referred to him as 'Agitator General'. In the wider community, he was attacked for his negative stance on transportation.

Returning to England in June 1841, Ullathorne took charge of the mission of Coventry, where he built a splendid new church dedicated to the Most Holy Sacrament and St Osburg, and befriended the remarkable Margaret Hallahan. Under his guidance, she founded a congregation of Third Order Dominicans that followed him to the Western District and the Diocese of Birmingham, finally settling at Stone in Staffordshire. Ullathorne threw himself into pastoral work at Coventry but it was clear that he was a bishop-in-waiting. In 1846 he was appointed as successor to Baggs in the Western District. He later wrote that 'my four years and a half at Coventry were the happiest and most fruitful years of my life, and I left it with extreme regret.'[7]

Ullathorne was consecrated Titular Bishop of Hetalona in Coventry on 21 June 1846, the day also of Blessed Pius IX's coronation. 'How glad I should be,' he later recalled, 'to be able to revive the sense in all its fullness that flowed in upon me, as the mitre was placed by the three Bishops on my head. My friends observed that at that moment my face underwent an extraordinary change, and assumed a singular expression.'[8] Among those present was Newman, who had recently converted and was making his first appearance at a large Catholic gathering.

Insisting that a bishop should live in the centre of his area's population, Ullathorne decided to move the episcopal residence from Prior Park to 7 King's Square, Bristol. He quickly asserted his authority by making a number of clerical moves and getting to grips with Prior Park, the great albatross round the neck of the Vicar Apostolic of that District. Within six months the new bishop had asked Rome to set up a commission, which included Bishops Griffiths and Sharples, although nothing was definitively decided during Ullathorne's brief rule. He also encouraged the building of the church at Clifton, started by Baines and eventually opened by Hendren, and divided Bristol and Clifton into five missionary districts. However, with the death of Bishop Griffiths in 1848 and the appointment of Walsh to London, Ullathorne was translated to the Midland District.

For his subsequent career, see pp. 137–8

Further Reading

D. A. Bellenger, *William Bernard Ullathorne* (2001)
C. Butler, *The Life and Times of Bishop Ullathorne*, 2 vols (1926)
J. Champ, *William Bernard Ullathorne: A Different Kind of Monk* (2006)
W. B. Ullathorne, *The Devil is a Jackass*, ed. L. Madigan (1995)

---

[7] Ibid., 278.
[8] Ibid., 277.

Joseph William Hendren, OSF

1791-1866

Titular Bishop of Uranopolis (1848)
Vicar Apostolic of the Western District (1848-50)
Bishop of Clifton (1850-51)
Bishop of Nottingham (1851-53)
Titular Bishop of Martyropolis (1853-66)

Joseph William Hendren was one of the last Vicars Apostolic to be appointed before the restoration of the Hierarchy, although his active episcopal career was one of the shortest. He was originally from Birmingham where he was born on 19 October 1791, his parents having recently come over from Belfast. Birmingham was then served by Franciscans, one of whom, John Pacificus Nutt, baptised the future bishop at St Peter's, Broad Street. The young Hendren was educated at the Franciscan school at Baddesley Clinton in Warwickshire and it was of little surprise that, on discerning a religious vocation, he decided to join the Order, with whom he was professed on 19 November 1807, taking the name 'Joseph'. He was eventually ordained priest by Bishop Milner at Wolverhampton on 28 September 1815, a few months after the battle of Waterloo.

At the time of his ordination, Hendren was teaching at Baddesley and the following year went to the Order's novitiate at Perthyre, Monmouthshire to teach philosophy and theology. Here he also served the nearby congregation at Courtfield once a fortnight when the Vaughan family (which later produced a Cardinal Archbishop of Westminster and several bishops) was away on the continent. In October 1818 the novitiate moved to Aston Hall, near Stone, Staffordshire, and Hendren supplemented his teaching duties there with serving the Catholics of Swynnerton. In 1823 he moved back to Baddesley Academy, this time as Director, and in 1826 transferred to the mission of Abergavenny in South Wales.

In 1839 he became confessor to the Poor Clares of Taunton, an English community that had originated in Flanders in 1619 but had fled to England following the French Revolution. He would remain close to the community for the rest of his life. He also looked after the Catholics of nearby Taunton Lodge. One of his converts during this period was William Thomas Gordon, a future Oratorian.

In 1847 Ullathorne appointed Hendren as his Vicar General and during the bishop's 'continental tour' of 1848 the Franciscan had effectively to administer the Western District. He looked forward to his master's return and little expected that Ullathorne was to be translated to the Central District and favoured him as his successor. The formal nomination was made by Propaganda on 29 July 1848 and Hendren was consecrated by Ullathorne on 10 September, the location of the ceremony having been moved from the unfinished church at Clifton to St Mary's on the Quay, Bristol. However, eleven days later he was able to officiate at the opening of Holy Apostles, Clifton, which would soon serve as the new diocese's pro-cathedral. Shortly afterwards he consecrated St Osmund's, Salisbury, and the following year the new church at Woodchester, which acted as a base for the Passionists and then the Dominicans.

Hendren's active period as a bishop was short. For three years he ruled the Western District and the newly-created Diocese of Clifton (from 1850). However, like his three most recent predeccessors, his rule was overshadowed by the debts of Prior Park. Ullathorne had appealed to Rome for help in the matter and the English bishops were divided over the future of the college – Hogarth, Briggs and Thomas Joseph Brown supported the continuance of the institution, while the powerful trio of Wiseman, Walsh and Ullathorne were against. The issue was complicated further when Propaganda decided that Hendren should work with Bishop Brown of the Welsh District to settle the dispute. Since Brown had opposed Hendren's appointment in the first place, the new bishop was reluctant to enter into this partnership and even offered to hand the direction of Prior Park completely into his colleague's hands. Hendren's authority was further damaged when the President, Dr Brindle, refused to resign without receiving the return of the £8,400 he had personally invested in the place. He eventually relented and left Prior Park in October 1849. Soon afterwards, a temporary solution was reached when the property was sold to Alexander Raphael, the Catholic MP for St Albans, who then let Prior Park back to the Church for the reasonable annual rent of £850.

On 29 September 1850 Hendren became Bishop of Clifton and, for the time being, administrator of the Diocese of Plymouth. Prior Park still hung above him like a dark cloud, especially when Mr Raphael died at the end of 1850 without making a will. He experienced further strife during the anti-Catholic hysteria that followed the restoration of the Hierarchy. The press seized upon the case of Augusta Talbot, a relative of the Earl of Shrewsbury, who had been a student with the Poor Clares of Taunton. In 1851 she applied to join the novitiate, despite still being a minor and a ward of the Chancery. The young Augusta was seen as the latest example of a 'young Virgin' kidnapped by a predatory Church and immured in a convent, which 'confiscated' her inheritance. Hendren had been involved, both as chaplain at Taunton and then as Ordinary, and he defended himself and the Church by writing a long letter to *The Times*. Despite this, the bishop became the subject of two cartoons in *Punch*. One portrayed him as a grotesque friar placing a white veil on a young girl, with the caption 'The Kidnapper: a Case for the Police', the other as the Big Bad Wolf, in soutane and clerical hat, waiting for Little Red Riding Hood.

Moves were already afoot to move Hendren to another diocese. On 16 June 1851, Propaganda decided 'that Bishop Hendren was to be translated to Nottingham. Cardinal Wiseman was to tell him how much Propaganda valued his work and that, wishing to discharge him from the heavy responsibilities connected with Prior Park, Propaganda was transferring him to Nottingham "so that he could be near his old Superior" [Ullathorne].'[1]

Hendren was relieved to be free from the troubles of Prior Park, although he still faced financial difficulties at Nottingham as well as the challenge of ruling a vast diocese that had no obvious centre. He erected a Chapter, established various important funds and encouraged the work of religious Orders. Ill health increasingly dogged him and he resigned his See in 1853, retiring firstly to the Birmingham Oratory, where he could be near his family, live in a congenial religious community and use Newman's extensive library. However, the onslaught of gout necessitated his departure from the Hagley Road to his beloved Poor Clares at Taunton. His last years were marked by declining health but his death, on 14 November 1866, turned out to be quite sudden. After the Requiem was sung by Bishop

---

[1] Bellenger (ed.), *Fathers in Faith*, 44.

Clifford of Clifton, the old bishop's body was buried in the nuns' cemetery at Taunton. Following the convent's closure, his remains were transferred to St George's, Taunton, on 4 October 1997 during a ceremony presided over by his successor in Clifton, Bishop Mervyn Alexander.

Further Reading

Maurice Whitehead, 'Educational Turmoil and Ecclesiastical Strife: The Episcopal Career of Joseph William Hendren, 1848-1853', *Recusant History*, Vol. 25, no. 2 (Oct. 2000), 263-280

The Welsh District

(1840–1850)

The Welsh District was carved out of the Western District in 1840. It consisted of Wales, together with the border counties of Herefordshire and Monmouthshire. Ten years later the Welsh District was divided into the Dioceses of Shrewsbury and of Newport and Menevia.

THOMAS JOSEPH BROWN, OSB

1798-1880

TITULAR BISHOP OF APOLONIA (1840)
VICAR APOSTOLIC OF THE WELSH DISTRICT (1840-50)
BISHOP OF NEWPORT AND MENEVIA (1850-80)

Thomas Brown, who was to become the first Bishop of Newport and Menevia, was born at Bath on 2 May 1798, the son of Thomas and Catherine Brown. He received his early education at a Protestant school, where he developed controversial skills in defending his Faith and, in the words of Bishop Hedley, 'never blushed or made a compromise; he argued and he explained; and I have often heard him say, in speaking of these young days, "I never was beaten".'[1] At the age of nine, Brown proceeded to the school at Acton Burnell, Shropshire, which was run by the English Benedictines who had formerly been at St Gregory's, Douai. Here he indulged in squirrel-hunting and, on 19 April 1813, received the Benedictine habit, taking the name 'Joseph'. The following year the whole community moved to their new house at Downside, Stratton-on-the-Fosse, near Bath, where Brown was to remain until 1840. On their journey to Somerset, the community stayed at the Star Inn, Worcester, and in later life Brown recalled the astonished look of the waiters when the monks sang Grace at dinner.

After his ordination to the priesthood on 7 April 1823 Brown quickly distinguished himself as a teacher of theology to the young monks. One of his students, the future Archbishop Ullathorne, wrote that in Brown 'I found a teacher who really taught systematically, and not only with method, but with considerable preparation and from an extensive accumulation of knowledge. I have always said that Dr Brown ... was the only person

---

[1] Bellenger, *Fathers in Faith*, 71.

from whose living voice I ever learnt much. All else was acquired chiefly through books.'[2]

Brown was a gifted speaker, debater and writer and enjoyed entering combat with the leading Protestant controversialists in the area. The most famous of these encounters was held in the riding school at Cheltenham where, for five days, the monk engaged in debate with representatives of the Protestant Reformation Society before an audience of 4,000 people, the whole gathering culminating in a riot. In 1834 he organized a similar convocation at Downside, which became the basis of a publication, the *Downside Discussion* (1836). Brown was the author of other works, mostly polemical, including *Catholic Truth Vindicated Against the Misconceptions and Calumnies of 'Popery Unmasked'* (1834).

While Brown was obviously capable of feisty dogmatic pugilism, he demonstrated that he was also amenable to the more subtle art of ecclesiastical diplomacy. In 1826 he attended the General Chapter of the Order and in 1829 he was sent to Rome to represent Downside in the disagreement with Bishop Baines, who was questioning the validity of the house's erection and the monks' vows in an attempt to seize control and open an episcopal seminary. Brown succeeded in his mission, leaving in his wake a favourable impression on Cardinal Cappellari, the future Pope Gregory XVI. It was said that his first memorial was 'couched in a Latin too classical for the judges at Propaganda' so that 'he submitted a completely different version in poorer prose.'[3] His sojourn in Rome also gave rise to an often-told anecdote, related here in the words of Cardinal Gasquet:

> During his stay in Rome he was lodged in the monastery of San Gregorio [al Celio], and his genial nature soon drew many friends to him. In the cold months he felt the want of an English fire very keenly, and to keep up the circulation of his blood he had recourse to a method very strange to the Romans. He obtained a piece of rope and made it do duty for skipping purposes, and whenever he felt particularly cold he would retire to his cell and go through this exercise till by degrees he became quite a proficient in the art. But now he began to perceive that the community were not so cordial in their manner towards him as before, and even at times they seemed to him to shun his company. He bore it for a time till his warm heart could stand it no longer, and prompted him to go to the Prior and ask for an explanation. The Prior received him most kindly,

[2] Butler, op. cit., I, 21.
[3] Van Zeller, op. cit., 37.

and after some difficulty he explained that the community had become persuaded that Dr Brown had great combats with the devil, or something of that nature, as they constantly heard the most unearthly noises in his cells, and blows which often shook the adjoining rooms. Dr Brown at once understood what had led to this misconception, and besought the Prior to come with him to his room, where he promised to explain the whole mystery. When there he produced his piece of rope, and much to the astonishment and subsequent delight of the Italian monk, went through his skipping evolutions. The Prior then insisted that Dr Brown must repeat the performance at the next recreation, which he, hoping to break down any wrong idea about himself, consented to do. The monks were delighted, and talked so much about the innocent amusement that their Cardinal Protector came to hear of it, and on his next visit insisted that the *monacho inglese* should give another performance in his presence.[4]

Having proved himself in so many ways it was unsurprising that the Downside community should have elected him Prior in 1834. He was given the honorific title of 'Cathedral Prior of Winchester' and a Doctorate in Divinity, the privilege of awarding three such doctorates having been granted to the General Chapter.

With the division of the four vicariates in England and Wales to eight in 1840, Wales became a District in its own right. Brown was appointed by Gregory XVI to the new District, despite his lack of practical pastoral experience and his own reluctance to exercise high office. He was consecrated by Bishop Griffiths at St John's Chapel, Bath, on 28 October 1840, having been assigned the Titular See of Apolonia.

The challenges that faced Brown were vividly expressed in his first Pastoral Letter:

> The field of labour allotted to us is extensive, and extremely necessitous … Since our very recent arrival here, the result of our inquiries into the state of the Missions in this county alone is most appalling. At Abersychan and Pontypool is a united congregation of 800 Catholics, having for their place of public divine-worship a room in a pub-house, used on the week-days by the customers of the house, and very kindly lent by the land-lord, on Sundays, for the celebration of Mass. At Merthyr Tydil [*sic*], there are at least 800 Catholics, for whose religious worship no better accommodation can yet be provided than an ill-floored loft, over a slaughter house. At Rhymney and Tredegar are numerous congregations without any chapel, or any resident Priest: depending for spiritual succour on the untiring zeal of the Missioner at Merthyr Tydil, for whom they are distant six,

---

[4] Bellenger, *Fathers in Faith*, 76-77.

and eight miles, and upwards. At Cardiff, on the borders of this county, the number of Catholics is not less than 1,200, having no more suitable temple for the tremendous mysteries of our Christian dispensation than a very small room, the window of which is taken out to accommodate the congregation, who crowd, as many as can find place, into a confined shed … We have hardly a school in any of our missions wherein faith and morals of multitudes of poor Catholic children who abound there may be formed and preserved. We have no means at our disposal. We have no seminary. We are almost without resources for the education of clergy. We, ourselves, are entirely dependent on the liberality and charity of those who can assist us.[5]

The District was so under-resourced that the cope presented to him by the students of St Gregory's was for many years the only one that existed in the entire Vicariate.

With the restoration of the Hierarchy in 1850, the Welsh District was divided between the new Dioceses of Shrewsbury and of Newport and Menevia, the latter being ruled by Brown for the remaining thirty years of his long life. Whereas south Wales boasted eleven missions and two chapels in 1840, the Diocese of Newport and Menevia could lay claim to 58 churches and 62 priests by 1880, the year of Brown's death. Betraying his Benedictine roots, Brown was the principal force behind the establishment of Belmont Priory near Hereford, which served as his pro-cathedral. Indeed, with the permission granted by the Holy See in 1858, he resurrected the old English practice of drawing the cathedral Chapter from the Benedictine monks. To some extent he succeeded where Bishop Baines had failed several decades before, in making a monastery the centre of a diocese. However, he also supported Cardinal Manning and the other bishops in petitioning Rome for greater control of parishes run by religious Orders.

Brown is often remembered for his explosive reaction to Newman's article in the *Rambler* of July 1859, 'On Consulting the Faithful in Matters of Doctrine'. Newman had discussed the disputes surrounding the Arian heresy in the fourth century when many of the bishops were heterodox and the true faith was, in many cases, preserved by the laity. Newman even referred to 'a temporary suspense of the Church's infallible authority'. Brown delated Newman directly to Rome, without reference to the Oratorian or his bishop (Brown's fellow Benedictine, Ullathorne). It seems that he assumed Manning had asked for a refutation in *The Rambler* but,

---

[5] Pastoral Letter 1840.

as Meriol Trevor put it, the former Archdeacon was 'so diplomatic on this occasion that he failed to make Newman understand that his orthodoxy was being called in question.' Brown declared that Newman's article was 'totally subversive of the essential authority of the Church in matters of faith.' Highly suspicious of those who had come to Rome via the Oxford Movement, he told Mgr Talbot that 'much evil' came 'from the herding together of converts.'[6] Newman remained under a cloud in Rome for years although Brown later made his peace with him. Indeed the bishop asked Newman four times to act as his theologian at the First Vatican Council and in 1874 persuaded him to write the *Letter to the Duke of Norfolk* in response to Gladstone's *Vatican Decrees*.

Having reached his mid-seventies Brown requested the assistance of an auxiliary bishop. This was granted in 1873 with the appointment of an Ampleforth monk, John Edward Cuthbert Hedley, who eventually succeeded him and won fame as a spiritual author.

Amidst all of his activity, Bishop Brown's deep faith and genuine piety could be witnessed at three o'clock each afternoon, when he would pause from whatever engagement was in hand and recall with those present the hour of the Saviour's death, commending the dying to His intercession. It was appropriate – and a gift to his obituary writers – that Brown's own end should come at three o'clock on 12 April 1880, which happened that year to be Good Friday. He died at his residence at Manor House, Lower Bullingham, Herefordshire and was laid to rest at Belmont.

Further Reading

Cardinal Francis Aidan Gasquet, 'Thomas Joseph Brown – Bishop of Newport & Menevia', *The Downside Review* (1880), 4-15, and reprinted in A. Bellenger (ed.), *Fathers in Faith – The Western District 1688-1988* (1991), 71-82

Bishop Cuthbert Hedley, *A Sermon preached at the funeral of the Right Rev. Thomas Joseph Brown OSB April 16th 1880* (1880)

Alban Hood, '"Stirring Up the Pool", Bishop Thomas Joseph Brown OSB (1798-1880) and the Dispute between the Hierarchy and the English Benedictines', *Recusant History*, Vol. 25, no. 2 (Oct. 2000), 304-324

---

[6] Meriol Trevor, *Light in Winter* (1962), 208-209.

General Bibliography

Titles relating to specific Vicars Apostolic are listed after each entry

Oxford Dictionary of National Biography (2004)

Amhurst, W., *The History of Catholic Emancipation* (2 vols, 1886)

Anstruther, G., *The Seminary Priests* (4 vols, 1968-77)

Aveling, J. C. H., *The Handle and the Axe* (1976)

Bellenger, D. A. (ed.), *Opening the Scrolls: Essays in Honour of Godfrey Anstruther* (1987)

Bellenger, A. (ed.), *Fathers In Faith: The Western District 1688-1988* (1991)

Bence-Jones, M., *The Catholic Families* (1992)

Birt, H. N., *Benedictine Pioneers in Australia* (2 vols, 1911)

Birt, H. N., *History of Downside School* (1912)

Bossy, J., *The English Catholic Community 1570-1850* (1975)

Buscot, W., *The History of Cotton College At Sedgley Park, 1763-1873, At Cotton, 1873-* (1940)

Chadwick, H., *St Omers to Stonyhurst: A History of Two Centuries* (1962)

Edwards, F., *The Jesuits in England* (1985)

Foley, B. C., *Some People of the Penal Times: Aspects of a Unique Social and Religious Phenomenon 1688-1791* (1991)

Foley, B. C., *Some Other People of the Penal Times: Aspects of a Unique Social and Religious Phenomenon* (1991)

Foley, H., *Records of the English Province of the Society of Jesus* (7 vols, 1875-1883)

Gilley, S., *Newman and His Age* (1990)

Gillow, J., *A Bibliographical Dictionary of English Catholics* (5 vols, 1885)

Hemphill, B., *The Early Vicars-Apostolic of England, 1685-1750* (1954)

Hill, R., *God's Architect: Pugin and the Building of Romantic England* (2007)

Kirk, J., *Biographies of English Catholics in the Eighteenth Century*, edited by J. H. Pollen and E. Burton (1909)

Leetham, C., *Luigi Gentili, A Sower for the Second Spring* (1965)

Leys, M. D. R., *Catholics in England, 1559-1829. A Social History* (1961)

Mathew, D., *Catholicism in England: The Portrait of a Minority: its Culture and Tradition* (1936)

Maziere Brady, W., *Annals of the Catholic Hierarchy in England and Scotland AD 1585-1876, With Dissertation on Anglican Orders* (1877)

Milburn, D., *A History of Ushaw College: A Study of the Origin, Foundation and Development of an English Catholic Seminary with an Epilogue 1908-1962* (1964)

Mullett, M. A., *Catholics in Britain and Ireland, 1558-1829* (1998)

Norman, E., *The English Catholic Church in the Nineteenth Century* (1984)

Norman, E., *Roman Catholicism in England from the Elizabethan Settlement to the Second Vatican Council* (1985)

Oliver, G., *Collections Illustrating the History of the Catholic Religion in the Counties of Cornwall, Devon, Dorset, Somerset, Wilts, and Gloucester* (1857)

Payne, J. O., *Old English Catholic Missions* (1900)

Schofield, N. and G. Skinner, *The English Cardinals* (2007)

Scott, G., *Gothic Rage Undone* (1992)

Van Zeller, H., *Downside By and Large: A Double Figure in Praise of Things Lasting and Georgian* (1954)

Ward, B., *History of St Edmund's College, Old Hall* (1893)

Ward, B., *Catholic London A Century Ago* (1905)

Ward, B., *The Dawn of the Catholic Revival in England, 1781-1802* (2 vols, 1909)

Ward, B., *The Eve of Catholic Emancipation: being the History of the English Catholics during the first 30 years of the 19th Century* (3 vols, 1911-12)

Ward, B., *The Sequel to Catholic Emancipation* (2 vols, 1915)

Ward, W., *The Life of John Henry Cardinal Newman* (1912)

Williams, J. A., *Bath and Rome: The Living Link* (1963)

Williams, M. E., *The Venerable English College Rome. A History 1579-1979* (1979)

Williams, M. E., *St Alban's College, Valladolid* (1986)

Wiseman, N., *Recollections of the Last Four Popes* (1856)

PICTURE CREDITS

The authors and publishers wish to express their gratitude to the following for permission to use images from their collections and to those who took photographs of the images:

Trustees of the Roman Catholic Diocese of Westminster – photos by Stefan Kaminski: Bonaventure Giffard, Richard Challoner, John Douglass, James Yorke Bramston.

Trustees of the the Diocese of Liverpool – George Hilary Brown.

Trustees of the Diocese of Leeds – photos by Philippe Lefebvre: John Briggs, William Hogarth, Peter Augustine Baines.

The Venerable English College, Rome – photo by Claudia Primangeli: Nicholas Wiseman; photos by Nicholas Schofield: Robert Gradwell, Charles Michael Baggs.

St Mary's College, Oscott – photos by Nicholas Schofield: John Milner, Thomas Walsh; photo by Chris Smith: John Milner (cover picture).

Downside Abbey – photos by Br Bartholomew Preston: Philip Michael Ellis, William Laurence York, Charles Walmesley, William Bernard Ullathorne.

Douai Abbey – photos by Philippe Lefebvre: George Witham, James Smith.

Lord Camoys – John Talbot Stonor.

Lord Petre – photo by Graham Hillman: Benjamin Petre's dog.

St Edmund's College, Ware – photos by Philippe Lefebvre: Thomas Griffiths, John Leyburn, William Poynter, Gregory Stapleton, Memorial of James Robert Talbot.